I0088242

Lightning Bolts
From Pentecostal Skies;
Or,
Devices of the Devil Unmasked

by

Martin Wells Knapp

First Fruits Press
Wilmore,
Kentucky
c2018

Lightning bolts from Pentecostal skies, or, Devices of the Devil unmasked.
By Martin Wells Knapp.
First Fruits Press, © 2018

ISBN: 9781621717799 (print), 9781621717805 (digital), 9781621717812 (kindle)

Digital version at http://place.asburyseminary.edu/
firstfruitsheritagematerial/153/

First Fruits Press
B.L. Fisher Library
Asbury Theological Seminary
204 N. Lexington Ave.
Wilmore, KY 40390
http://place.asburyseminary.edu/firstfruits

Knapp, Martin Wells, 1853-1901.
  Lightning bolts from Pentecostal skies, or, Devices of the Devil unmasked /
by Martin Wells Knapp. – Wilmore, KY : First Fruits Press, ©2018.
    304 pages ; 2 cm.
    Reprint. Previously published: Cincinnati, Ohio : The Revivalist, c1898.
    ISBN: 9781621717799 (pbk.)
    1. Pentecostalism. I. Title. II. Devices of the Devil unmasked.

    BX8763.K56 2018

Cover design by Jon Ramsay

asburyseminary.edu
800.2ASBURY
204 North Lexington Avenue
Wilmore, Kentucky 40390

First Fruits
THE ACADEMIC OPEN PRESS OF ASBURY SEMINARY

First Fruits Press
The Academic Open Press of Asbury Theological Seminary
204 N. Lexington Ave., Wilmore, KY 40390
859-858-2236
first.fruits@asburyseminary.edu
asbury.to/firstfruits

Martin Wells Knapp.

LIGHTNING BOLTS

FROM PENTECOSTAL SKIES;

OR,

DEVICES OF THE DEVIL UNMASKED.

By MARTIN WELLS KNAPP,

Author of "Christ Crowned Within," "Out of Egypt Into Canaan," ' Revival
Kindlings," "Revival Tornadoes," "Impressions," and "The
Double Cure"; Editor of "The Revivalist";
Publisher of "Full Salvation Quar-
terly" and "Pentecostal
Holiness Library."

"*He shot out lightnings and discomfited them.*"
(PSALM xviii. 14.)

OFFICE OF

The Revivalist, Full Salvation Quarterly, and Pentecostal Holiness Library,

CINCINNATI

CONTENTS.

ILLUSTRATIONS.

[Designed by the Author and executed by J. A. KNAPP.]

"STRUCK BY LIGHTNING."

LIGHTNING BOLTS.

CHAPTER I.

PREFATORY.

The lightning bolts of the Bible and of this book are destructive only to error and its adherents.

Those whose souls are protected by the lightning rods of God's truth are safe, and can shout and sing while the lightning leaps and the cyclones of Pentecostal purity and power sweep the earth.

We live in the electric age in both the material and spiritual worlds. Light, heat and motion have been drawn from electricity until old customs and appliances have been revolutionized.

From the Pentecostal dynamo there has also burst forth into the spiritual world, light and love and power which is causing multitudes to rush from the old candle-lighted stage-coaches of forms and ceremonies and dry creeds and crooked experiences into the brilliantly lighted, swiftly propelled cars of full salvation, which, by divine power, are bearing their inmates triumphantly on and up from "glory unto glory."

They startle. Lightning bolts startle by their vividness, intensity and death-dealing power. In all ages the lightning which has fallen from Pentecostal skies has startled the nations. The prayer of the writer of this book is that these bolts may startle and awaken all its readers who are not securely building on the Rock which no storms can shake.

They hit. Lightning bolts always hit somewhere. Sheet-lightning entertains by its beauty and by the fact that it is just "playing at lightning," but lightning bolts always hit. God never sends them in either world for amusement. At Pentecost they hit the crucifiers of Jesus, and they have continued to fall with gleeful fury upon Pharisees and hypocrites ever since.

They awaken. The thunder which is born of the bolt is a mighty awakening agency. So the life and power and zeal which follow from one person who, like Paul, Wesley, or Finney, has become a lightning bolt of Pentecostal power, often awaken thousands from the sleep of sin and lead them into the kingdom of God.

They reveal surrounding objects. Their vivid light banishes darkness and reveals every enemy lurking beneath its shadows. The prowling wolf, the cowardly assassin, the treacherous pitfall as well as the place of safety, is seen under its searching light. In the dark night of sin, formality, worldliness and error in which the church is befogged, Pentecostal lightning bolts make surprising and often terrifying revelations. They show lost men where they are and warn them of spiritual foes, and reveal Him who only is able to save.

They frighten. People fear their fury. They dread being hit. Yet a God of infinite love creates them, and continues to hurl them where He sees that they should fall. Just so people fear spiritual lightning. The opposition to ministers who are charged with it is from this source. A gifted preacher of my acquaintance was recently moved from a four thousand dollar appointment to one of three hundred for this cause. Tidings come to-day from another, isolated for the same reason.

People who have not Pentecostal protection fear Pentecostal bolts and the storm-centers of Pentecostal ministers, from which they often leap.

They are no respecters of persons. They fall in defiance of color, clime, creed, and social, political or ecclesiastical position, dealing death and doom wherever God sees fit to send them, asking no leave, making no apologies. In like manner, Pentecostal bolts fall wherever shams and sin are found, and give light and comfort to all who, irrespective of names and creeds, love to see error die.

They shock people. This is a sure sign that they fall near where they live. Scribes and Pharisees were fearfully "shocked" when this kind of lightning first fell, and formalists and worldlings and hypocrites are always thus affected by it, while God's true children

> "Can brave the wildest storms,
>   With His glory in the soul;
>   And can shout amid the tempest:
>   'Praise the Lord!'"

It is a department of celestial fire-works with which God entertains His children, and others are apprised of their real spiritual character by the way it affects them.

Sometimes they kill. When they do, we do not blame them or the God who sends them, but say, "He doeth all things well." Thus they leaped upon Achan, Ananias and Sapphira, to the alarm of evil-doers and the defense of God's people; and thus they sometimes fall upon like characters to-day, with similar results.

They are extraordinary. They are extraordinary compared to the constant shining of the sun and the quiet power of gravitation, but are of God, and have their place as truly as these. In a like manner, the sunshine of grace and the fragrant breezes of salvation is the normal state of the spiritual world, but in it lightning bolts have a place as really as in the physical. They are not the normal state in either. In both they are the exception and not the rule, yet a force that God will not dispense with. The writer has written five books full of light and food and warmth to only this one charged so heavily with lightning.

They attract attention. Lightning bolts attract public attention. The thunder which follows vibrates far and near. So with spiritual bolts. The howls of people who are hit often reverberate through a whole city, and, by the aid of the sounding-boards of the press, through an entire nation. It was these that filled Jerusalem with an uproar in the days of Jesus, and which are to thus fill modern Jerusalems as they leap again with like precision and fury upon the children of those whom they thus destroyed.

They are unpopular. Lightning bolts are unpopular. People, as a rule, dread them. They awaken and startle and kill in such a way as to be a source of alarm, yet they are a part of God's plan, and have a mission which no other force can fill. The lightning bolt phase of Christianity is just as unpopular for similar reasons, yet none the less needed. The bolts of this book leap from the great storm cloud of divine truth, which has its source in God's Word.

They never apologize. No matter who is hit, or how many, or how terribly people are ''shocked'' or criticise, they never take anything back. If the writer expresses any erroneous views of his own, he will gladly welcome correction, and publicly confess; but for the bolts of divine truth which leap from the Word of God, and of which this book is full, there can be no apologies, no matter how severely and by whom criticised.

They appear cruel. Their work often seems cruel and destructive. Such to limited human sight it may seem. But such, tried by God's standard, it never is. For in both the physical and spiritual world no bolts leap but from the bosom of infinite love. In the Universities of Eternity, if not before, we will doubtless learn that even the "wrath of the Lamb" is but one form of love divine.

They are sudden. "Quick as lightning." In a similar way the truth leaps upon its foes, until they perceive they are "in the gall of bitterness and bonds of iniquity"; or, Ananias-like, are quickly summoned to a higher court than earth's; or are, like Pharaoh's hosts, suddenly drowned in some Red Sea, while those whom they seek to crush sing pæans of victory upon its shores; or, like the antediluvian world, see their folly when too late, and sink beneath their sins.

They are unchangeable. They are just the same now as in the days of Adam, of Moses, and of the primitive church. So with the electric current of Pentecostal truth. The same wires that gave light, and heat, and motion to the salvation cars, in which patriarchs, prophets and apostles sped triumphantly to the skies, will bear their children of this age to the same pearly portals. And the bolts which fell on false prophets, and people, and Pharisaical hypocrites of old, leap with kindred fury upon their followers to-day.

They appear sacrilegious. They often strike churches, and sometimes kill preachers. Indeed, the tall steeples of many modern temples invite them. Sham churches and preachers in a similar way draw down bolts of burning rebuke and exposure from Pentecostal skies. No false plea of sacred place and office can keep them off. No place is sacred where God is disobeyed and insulted, and no man is sacred who profanes his office by betraying sacred trusts. Such places and such ministers are, and ever have been, subjects of Divine Lightning Bolts, such as are magnified in this book.

Protection provided. There is perfect protection from them. A person perfectly insulated is as safe from lightning in a storm as in the sunshine. Lightning rods of a sham profession have been tried in vain for this purpose, as they draw the lightning instead of diverting it; but all who are insulated from the world by a Holy Ghost experience, fear no bolts from either above or below. If you get "shocked" or killed it will be because you are not properly insulated.

They herald refreshing showers. These showers banish drought, refresh nature, and are a precious, heaven-sent boon. So with the showers of salvation which attend the lightning bolts of Pentecostal power; they turn Saharas of formality into blooming gardens of Christian experience and activity, banish the malaria of worldliness and sin, making the spiritual atmosphere fresh and healthful and laden with the beauty and fragrance of heaven. Showers of blessings have fallen upon the writer as he has penned these pages, and he prays and believes that God will pour them down upon all who rightly read the book. "Now unto Him who is able to do exceeding abundantly above all we ask or think, according to the power that worketh in us, unto Him be the glory in the church and in Christ Jesus unto all generations for ever and ever. Amen."

CHAPTER II.

Someone has said that there is a scarlet thread running clear through the Bible, and that this thread is the blood of Jesus. There is another thread running through it. It is the white one of the promise of the Pentecostal outpouring of the Holy Ghost. Of all the promises of the Bible, God exalts this as "THE PROMISE" of all the ages. Of this the prophets wrote and sang, and when the kingdom of heaven came its great prophet proclaimed not only the advent of the King, but the coming of the Holy Ghost. Above all other truths Jesus himself heralded the fulfillment of this promise, which should be the artesian well of water overflowing and transforming the deserts of sin and formality into gardens of Paradise. This incoming and indwelling, and cleansing and filling of the Holy Ghost was to be an epochal experience in the lives of his people. Among the many names divinely given it is that of a "baptism." "He shall baptize you with the Holy Ghost and with fire" (Matt. iii. 11).

It is a promised baptism. "I send forth the promise of my Father upon you" (Luke xxiv. 49). Even the promises which found fulfillment on Calvary are no more numerous or strong than those which center at Pentecost. (See John xiv. 16; xv. 26; xvi. 13; Acts xviii. and references.) After such strongly repeated promises, God would cease to be God were they not fulfilled. The veracity of the Godhead is at stake; the Holy Ghost must be poured out upon the Church, or the Eternal Throne crumbles.

It is a commanded baptism. "Be filled with the Spirit" (Eph. v. 18). Believers are under as great obligations to obey this command as any other in the Bible. All who refuse to thus "tarry" until filled disobey God and imperil, not only their own souls, but those of all whom they might win if thus filled. We can not teach obedience unless we exemplify it. A citizen who disregards the supreme requirement of the government never would be commissioned to represent it. All who knowingly ignore this commandment are thus guilty. Hence multitudes of self-constituted ministers, where there should be God-called, heaven-qualified flames of fire.

It is a spiritual baptism. "John indeed baptized with water; but ye shall be baptized with the Holy Ghost not many days hence" (Acts i. 5). John's was with water. This is with God. The disease which this baptism cures is spiritual, and deeper than skin, bones, blood and nerves, hence the remedy must be spiritual and efficient. The dross which it is to eliminate permeates the entire soul so that nothing but celestial fire can melt and purge it. It is the glorious spiritual reality of which water is the outer sign.

It is administered by Jesus. "Being therefore by the right hand of God exalted, and having received of the Father the promise of the Holy Ghost, he hath poured forth this, which ye see and hear" (Acts ii. 33). Hence all cavil at it, is cavil at Him. All criticism of it, is criticism of Him. All opposition to it, is opposition to Him. As John administered water, so Jesus administers the Holy Spirit.

It is one baptism. Some have supposed the baptism

with the Holy Ghost to be distinct from the baptism with
fire — two baptisms, one with the Holy Ghost, and one
with fire.   That this is a mistake is seen from the fact
that Jesus, in Acts i. 5, referring to the fulfillment of the
promise, made no mention of fire at all, and that when it
came the tongues of fire were simply attendants of the
Spirit, and that it was never again repeated.   Fire evidently was the outer token that the promise was fulfilled.
When Jesus came, His advent was signalled by a star;
when the Holy Ghost descended, His was by these
tongues of fire.   In answer to the question, "Is there a
second baptism of fire for truly sanctified people?" Commentator W. B. Godbey says: "No.   There is but one
baptism (Eph. iv. 5).   But you may have many revivals
of the fire already in your heart.   II. Tim. i. 6, Greek:
'Therefore I remind thee to revive and refire the gift of
God in you.'   Timothy had received the gift of the Holy
Ghost, which is sanctification.   Here Paul admonishes
him to revive and refire it.   The Greek *anazoopureo*,
translated 'Stir up' in English, is proven, and again,
Zooe, life, and *pur*, fire.   Hence it means to revive and
refire.   These Scriptures certainly relieve us of the difficulties.   If you have not received the baptism of fire,
you are not sanctified.   If the fire has gone out, you
have lost your experience.   Timothy was no backslider.
He was in the sanctified experience.   Yet Paul reminds
him to revive and refire his experience.   Regeneration
gives life, and sanctification gives purity and energy.   If
Timothy needed showers from the heavenly ocean to
revive the divine life in him, and showers of fire from
heaven's altars to keep his sanctification red-hot, would
we not do well to profit by Paul's advice to Timothy?
The fact that you enjoy spiritual life does not contravene
the conclusion that you can be refreshed and revived indef-

initely. The fact that you have been baptized with the Holy Ghost and fire, and have the fire of God burning on the altar of your heart, in sin-consuming flames going through your entire being, does not disqualify you to receive more fire. Get hotter and more zealous for God and souls. We all, like Timothy, need to be 'revived and refired,' ever and anon, from God and of heaven. No danger of getting too hot.''

It is a verified baptism. When the long-looked-for day of Pentecost had come, and the conditions were all met, the promise was fulfilled; the baptism fell upon the waiting people, and they were all '' filled with the Holy Ghost.'' This, with Cornelius and his company (Acts x.), the Ephesian converts (Acts xix.), and with others, was repeated, making the early churches pre-eminently Spirit-baptized churches, and thousands of witnesses, some living, many now translated, attest to the same blessed baptism. Thus the reality of the baptism and its obtainability by the believer has been settled. In the mouths of multitudes of unimpeachable witnesses all has been established. It is a verified baptism.

It is a purifying baptism. Peter, divinely inspired, declaring the nature of its effect upon himself and others, said: '' God, which knoweth the heart, bare them witness, ... cleansing their hearts by faith '' (Acts xv. 8, 9). This is a deathblow to the popular notion that the baptism with the Holy Ghost does not eliminate car-, nality or inbred sin, but that one may be fully sanctified, and still have pride, lust, fear, envy, temper, impatience in the soul. No, no; a thousand times, no. Away, forever away, with the travesty on the work of the Holy Ghost, which would thus paralyze His power to expel the hornet's nest of depravity from the human heart. The purifying fire of the Holy Ghost eliminates all the dross of inbred sin, expels the seed of sin's disease, ejects the "old man" of indwelling evil, and fully sanctifies the soul. As regeneration, of which water baptism is the type, purifies the outer life and washes away all actual transgressions, so this baptism, symbolized by fire, melts and burns until all inner dross is purged away, and the soul thus purified is made "whiter than the snow." Glory!

It is an empowering baptism. It is the promised "power from on high," the "power of the Holy Ghost," eliminating the cancer of carnality that was sapping away the very citadel of the forces of spiritual life. It not only does this, but also imparts perfect soul-health; and not only this, but so enthrones Jesus within that His wisdom and power become continually available. Then when the enemy assaults or is charged, he finds One greater than himself or ourselves within, and in Jesus' strength through this blessed baptism we become "more than conquerors." This baptism transforms weaklings into giants, imparts all needed power to effectively witness, work, pray, preach, give, endure, deny, suffer, sing, write, shout, vote, or die for God as He may will. Henceforth the soul is so "strengthened with all power, according to the might of His glory, unto all patience and longsuffering with joy" (Col. i. 11), that in Jesus' name it is invincible.

It is a liberating baptism. Under its influence, the believer fully realizes "whom the Son makes free is free indeed," and emerges from a lower plane into the "glorious liberty," which is the privilege of every Christian. All bondage is henceforth broken. The soul at last is liberated. The cage of conventionalities and opinions and preconceived notions and dreaded censures is broken, and soaring away up into its native air, it mounts upon wings as eagles, and is sweetly, blessedly, fully *free*.

It is a joy-bringing baptism.   It is included under the
"these things" which Jesus revealed unto His disciples,
that "their joy might be full."   God wants glad people.
Sin has made them sad, the Holy Ghost will make them
glad; so that, under all circumstances, the joy of the
Lord is their strength, and they can take joyfully anything God sends or permits, from the snapping of a cur
to the "spoiling of their goods," or even the execution-
er's ax.

It is a fear-dispelling baptism.   Under its influence
cowardly Peters became bold conquerors.   Fear of the
world, of the dark, of robbers, of poverty, of enemies,
of death and the future, like howling wolves, all flee
before the Pèntecostal fire.   The "perfect love" which
it, and only it, imparts, indeed "casteth out all fear,"
that we "may have boldness in the day of judgment."

It is a carnality-killing baptism.   In a preceding paragraph we showed that it cleanses from all inbred sin.   A
stronger figure is needed and given in the Word.   Sin
within is represented as being "dead," that the "body
of sin might be done away" (Rom. vi. 6).   The electric
current from the Pentecostal battery completely electrocutes the "body of this death," so that the believer henceforth becomes dead indeed unto sin and alive unto God.
It is as if a defiant and boastful robber, chained in the
cellar, should suddenly be executed and his body ejected.

It is an establishing baptism.   Its recipients become
"steadfast in the faith," "rooted and grounded in love,"
"able, having done all, to stand."   It puts to shame the
shallow counterfeit of holiness which imparts no back-
bone, and yields easily to enticements and opposition.
The gifts of an empire, the allurements of pleasure, or
threats or tortures of the world, can neither move nor
confound those who possess this transforming gift.

Hence the primitive preachers proclaimed this experience early to believers. If such a course, as many false teachers claim, is calculated to "discourage young converts" then the Apostles were guilty of a great wrong. How Satan delights to substitute the nonsense of the schoolmen for the practices of the Pentecostal Church. Multitudes of saints who might have been confirmed, established, and mighty through God have been wrecked through this strategem of hell. Somebody will have their blood to answer for at the judgment. The plea that one might be accused of being "cranky" or a "hobbyist" will bring little comfort then.

It is an exhilarating baptism. It caused such intense spiritual intoxication that the people thought its possessors were drunk. They laughed and shouted so uproariously that it brought multitudes of people to see the strange new sight. It so planted the ecstasies of heaven in human hearts heretofore strangers to such soul-thrilling vibrations that they could not control their transports, and evidently they did not care to. Doubtless Rev. I. Culture was confused and disgusted at such a spectacle, Rev. F. O. R. Mality was shocked beyond expression, and Mr. and Mrs. H. Y. Pocrisy could not conceal their rage, and the whole Love Sin and Self Indulgent families, then, as now, could not "see that there was any religion in it"; but the saints rejoiced, Peter preached, God took care of the consequences, three thousand were converted in a day, and heaven and earth rejoiced. The disciples were so "drunk" that they were oblivious to "reputation," "dignitaries," political and ecclesiastical perils and persecutors. Is not a joy like that worth having? How the devil and his aids would like to persuade us that this was only for ministers and primitive times! Woe to the sham preachers who are propagating such a lie!

It is illuminating. It clarifies the spiritual vision, so that great Bible truths, which before were seen only in dim outline, appear to be gigantic Rocky Mountain ranges; what before seemed like narrow channels and little lakes of grace are transformed into Amazons, Niagaras and Atlantic Oceans. It puts people where they see in every sinner the possibility of a saint, and in every believer, of every clime and color, a near relation. It sweeps the soul suddenly into a glorious suntide of celestial light, where, walking in the light as God is in it, it realizes fellowship with Him and His family, and continually sees and feels and magnifies the cleansing blood.

It is the mainspring of true liberality. " Neither was there among them any that lacked: for as many as were possessors of lands or houses sold them, and brought the prices of the things that were sold, and laid them at the apostles' feet" (Acts iv. 34). Real Pentecostal fire consumes penuriousness and stinginess and closefistedness like a forest fire dry leaves. It melts the soul into a Pacific Ocean of divine love, on which fleets of salvation vessels continually move to save the lost. Niggardliness in a person who claims to have this baptism is like the eruption of small-pox on a man professing perfect health. (See chapter on " Pentecostal Giving.")

It is a drawing baptism. "And when this sound was heard, the multitude came together" (Acts ii. 6). For weeks people have been coming, afternoon and evening, to a Pentecostal meeting in this city. Where there is Pentecostal preaching, Pentecostal testimony, prayer, exhortation, convictions, conversions, sanctification, shouts, tears and triumph, there will the people be drawn together. A young man spoke in our yesterday's meeting who had been drawn all the way from Pennsylvania, for he knew not what, until he received this baptism.

It is a convicting baptism. "Now when they heard this, they were pricked in their heart, and said unto Peter and the rest of the apostles, Brethren, what shall we do?" (Acts ii. 37). This is a standing answer to the twaddle that this baptism should not be preached before the unsaved. Because John Wesley taught that only believers were eligible to this gift, many have perverted this into the error that the doctrine should not be preached in their presence. This is a device of the devil, as its preaching and testimony is one of the mightiest of convicting agencies, not only to unsanctified believers, but to the unconverted, as illustrated at Pentecost. How can a rebel be more effectively conquered than by telling not only of a pardon but of position and enjoyment in a life of complete loyalty? A drowning man will not slacken his efforts to board the life-boat if told that there is not only life in it, but clean clothes and an abundance of provisions. Conversion puts a man in the life-boat of salvation; this baptism clothes, arms, feeds and furnishes with a life-preserver. Hence its proclamation deepens conviction for these things.

It is a unifying baptism. "For in one Spirit were we all baptized into one body" (I. Cor. xii. 13). It burns away all barriers of creeds and color and clime, and cements in sacred bonds of holy love. Regeneration brings the believer into the family of God. This baptism eliminates all elements that would separate and alienate the members of the family. In meetings where this baptism is honored, all denominations mingle, of one heart and mind. Like a fierce, fiery furnace, it melts believers into one stream of liquid love.

It is essential to prevailing prayer. "For we know not

how to pray as we ought, but the Spirit himself maketh intercession for us with groanings which can not be uttered '' (Rom. viii. 26). Only Spirit-filled believers can be giants in prayer. Carnality in the heart, which is destroyed only by this baptism, obstructs the wires between the soul and God and often hinders communion with Him. Spirit-filled, Spirit-prompted, Spirit-answered, is God's order in the realm of prevailing prayer.

It is a tongue-loosening baptism. ''And they were all filled with the Holy Spirit, and began to speak with other tongues as the Spirit gave them utterance.'' Wherever the waters of a Pentecostal experience are turned on, the wheels of Pentecostal testimony begin to move. It was so at the upper chamber, with Cornelius, with the Ephesian converts, and is in all instances where it is received. It is God's cure for the spiritually tongue-tied and the spiritually dumb.

It is a confirming baptism. ''And they continued stedfastly in the apostles' teaching and fellowship, in the breaking of bread and the prayers'' (Acts ii. 42). Paul ''confirmed the churches'' by leading them to receive this experience. One reason why so many professed converts lapse is because so few ministers follow the Pauline example. And the reason why they do not follow this example is that they do not possess the experience. If all who aspire to be Joshuas and Pauls in leadership would actually follow their example in experience, they would swiftly lead multitudes up into the Canaan land of Pentecostal purity and power.

It is a soul-winning baptism. ''And the Lord added to them day by day those that were being saved'' (Acts ii. 47). It enables to so ''teach transgressors'' that sinners ''shall be converted unto God.'' It is to real revivals what steam and fire are to the engine—

the power that makes them go. The customary protracted meetings where this imperative Pentecostal condition is ignored thus advertise a deplorable lack of Scriptural
knowledge and experience, and their meagre, transient
and frequently fraudulent fruits are a forceful comment
on the folly of substituting human manipulation for
celestial dynamos.

It is abiding. "That he may be with you forever"
(John xiv. 16). The incoming of the Holy Ghost
cleanses the temple and adorns it. This is the baptism
with the Spirit. His indwelling, like the constant flow
of an artesian well, keeps it clean. Unless the conditions
of His remaining be violated, He will abide forever.
The soul-temple was created for this, redeemed for this,
and possessed by Him for this. He never will leave it
unless He should be grieved away. (See "Pentecostal
Light," by Rev. A. M. Hills.)

It is essential to final glorification. "But if the Spirit of
him that raised up Jesus from the dead dwelleth in you, he
that raised up Christ Jesus from the dead shall quicken also
your mortal bodies through his Spirit that dwelleth in you"
(Rom. viii. 11). Unless first baptized and purified by the
Spirit, He can not dwell in us, and if He dwell not
in us He can not quicken these bodies and glorify them
when Jesus comes, and thus culminate and climax all the
work of redemption which has preceded this.

It is a wonder-inspiring baptism. "And they were all
amazed and marvelled" (Acts ii. 7). The multitude
could neither understand the source of it nor the methods
of its operations. "Spiritual things are spiritually discerned." We have often seen crowds gather at Pentecostal meetings to look on with like amazement at manifestations which were Spirit-born. One of the proofs of

the defectiveness of much which is now called Pentecostal is that it excites no wonder.

It is a perplexing baptism. "And they were all amazed,
and were perplexed, saying one to another, What meaneth
this?" (Acts ii. 12). This baptism is supernatural. It
is as mysterious as the incarnation of Jesus. It is as high
above unenlightened human thought as the heavens are
above the earth. Spiritual-minded people accept it and
proclaim it as a divine revelation and work; unspiritual
people, whether in the ministry and church or out,
try to analyze it, and are always amazed, perplexed and
confounded at its essence and manifestations. As well
attempt to fathom infinite space, or understand all the
mysteries of creation, as for the natural man to know
this work of God.

It is a derided baptism. "But others mocking said,
They are filled with new wine" (Acts ii. 13). Derision
is usually an advertisement of weakness and lack of
argument. It is one of the world's favorite weapons.
It accused a Spirit-baptized people of being on a drunken
spree. It attributed the work of the Holy Spirit to the
work of unholy spirits. Modern formalists are guilty of
the same sin. If you laugh or weep or shout or leap
under the effect of this new wine of the kingdom, marvel
not if false professors at once turn upon you the gatling
guns of devilish derision, and rejoice that you are in good
company; for so persecuted they the prophets that were
before you.

It may be quenched. "Quench not the Spirit" (I.
Thess. v. 19). As water quenches fire, so the holy fire
kindled by this baptism may be quenched by turning upon
it the cold water hose of neglect of duty, failure to confess and disobedience to its promptings. (See "Quench
not the Spirit," by Rev. A. M. Hills.)

It is a death-dealing baptism.   First, it electrocutes the
"old man" of carnality in the believer's heart; and,
secondly, it, like a live electric wire, deals death to all
who tamper with it.   Witness the victim who tried to
steady the ark, Korah and his companions (Numbers
xvi.), Ananias and Sapphira and King Herod.   It is far
safer to play with lightning rods in a thunder storm than
to oppose this baptism or any of its manifestations.

It is limited to neither rank, sex, office nor nationality.
"For as many of you as were baptized into Christ did
put on Christ.   There can be neither Jew nor Greek,
there can be neither bond nor free, there can be no male
and female: for ye all are one man in Christ Jesus"
(Gal. iii. 27, 28).   The women received it at Pentecost,
and are divinely exhorted to use the gifts which it
imparts.   Stephen was one of its first fruits among the
laymen, and the baptism of Cornelius and his house is
Heaven's object lesson that it is for every name, age and
nationality.   Sammy Morris, the Kru boy; David of
India, and Amanda Smith, the sanctified slave, are among
the many modern proofs of this truth.

It is a transforming baptism.   "Now when they beheld
the boldness of Peter and John, and had perceived that
they were unlearned and ignorant men, they marvelled;
and they took knowledge of them, that they had been
with Jesus" (Acts iv. 13).   It transforms spiritual
weaklings into giants, spiritual simpletons into philoso-
phers, spiritual cowards into fearless captains of King
Jesus, that shout victory, breasting the combined assaults
of men and demons, of church and state.

It is subsequent to conversion.   It is promised only to
God's children.   All whom the Scripture records as
receiving it were already believers, like those at Pentecost, Cornelius and his family, the Ephesian converts,

and others.　All who really have it witness that they were convicted of the need of it, and received it after they were converted.　To confound it with conversion is like confounding the planting of a garden with the destruction of the weeds in it.　All who claim that the two are identical thus advertise both their own ignorance and lack of it, for all who feel its fiery flow have no trouble in telling the difference.

It is for believers only.　" Whom the world can not receive " (John xiv. 17).　" Now the natural man receiveth not the things of the Spirit of God: for they are foolishness unto him; and he can not know them, because they are spiritually judged " (I. Cor. ii. 14).　Both Christ and Paul agree that this baptism CAN NOT be received by worldlings.　God builds His spiritual temples only on the foundation of a regenerate life.　He resurrected Lazarus before He liberated him.　He does not propose to cleanse and furnish the devil's houses.　John did not baptize corpses with water, nor will Jesus baptize dead souls with fire.　Only believers living in the glorious light of conscious sonship of God received this baptism at Pentecost, or ever have since.　Others " CAN NOT."　God says so.　Hence the question is forever placed beyond controversy.　Hence the folly of pressing it upon the unconverted inside of church membership or out.　Yet it may be preached in their presence, and is one of the mightiest agencies for their conviction

It is instantaneous.　The three great works of Redemption which redeem man from the wreckage of sin, and restore him to final perfection are all instantaneous.　First, the Birth of the Spirit which embraces the pardon of all his actual sins, the resurrection of his soul from spiritual death and the enrollment of his name in the Lamb's book of life.　Second, his final glorification when

Jesus comes, by which all the effects of sin on his mind and body are to be eradicated, and his whole being celestialized. This is divinely declared to be wrought in the "twinkling of an eye." Third, the baptism with the Holy Ghost, by which inbred sin is eliminated and he is filled with God. This, like the two other epochal works above mentioned, is always instantaneous. It is preceded and followed by gradual unfoldings and enlightenments, but is, in the very nature of the case, wrought in an instant. "The Lord whom ye seek shall *suddenly* come to his temple" (Mal. iii. 1). "And *suddenly* there came from heaven a sound, . . . and they were all filled with the Holy Spirit" (Acts ii. 2-4). It is represented as a baptism to be administered, a "gift" to be taken, "water" to be drank, medicine to be administered and a Person to be received. Hence, as quickly as one may be baptized with water, reach out the hand and take a present, drink a draught, or "open the door" and welcome a friend, just so quickly may this baptism be obtained, yea, even quicker, as spiritual movements are more swift than physical. Every Scripture example of persons receiving it like the commandments, promises and figures, which teach its obligations, proclaim its instantaneousness, while the experience of all believers in all ages, of all names and ranks, which have verified its reality, like a mighty Niagara, unitedly and overwhelmingly testify to the same fact. Satan, through the teaching of "gradualism" by befogged schoolmen, has beguiled multitudes into the malarious fogs of indefiniteness who otherwise might have been rejoicing on the mountain tops of Pentecostal victory. One reading of the Bible through should convince the most stupid that this glorious spiritual baptism can not be obtained by growth or death or works or degrees, but must be an instantaneous act administered by Him whose right it is to baptize believers "with the Holy Ghost and fire." Beware, lest Satan and his preachers befog you, as all hell unite with him and his ministers to blind believers as to the present obtainability of this "inheritance of the saints in light."

It is conditioned on absolute abandonment to God. "Given to them that obey him" (Acts v. 32). If the ore refuses to submit to the fire it never will become pure gold and receive the governmental stamp. The great Teacher can not award this great prize to refractory pupils. They may seek it, pray for it, fast for it and sacrifice for it, but while a spark of dictation remains it never will be bestowed. Whatever the will is set on must be relinquished to the wiser will of God. It may be a friend, or a position, or reputation, or an anticipated feeling or experience, or unwillingness to go to the altar, or to meet some similar test. God must be obeyed or this baptism must be given up. It is divinely declared that only those who OBEY HIM can inherit this priceless legacy.

It is received by faith. "That upon the Gentiles might come the blessing of Abraham in Christ Jesus, that we might receive the promise of the Spirit through faith" (Gal. iii. 14). Like justification, this baptism is not through works nor growth, nor death nor creeds, but THROUGH FAITH. As Israel crossed the Red Sea and the River Jordan by faith, so the penitent's sins, through HIS FAITH, are drowned in the Red Sea of the Saviour's blood, and the believer, by FAITH, sweeps triumphantly through the Jordan of death to carnality into the spiritual Canaan-land promised to all the true children of Abraham. It is only those who BELIEVE that enter in to this "rest." When the soul dies to all but the will of God, drops every toy and treasure and grasps this promise in both hands with present abandonment to all of its conditions, then and thus its power is proved and benefits appropriated. Beware, reader, lest like backsliding Israel at Kadesh-barnea, you harden your heart by drawing back and so "enter not in because of unbelief."

It is received by earnest asking. "If ye then, being evil, know how to give good gifts unto your children, how much more shall your heavenly Father give the Holy Spirit to them that ask Him?" (Luke xi. 13). "These all with one accord continued stedfastly in prayer" (Acts i. 14). Importunate, united, believing, expectant prayer was the key that unlocked the Pentecostal chamber, and it is the only key that will unlock it. Jacob-like, the candidate for this degree must pray and fast and moan, "I will not let thee go, except thou bless me." When God's children, with a complete and reckless abandonment to Him, ask for this blood-bought gift, He will not say them nay. So His Word declares, Pentecost proves, and scores of living witnesses testify. Hallelujah!

The need of it must be confessed. Pardon and sonship are obtained on confession and abandonment of actual sins, and by faith in extended promises. The baptism with the Holy Ghost is received by the confession of inbred sin, death to everything contrary to God's will, and faith in the promises which offer it. As water baptism is administered to a yielding subject by the baptizer, so this baptism from the skies is bestowed by Jesus upon all who meet the conditions upon which it is promised. It is not received by growth or works, but by meeting the conditions above named. Reader, are you meeting them?

It is an indispensable baptism. Else God would not have preached it, provided it and commanded it; else

Jesus would not have purchased it and stand ready to administer it to all who will meet its conditions; else the Spirit would not create a hunger for it, and deepen conviction for it until all other lights grow dim if it be not possessed. Without it the old serpent of inbred sin, with all his children — Pride, Unbelief, Fear, Envy, Unholy Temper, Impatience and Selfishness — will lurk and coil and hiss in the dark jungles of the unsanctified heart. Without it there may be love, but never perfect love; peace, but not perfect peace; joy, but not fulness of joy; boldness, but not without fear; patience, but not perfect patience; life, but not fire; growth, but not without disease. Without it God is displeased, His commandments and promises unappropriated, spiritual gold mines of opportunities neglected, and souls lost that, with it, might be won, and the believer a burden for others to nurse and carry, when he should be an electric motor, radiating spiritual light and heat and motion. Reader, have you received this baptism? Are you now enjoying its glorious impartations? Are you heralding its blessedness?

LOST, SAVED, SANCTIFIED.

CHAPTER III.

By Pentecostal sanctification is meant sanctification as preached, professed, experienced and lived in the primitive Pentecostal church, and by all who now really possess it, in contrast with the dry, cold, argumentative, critical, dictatorial, theoretical or fanatical substitute which Satan is trying to palm off for the thing itself.

Pentecostal sanctification is the work which Jesus does in a believer when He baptizes him with the Holy Ghost.

All who have this baptism have Pentecostal sanctification; all who have Pentecostal sanctification have this baptism. Jesus is the Baptizer and Sanctifier; the believer, the subject; the Holy Ghost, the element; the Word, the baptismal bowl; the blood, the purchase price; and God the Father designs it, wills it and gave the Son to effect it.

The believer submits to the Baptizer, obeys the Word, trusts the blood, receives the Holy Ghost, and praises God the Father for the glorious results.

It is bestowed by Jesus. "But of him are ye in Christ Jesus, who was made unto us wisdom from God, and righteousness and sanctification, and redemption: that, according as it is written, He that glorieth, let him glory in the Lord" (I. Cor. i. 30, 31). Christ bestows it, and all the glory of it should be given, not to self or others, but to him. Even the Word itself may be so unduly magnified as to rob Him of glory due for doing the work which it represents.

It is through the Spirit. "In sanctification of the

Spirit, unto obedience and sprinkling of the blood of Jesus Christ'' (I. Pet. i. 2). Thus Peter unequivocally declares it to be through the Spirit.

It is received by obeying the truth. ''Seeing ye have purified your souls in your obedience to the truth unto unfeigned love of the brethren, love one another from the heart fervently'' (I. Pet. i. 22). Jesus prayed, ''Sanctify them in the truth: thy word is truth'' (John xvii. 17). Peter declared the Saviour's prayer answered in its verification among those to whom he wrote.

It is through the blood. ''Wherefore Jesus also, that he might sanctify the people through his own blood, suffered without the gate'' (Heb. xiii. 12). Thus sanctification is the great object of the atonement, and the blood is its purchase price. He who rejects it rejects the blood. He does not believe, and is therefore an infidel. The paralysis of the church is largely due to practical infidelity at this point, in both pulpit and pew.

It is the will of God. ''For this is the will of God, even your sanctification, that ye abstain from fornication'' (I. Thess. iv. 3). Here is clearly declared: First, that sanctification is the will of God. Who then dare criticise it, or oppose it, or even be indifferent about it? Second, that it is God's remedy for fornication. Worldliness is spiritual fornication. Regeneration gives up the world; entire sanctification burns inbred sin with all its worldward bents out of the heart and imparts such a love for celestials as to make one loathe the insipid water from the stagnant pools of worldom. All truly saved people renounce the world—dancing, circuses, theaters, horse races, etc., but all really sanctified people abominate them.

It was a source of apostolic rejoicing. ''But we are bound to give thanks to God alway for you, brethren, beloved of the Lord, for that God chose you from the beginning unto salvation in sanctification of the Spirit and belief of the truth" (II. Thess. ii. 13).   Paul did not bewail its possession by his people, but "was bound to give thanks" because of it; hence different from many of his spurious followers.

The Pentecostal gallery not only gleams with the electric lights of Pentecostal doctrines, but is vocal with the songs and shouts of Pentecostal experiences.   The truth of entire sanctification not only dazzles by its brightness, but its experiences attract by their beauty and power.   In studying them we see the doctrine in-carnated in human beings of like natures with our-selves, and thus behold what it is able to do and what we, the Church, the world, and God have a right to expect of it in us.   Let us examine them, and if our experience can meet the test we may rejoice in what God has done for us; if it does not, we can be glad for what he is able to do and has made provision for.   As there is no Scriptural statement to the contrary, but many facts to prove it, we may rest assured that the heart experi-ences of the primitive Church are available to believers to-day.   Even a casual reading of Scripture shows the following facts in regard to Pentecostal Sanctification:

It was not a work which exempted from infirmities, temptation, danger of falling, or mistakes; for it is divinely recorded that the best of Apostolic people were "in heav-iness through manifold temptations," "encompassed with infirmities," needed to "take heed" when they thought they stood "lest they fall," and, like Peter, had to be rebuked for mistakes.   It is not a work that dispenses with growth in grace nor Christian activity, for its pos-sessors exemplified both and exhorted others to do like-wise.   It imparts no new graces, but it eradicates all the weeds of carnality which hinder the flowers planted at Regeneration, and also insures the abiding presence of the indwelling Comforter, which amazingly facilitates their growth.

It is not a work that in any way fosters fanaticism, for the Pentecostal church was largely free from that, howbeit much in it now and then is termed fanaticism by formalists.

It is nowhere in the New Testament called a " deeper work " or "higher life " or "more religion," but was indicated by terms chosen by the Holy Ghost, upon whose words human vanity has so often felt that it could improve.

It is not obtained by works, growth, repression, imputation, death nor degrees. No hint of its obtainment in any of these ways can be found between the two lids of the Bible, nor in any New Testament example. These notions were born in hell, and have been palmed off on dead or sleeping professors, to keep from receiving this fire.

It is not confined to the ministry or to the Jews. It was promised and received by all who would meet its conditions. "The promise is to you and your children."

Those who teach that it was only for the apostles advertise an ignorance of sanctification inexcusable. Its possession by Cornelius and his house (Acts x.), the Ephesian converts (Acts xiv.), and the whole tenor of Scripture commands, promises and provisions all combine to rebuke the ignorance and sin of such teachers. It would be no less absurd to teach that air and sunshine was confined to them alone.

It is not identical with conversion. Only persons truly converted can receive it, or are urged to seek it.

It confers the following named benefits, which regeneration, as high as its standard is, does not impart. As this subject is embraced in "Pentecostal Baptism," treated in the preceding chapter, much there magnified applies also to it.

It is a badge of brotherhood. "For both he that sanctifieth and they that are sanctified are all of one: for which cause he is not ashamed to call them brethren" (Heb. ii. 11). Worldly persons are ashamed of this badge, but Jesus is proud of it. Keep your eyes on them and you will be tempted to hide it. Keep your eyes on Him and you will gladly and openly wear it and welcome any odium that thus may come from those who do not see its work. Those who have this badge and grip are initiated into spiritual secrets compared to which those of secret worldly orders are as dross.

The following are among its transcendently glorious accompaniments:

A clean heart. "Blessed are the pure in heart, for they shall see God" (Matt. v. 8). "Cleansing their hearts by faith" (Acts xv. 9). Thus the Word settles beyond all controversy that entire sanctification through baptism of the Spirit completely cleanses the soul.

Perfect peace. "And peace from God" (Phil. i. 2). Peace be "multiplied" (II. Pet. i. 2). Regeneration implants peace with God; sanctification eliminates all discordant elements from the heart, so that the peace of God and the maturity which follows continue to multiply until they reach degrees beyond expression. Glory! What a contrast to the spurious profession that bristles at a single rebuff.

It is an overcoming experience. It imparts the power which Jesus promised "over all the power of the enemy," so that one may quench every fiery dart and his shield still be strong enough to have turned them had they been a millionfold more furious and frequent. Made "more than conquerors through him that loved us"; the devil is defeated, his weapons captured, his hosts subdued and there remains enough reserve force in God to have more than whipped ten million devils, though they had assaulted in men mightier than Goliath, or enticed by beauty a thousandfold greater than that of Delilah. Glory! A marked contrast to much modern stuff labeled entire sanctification, which falls under the first round from the devil's batteries.

It imparts perfect love. "Unto unfeigned love of the brethren" (I. Peter i. 22). It expels everything from the soul that is contrary to perfect love. It melts envy and malice and pride and all kindred passions, and keeps the soul too warm for their return. It not only loves its enemies, and prays for them, but would do it were they tenfold more bitter than they are, and then have an exhaustless reserve left. This grace is beautifully manifest in the life of Jesus by His prayer for His enemies upon the cross, and in the similar prayer of Stephen for his persecutors.

It gives a surplus of holy courage. Regeneration brings a sort of daring, but, like Peter's, it fails when needed most. The baptism with Holy Ghost and fire destroys all carnal fear, and places dauntless Courage on the throne. It enables its possessor to look his enemy in the face with perfect confidence of victory. Ecclesiastical and political Sanhedrims lose their terrors, and can be met with a smile and shout of victory, with the battle-cry, "If God be for us, who can be against us?" It can face all earth and hell in arms, and so meet them that they will quake and fly. It glories in cutting loose from all worldly moorings, that the divine source of its strength may be known and magnified. Gideon-like it sends to the rear thousands of faint-hearted followers, crucifies every questionable desire, and shouting, "The sword of the Lord and Gideon," puts every foe to flight. The counterfeit thing shows the white flag to save its own scalp.

It gives a surplus of delight in the path of duty. No matter how arduous the task or threatening the pathway, people possessing the Pentecostal blessing have an intense longing for it. It may be the thorn every step of the way and fagots and the stake at the end, but they welcome it as a bride the bridegroom, with open arms. It is a fact that laws had to be enacted in the early church to keep Christians from needlessly exposing themselves to martyrdom, so ardent was their love for the way that Jesus went. Temporal rewards and salaries for service were unasked in the presence of this primitive grace. The bliss of the labor was love's sweetest reward, and the harder the discipline the brighter the crown. Under such an administration a hireling ministry could not well be. Many to-day enjoy a similar experience. All who possess Pentecostal sanctification are proving its reality. An empty profession can not bear this test, but prefers being fed to fighting, and deems self-denial and hard work drudgery.

Fulness of spiritual joy. Not that there will be no sorrow, but that one may be "sorrowful yet always rejoicing." This joy may manifest itself in many ways —in smiles, laughter, songs, shouts, praises, or leaping. True religion does not consist simply in joy and its manifestations, but a religion which has no spiritual joy in it is the devil's cheat, and he has palmed it off on many hell-bound victims. Those who feel its ecstasies will always disdain the jokes, jests and worldly amusements which worldlings inside the church and out love

so well. The "amusement apostasy" in the churches is
an advertisement of spiritual death. With a fulness of
unspeakable, everlasting joy believers have no desire for
Satan's rib-tickling substitutes, such as are frequently
vended under the cloak of religion by spurious churches.
What a contemptible farce! And if such be the stream,
how deplorable the fountain from which it flows! How
vitiated the tastes of those who drink! How criminal
the action of those who, by their presence or silence, say
amen to such a desecration and fraud! How disappointed
the husbandman who finds these "Apples of Sodom"
where there should be Holy Ghost fruit! Not only does
Pentecostal sanctification impart the joy that despises
all worldly substitutes, but a joy that could rejoice in
the midst of famines and persecutions greater than ever
known, and then have a surplus not exhausted. It can
take "joyfully the spoiling of its goods," and has been
known to shout at the funeral of a loved one. A letter
from one who has it lies before me. It reads: "I am in
the burning, fiery furnace, but the form of the Son of
God is with me, so I sing, 'Hallelujah to the King!'"
What a contrast to the spiritual life that wilts when the
weather is warm and to the detestable, sinning religion
which Mr. and Mrs. Mirth, Mr. and Mrs. Hypocrisy,
Mr. and Mrs. Pride, Mr. and Mrs. Formality, and all
their relatives, with the endorsement of the men of Big-
Head Theological University, have substituted instead
of Bible religion. A puny corpse twitched by an electric
current where God would have a panoplied spiritual
giant putting ten thousand foes to flight.

Perfect assurance. "Unto all riches of the full assurance of understanding" (Col. ii. 2). The Ishmael of
doubt being electrocuted, the Isaac of full assurance rejoices in the fulness of faith.

> " Perfect assurance, Jesus is mine.
> O what a foretaste of glory divine,
> Heir of salvation, purchased of God,
> Born of His Spirit, cleansed through the blood."

People who live in Doubting Castle, yet profess Pentecostal sanctification, by their words and looks give the lie to their professions.

Perfect patience. "Unto all patience and longsuffering with joy" (Col. i. 12). Entire sanctification eliminates all the dross of impatience and leaves the pure gold of perfect patience, which can endure the most vexatious trials with joy. I. Cor. xiii. declares that love endureth all things. Before entire sanctification this endurance is marred by protests of the carnal mind; afterwards it reigns with no such rival. The professed experience of entire sanctification that gets miffed and provoked and irritated is a libel on the name, and should lead its possessors to tarry at the chamber where all such chaff is burned up.

It is accompanied by an exuberance of fruitage. "Bearing fruit in every good work" (Col. i. 10). "Every branch that beareth fruit he cleanseth it, that it may bear more fruit" (John xv. 2). "Herein is my Father glorified, that ye bear *much fruit*" (John xv. 8). In regeneration the branch bears some fruit; the Pentecostal purgation promotes it into a realm of "fruitfulness in every good work." The indwelling Spirit gives point, **power** and success to every prayer, praise, testimony, sermon and article, so that "*Whatsoever* he doeth shall prosper," is verified in the believer. It may not always *look* so, but it always *is* so. Bishop Taylor, spending his old age in Africa winning thousands for God, is one of many illustrations of this truth.

It appropriates abounding grace. "But where sin

abounded, grace did abound more exceedingly" (Rom. v. 20). It sings and feels,

> Plenteous grace with thee is found,
> Grace to banish all my woes.
> How the healing stream abounds,
> SAVES and FILLS and OVERFLOWS.

It remembers with embarrassment when it was skeptical about God being able to give a "know-so conversion" and would not entertain the thought of his power cleansing completely, sanctifying wholly and imparting a Pentecostal experience of constant victory. Such was its former contemptible conception of the God of nature and of Grace! Once Grace seemed like the glimmer of a candle, now like a whole universe of light in which it floats and flies and works. Instead of croning, "I can't help sinning," as it did before conversion, or "It's hard to keep sin down," like it did before the Pentecostal baptism, it now shouts, "God makes all grace abound towards me, so that always having *all sufficiency in all things*, I abound in every good work." He "supplies every need," and were trials and needs and distresses a millionfold greater, his grace would still be sufficient with an infinite and exhaustless surplusage. This view inspired the early Church with the spirit of resistless conquest on every battlefield. Such a God can just as easily cast out one million devils as one; forgive the blackest sinner as any other; cure a disease or depraved appetite as a "nervous spell"; sanctify wholly as to save in spots. In the might of this experience the early Church unreservedly and uncompromisingly planted itself right in the centers of heathendom, and rescued men from stronger than iron chains of habit, customs, superstitions and sins which Satan had been forging around them for ages. Who shall say that when the Pentecostal experience becomes as frequent as then, that the Church will not possess its former power? The devil says no, and opinionated schoolmen have echoed his answer until multitudes believe it. This notion was born in hell and is welcomed by people with no experience or low stock to apologize for their own destitute condition. Rejecting this pessimistic view of grace, let it be remembered that its infinite provisions can redeem, and save, and sanctify, and glorify a million of little worlds like ours, and that this would be but a single drop out of its infinite ocean. Glory! Under its influence the apostolic church belted the globe with salvation without any appeals for financial help from either Jews or Romans, or the aid of a single "patent pill" advertisement. They lived, as an old saint testified, "Away up in the exceedinglies." Pentecostal sanctification cuts all restraining cords, so that, balloon-like, one sweeps right up into this sweet atmosphere. Wanted—millions of souls who will make the ascent.

It makes its possessor like Jesus. Any professed Pentecostal sanctification which fails at this point is a spurious, broken bridge. One of God's servants says:

"Jesus loved and prayed for His enemies. Do you? He did not complain, though He had nowhere to lay His head. Do you? He did not murmur when all forsook Him and fled. Do you? He went among the poor and lowly to lead them to God. Do you? He denied Himself comfort and ease that others might find peace to their troubled souls. Do you? When Jesus met a person or company of persons He talked to them of eternal things. Do you? He that said for 'every idle word men should give account to God,' never engaged in foolish talking or jesting. Do you? Jesus said that 'men should pray everywhere'; and He prayed much, sometimes whole nights. Do you? Jesus was so earnest in prayer for a lost world that He prayed, 'being in agony.' Are you? Jesus, like a 'lamb before his shearers,' was dumb, and patiently endured mocking and shame. Do you? Jesus was 'separate from sinners.' Are you? Christ was 'holy, harmless and undefiled.' Are you? Jesus had such love for those who crucified Him that He prayed, 'Father, forgive them, for they know not what they do.' Have you? It is written, 'If any man have not the spirit of Christ he is none of his.'"

Pentecostal sanctification places its possessor where by grace he meets the Scriptural tests named in this and the preceding chapter. Tried by these, much under its name may be found wanting. All who have mistaken conversion or reclamation for Pentecostal sanctification doubtless will be tempted to pull this Scriptural standard down to the level of their own experiences. Reader, do not do this. *Get your experience up to the standard.* Others who are tugging away at the cracked pump of a mere theoretical profession will be exposed to a similar temptation, and should at once abandon the pump and apply to the celestial water-works for the artesian well of a Pentecostal experience.

All is not Pentecostal that sails under that name. All may not be fully sanctified who fight in its defense. Its possession is its best defense. Its proclamation and testimony will convince and conquer where learning and logic are lame.

Satan pales at the havoc which the advance of genuine Pentecostal experiences are making in his territory. Hence all earth and hell are moved to divert from its possession. Through this Satanic influence it is largely rejected, ignored or opposed by professed Christian pulpit and press. It is frequently misrepresented and derided.

Men who are loyal to it are degraded from influential to humbler spheres. I recently met an able, eloquent and scholarly minister who had been changed from a four thousand dollar to a three hundred dollar charge for this cause. Its obtainment is not only discouraged, but its testimony opposed. Another favorite strategem of Satan is to palm off a spurious profession for the genuine work. Hence he bends his best energies to dupe people into the absurd, unscriptural belief that regeneration bestows it, or that it is simply an experience of "more power," but does not eradicate inbred sin. He succeeds in getting influential men to help him propagate this lie, and thus deceive the multitudes. One mark of those who profess the defective work is that at some point under Scriptural tests of the genuine work their experience fails. There is reason to believe that there are many who profess this grace whom Satan has thus deceived. Reader, are you among that number? Now, as in Elijah's crucial hour, God's answer is by fire. Does it fall upon you? Is it burning in your heart?

> "Refining fire, go through each heart,
>   Illuminate each soul;
>   Scatter thy light through every part
>   And sanctify the whole."

It embraces the crucifixion and death of self. "Knowing this, that our old man was crucified with him, that the body of sin might be done away" (Rom. vi. 6). A sanctification that does not electrocute indwelling evil is a Satanic humbug, and its advocates among the most effective obstructors to the genuine work of Christ.

> "My friends may say I'll ruined be,
>   If I die.
>   If I leave all and follow Thee,
>   But I'll die.

Their arguments will never weigh,
Nor stand the trying judgment day;
Help me to cast them all away,
  Let me die.

"Oh, I must die to scoffs and jeers,
  Let me die.
I must be freed from slavish fears,
  Let me die.
So dead that no desire shall rise
To pass for good, or great, or wise,
In any but my Saviour's eyes:
  Let me die."

It is by faith. "An inheritance among them that are sanctified by faith in me" (Acts xxvi. 18). Like the baptism with the Spirit, with which it is identical, it is by simple faith. See preceding chapter. Not by growth, or works, or rites, or time, or death, but by simple faith in Jesus. Faith is the golden key that opens the windows of heaven to let the blessing fall. This faith must be accompanied by absolute abandonment to God in everything, otherwise it is false.

Obedience and faith are one at this point. "And we see that they were not able to enter in because of unbelief" (Heb. iii. 19). Unbelief was the fatal key with which the children of Israel locked themselves out of the promised land into the burning wilderness, and with the same key many are now doing the same thing. "Take heed lest there be in any of you an evil heart of unbelief."

Reader, are you in possession of this priceless pearl? Like gold hidden in the mine, it must be sought if found. Jesus deposited an infinite price in heaven's bank to purchase it for you. Satan is seeking to keep you from its possession. It will prove a balm for all your wounds, a solace for all your sorrows, an invulnerable defense against all your foes.   If it is not yet yours, will you not NOW, in view of God's requirements and provisions and your own needs, the fearful consequence of neglect both here, at the Judgment and through eternity, seek until it is yours — fast, pray, abandon, die and believe until God shall open the "windows of heaven, and pour you out" this priceless gift?

For fuller treatment of the subject of this chapter, the reader is referred to "The Double Cure," "Christ Crowned Within," and "Out of Egypt," by the writer of this book, and the works of Carradine, Keen, Godbey, Pickett, Hills and other standard writers on this theme.

CHAPTER IV.

PENTECOSTAL CONVERTS.

Pentecostal converts are those who are "born of the Spirit." Their lives witness to the electric character of their birth. They are as different from the superficial, spurious professions which abound on every hand as a strong, noble man is from a sawdust dummy. A Pentecostal church and ministry naturally bring forth the offspring of stalwart converts. Counterfeit converts shrink from Scripture tests, but these welcome them, and always bear the following marks:

They possess spiritual life. Their lives are hid with Christ in God, and this life "no man taketh from them," for it is the life of God in the soul.

They are full of spiritual activity. The life within manifests itself in many ways. They are ever engaged about their Father's business, and glad to "go work," in even the humblest place in His vineyard. Spiritual inactivity is positive proof of spiritual sickness or death.

They are loyal converts. Not always loyal to ecclesiastical church committees and worldly methods of backslidden churches; but they are loyal to Christ, and love Him and keep His commandments, and do those things that are "pleasing in His sight." They are living comments on the truth of the divine declaration that "he that is born of God doth not commit sin." They are committed to everlasting loyalty to the Son of God, the Word of God, the Spirit of God and the Church of God.

They are transformed converts. With them old things

have passed away, and all things are become new. Old companions, old books, old thoughts, old habits and old amusements have all given place to new songs, new thoughts, new companions and new associations. Professed converts in whom no such changes have taken place labor under a terrible delusion.

They are convicted converts. The light of the Holy Spirit shining in their hearts and the life of Jesus there soon reveals the presence of inbred sin. Its uprisings of fear, and sin, and pride, and envy, and unbelief, and temper, sooner or later reveal to them the need of the sanctifying baptism with the Holy Ghost, which will utterly expel these noxious weeds and make the soul a blooming garden of the Lord; for this they hunger and thirst, and pray and seek, and confess their need until the work is wrought and they rejoice in all the "fulness of the blessing of the Gospel of peace."

They are soul-seeking converts. One of the first tendrils that shoots from the vine of a truly converted soul is the desire to see others saved. This desire prompts to earnest effort and prayer, to awaken others and lead them to the Saviour. This leads to fasting and personal warnings, and invitations and the distribution of books and tracts and papers designed to lead into experiences of salvation. Professors who are asleep to the peril of those surrounding them, and make no efforts to save them, thus give positive proof that they themselves are not regenerated.

They are illuminated converts. Jesus, the light of the world, is shining in their hearts and on their pathway. All lesser lights are now dim, as they have turned to follow Him wherever He may lead, and walking in the light as He is in the light, they taste the blessedness of

His fellowship, and will never rest until they know the blood applied which cleanses from all sin.

They are rich converts. Their names are enrolled among the number of whom it has been divinely declared that they shall "inherit all things." Their treasure is laid up, not in the breaking banks of earth, but in the vaults of the skies, where robbers can not come nor rust destroy. When earth shall melt and suns and systems disappear, their wealth will keep on increasing in values which figures can not measure.

They are divinely protected converts. He who toucheth them "toucheth the apple" of God's eye. It were better for all such that a millstone were hanged about their necks and they were cast into the sea. God holds them in the hollow of His hand and no man is able to pluck them out. In the presence of wicked men and devils they can triumphantly sing and shout, "Thanks be unto God, who giveth us the victory."

They are unworldly converts. They can not be otherwise, for it is divinely declared that if "any man love the world, the love of the Father is not in him." They have renounced its pomp and glory, "with all covetous desires for the same, so that they will not follow" or be led by it. Worldly fandangoes and fraternities inside the church or out have lost their charms to them, for a bright and morning Star has risen on their sight which dims their vision to all lesser lights. The worldly convert is always a counterfeit convert. Worldliness is spiritual treason, and worldly churches are the devil's churches, worldly· preachers his ministers, worldly professors his members.

They are Christlike converts. Jesus was born in a manger, and His dying couch was a rugged cross. He came to minister to others, not to be coddled. He stooped to the vilest, and no place was too humble if His Father's interests could be served. How different from His professed followers, who shun the cross, evade missions and meetings that are lowly and unpopular, and substitute starch and sentiment for sanctity.

They are church-going converts. "Not forsaking the assembling of ourselves together, as the custom of some is" (Heb. x. 25). Professed converts, who have no affinity for public services, are deceived. God's true children love to mingle and unite in their praises, prayers and professions. Lukewarmness at this point is a certain symptom of a fatal disease.

They are Sabbath-keeping converts. They realize that the Sabbath law is not abrogated, and so delight in keeping it holy. Sunday newspapers have no welcome in their homes. They plan to dispense with all needless labor on that day, and to spend it in restful, worshipful service, such as God delights to bless. Spurious converts seek their own pleasure instead of God's glory on this holy day. True ones find their highest joy in its glad observance.

They are the product of a live church. A cold, dead, formal church will freeze converts to death. Babies, however well born, would soon die on an iceberg. A mother who does not love children can not mother them. The church that does more to fill her ranks with worldlings, who will give her social influence and money, than with souls born of God can have no spiritual children. Many modern revival reports should read, "One hundred bastards born," instead of "One hundred conversions." Whether there should be weeping or rejoicing over revival statistics depends upon their character. If the quality is bad, the bigger the worse. If its converts are not born of God, and yet think they are and profess to be, as in many instances, the revival is one of deception and hypocrisy, instead of true religion. Such are not converts of Pentecostal ministers and churches. Now as then true converts bear the marks of divine and heavenly birth. All who lack this should forsake every false way and fly to God for salvation.

They are in God the Father. "Paul, and Silvanus, and Timothy, unto the church of the Thessalonians in God the Father and the Lord Jesus Christ: Grace to you and peace" (I. Thess. i. 1). Bible regeneration takes the soul out of the world and makes it a living branch of the true vine. He who is not in God is in the world. When such persons profess to be saved they call God a liar, and, as a rule, deceive no one but themselves. The threshing machine of conviction and conversion separates the soul from the straw of sin and the world, and stores it safely into the granary of God's justifying grace. Entire sanctification cleans out the chaff and cockle, and fits it for use or market.

They are a source of joy to true ministers. "We give thanks to God always for you all, making mention of you in our prayers" (I. Thess. i. 2). The greatest weight to Pentecostal pastors is unconverted church members. They can not rejoice in them, for they are the devil's most effectual barriers to the advancement of God's kingdom, and the only ray of hope the preacher has is that God's grace is able to transform them. Truly converted souls are sources of comfort, strength and inspiration. They have the faith which prompts them to work. It is the mainspring of ceaseless activity in God and for God. The base substitute of worldly works with which Satan counterfeits this in sham professors is one of his shrewdest traps. Thus duped people run a ceaseless round of worldly activities trying to palm this off under the label of "church work," for the genuine. But God is not mocked, and there is no place for such converts in His Church. Fairs, festivals, card socials and other schemes for worldly amusements in the church are an offence unto God, an abominable stench which he will not tolerate in His Church. They are the sickly offspring of spurious faith, a decaying corpse of dead "works," usurping the place of Spirit-inspired activity. Prayer, and praise, and liberality, personal appeal and testimony bud, blossom and ripen from every truly converted soul as naturally as fruit from a healthy peach tree.

Love is the mainspring of their labor. "Remembering without ceasing your work of faith, and labour of love, and patience of hope in our Lord Jesus Christ, before our God and Father" (I. Thess. i. 3). Divinely imparted love impels them. Loving God, they desire to please Him; loving man, they try to be a blessing to him; loving their enemies, they pray for them. Love to God and man is an incentive of all the efforts of the truly saved. Zeal for the church, and its societies and some of its members may exist where this love is wholly lacking. True love lives for God and others, sham love for self.

They are hopeful converts. "And patience of hope" (I. Thess. i. 3). They do not hope that they are saved, for this they *know*, but that God will keep them to the end, and that soon the Saviour will return, and that they shall reign with Him forever. This hope has a good foundation in every truly converted person, and is an anchor to the soul, both "sure and steadfast." What a contrast to the "hope" of sham religionists, which is built on the quicksands of self or church or creed, and destined soon to perish!

They are "know-so" converts. "Knowing, brethren beloved of God, your election" (I. Thess. i. 4). Not a hope-so, think-so, guess-so, maybe-so delusion, but the certain knowledge of their enrollment in the book of life. An assurance which neither men nor devils can take from them.

They have peace with God. They have been at war with Him, but now have fully surrendered, and made their peace with Him. It is the sweet, restful peace that Jesus gives to all who serve Him, in contrast with the false, deathly peace with which Satan tries to comfort those who try to believe they are saved when they are not.

They are followers of Jesus. They follow others only as others follow Him. "And ye became imitators of us, and of the Lord, having received the word in much affliction, with joy of the Holy Ghost" (I. Thess. i. 6). They not only eulogize the Saviour and His ministers, but exemplify them. The will and smiles of Jesus are worth more to them than the honors, pleasure and wealth of all the world. They will go nowhere that Jesus and His true ministers can not go. This principle keeps from circuses, godless lodge-rooms, church fandangoes, dances, saloons, theaters and kindred places of evil. Many people, like a guide-board, point the right way, but never go that way themselves. They profess a truth and act a lie at the same time. The Pharisees of all ages do this, and in so doing sink to their doom. Pentecostal converts, warned by their example, shun their fate.

They provoke and endure persecution. Because they are not of the world, the world hates them. They renounce the world so completely that the world in turn renounces and denounces them. A regeneration which provokes no such persecution is not from God. A conversion that can not endure persecution for Christ needs to be reconverted. The Thessalonians "received the Word in much affliction," and all who really receive it must prepare for similar experiences. The enemy is restrained now, as not then, but still harbors the same hatred towards the sons of God. People in this city endure martyrdom for Him as truly as did those of the apostolic church. Justification brings the grace to *endure* persecution, the baptism with the Holy Ghost enables to *rejoice* and be exceedingly glad in it. Those who can do neither are not the children of God. Early Christians were disowned, betrayed, threatened, arrested, tortured and killed; all but the last are of common occurrence to-day among converts of the Pentecostal type.

They are joyful converts. "Having received the Word in much affliction, with joy of the Holy Ghost" (I. Thess. i. 6). Birth of the Spirit always brings joy of the Spirit. A joyless religion is a Christless religion and a hopeless religion. Conversion brings joy; entire sanctification eliminates from the heart every weed that would choke it. Growth develops and matures it. "No joy, no salvation" is as true as "twice two are four." It is not a condition of salvation, but an inevitable result of it. When the great Musician touches the keys of the soul with salvation, it is one of the sweetest notes which thrill it. Though afflicted, they rejoice in it. The first work brings rejoicing Isaac into the heart, the second banishes mocking Ishmael and enables to shake jails with songs and shouts of joy. What an enigma to cruel, persecuting and intriguing priests. How different from the glum, sad, resentful, sanctimoniousness of spurious professors. What a contrast to the superficial, worldly, carnal jollity which blind devotees of worldliness seek to substitute for it! The first is a stream pure and exhaustless, its fountain, God Himself. The other is surface water oozing from the swamps of

sin, soon evaporated and gone forever. Reader, which
have you?

They are missionary converts. "For from you hath
sounded forth the word of the Lord, not only in Macedonia and Achaia, but in every place your faith to God-
ward is gone forth; so that we need not to speak anything" (I. Thess. i. 8). The Word of God "sounded
out" from them. Salvation saves from selfishness.
Saved themselves, they speed to bring others to their
great Physician. A saved man, who has been cured of
a fatal disease, free of charge, will commend the physician to others thus afflicted. His neighbors will hear of
it. Live grapevines send out new shoots and tendrils;
dead ones do not. All of God's children are born with a
missionary spirit. One positive proof of the alarmingly
prevalent dead branches in the churches is the indiffer-
ence to missionary appeals and small offerings for missions. Hundreds of thousands of professed Christians
give nothing at all. Truly, such shall be cast forth
as branches, and gathered and burned. No interest or
investment in mission work is positive proof of no title
to heaven. Better writhe under this truth now and get
right than to reject the warning and writhe forever when
it is too late.

They are not sanctified wholly. All of Paul's epistles
are largely exhortations to the churches to be fully sanctified, and are full of facts which prove that truly converted people in them were not thus baptized. They
were "yet carnal," showing that carnality had never
been eradicated. Pentecostal converts always have a
parallel experience. The light imparted at regeneration
very soon reveals to them inbred sin and the need of the
cleansing baptism. Pentecostal preaching now, as then,
keeps this truth before them. Converts who claim that

they were fully sanctified when converted, are unenlightened, or never were regenerated. Paul calls his converts his "glory and joy," yet longs to "perfect that which is lacking in their faith," to the end that he may establish their hearts "unblamable in holiness before God." Whatever is loved more than God is an idol, and must be abandoned to enter God's kingdom. Repentance renounces all idols; regeneration enthrones the true God, while sanctification eliminates all within which does not harmonize with Him.

They have no idols. It matters not whether an idol be self, or wife, or child, or reputation, or money, or dress, or fame, or gods of wood or stone, it must be dethroned before Christ can be enthroned. This subtle sin is secretly ensnaring more than drink. Men and women guilty of the grossest heart-idolatry pose as worshipers of the true God. They hire godless choirs to entertain themselves and popular preachers to please themselves, and dare to flaunt such insults in the face of Omnipotence for worship. For answer, He thunders back in His righteous wrath: "I hate, I despise your feasts, and I will take no delight in your solemn assemblies. Yea, though ye offer me your burnt offerings and your meal offerings, I will not accept them" (Amos v. 21, 22).

They are Bible-reading converts. "Now, these were more noble than those in Thessalonica, in that they received the Word with all readiness of mind, examining the Scriptures daily, whether these things were so" (Acts xvii. 11). They both searched the Scriptures and conformed to them. No human say-so with them could be substituted for a "thus saith the Lord." A true Christian welcomes all the light which shines from the Word, let the consequences be what they may. It is a delusion to place feelings, imaginations, human counsels and aids in its place. They searched the Scriptures. Some read them, others study them, and still others search them. There is no more infallible mark of the spuriousness of many professed conversions than this lack of love for the Word. People who are unscriptural in their practices, and have no love for searching the Bible, may be professors of religion, but are in no wise possessors of salvation. Pentecostal converts need this unmistakable New Testament test.

They are penitent converts. Repentance is the first step up the ascent which leads into the temple of regeneration. None can enter without taking this step, and none can abide herein without keeping it. The hope of a professed Christian who has not done this is a damning delusion, which will, unless dispelled by the truth, drown in the depths of eternal despair. "He that doeth sin is of the devil" (I. John iii. 8), "Whosoever is begotten of God doeth no sin" (I. John iii. 9), are divine declarations which frequently fall on deaf ears. Yet they are solemnly and awfully true. They unmask millions of the devil's dupes with which the nominal churches are crowded, but that does not invalidate them. "Let God be true, though every man a liar." A repentance which holds on to a single sin is a fraud, which must be abandoned here or exposed at the Judgment. Pentecostal converts attested the genuineness of their repentance by burning the bad books in their keeping, though it cost them thousands of dollars. Barrels of whisky poured in the streets and bonfires of tobacco and kindred Satanic property would signify a similar work to-day! When people genuinely repent of all sin they welcome such sacrifices. Yes; this is severe on professors who drink on the sly or are themselves slaves to tobacco. But it will be harder still for them at

the Judgment unless they repent. Genuine repentance, such as must exist to possess salvation, accepts
the justice of eternal punishment and renounces every
sin. It also embraces restitution and complete reformation
of life and character. False repentance is the devil's substitute which he seeks to palm off on souls to their ruin.
It professes to break off sins that are known, but covers
those that can be hid from human eyes. It is ashamed
of itself, and seeks self-justification by sham excuses. It
leads to false security, hardness of heart and conscience,
self-righteousness, false peace, false hope, hypocrisy and
hell.

They confess their sins. "Pricked to the heart" instead of "tickled in the head," as they saw the awful
wrong of sin to themselves, to others, and above all to
God, and crying out in agony, they confessed their lost
condition and need of a Saviour. All true converts have
passed through a parallel experience. Sham confession
is sometimes extorted because of exposure or fear of it,
but is afraid of going too far, anxious to hide as much as
possible, and has dry eyes, or if it weeps at all it is
because of shame or fear of exposure, and not because of
its own wickedness. Genuine confession owns up all,
humbles itself completely, renounces all excuse-making
and self-justification, and abandons all utterly to the
unmerited mercy of God. Pentecostal conversions require Pentecostal confessions. "Whoso covereth his sins
shall not prosper, but whoso confesseth and forsaketh
them shall find mercy." Unconfessed wrongs are chains
with which Satan is fettering multitudes.

They are honest converts. "Let us walk honestly"
(Rom. xiii. 13). If they have wronged any man they
are willing to restore fourfold. Restitution to the extent
of ability is one of the characteristics of genuine repent-

ance.   Tears of sorrow are unavailing if they fall on
hands which hug stolen goods.   Old debts disowned are
damning thousands.   Under this crime people snivel
over their lack of faith and religious feeling who should
be in jail.   When a man refuses to right a wrong within
his reach he bolts the door of mercy to his own soul.
"With what judgment he has judged, he shall be
judged; and with what measure he has meted, it shall
be measured to him again."   Dishonesty in business is
stealing.   A dishonest man is a thief.   Lip profession
adds lying to robbery.   Repentance makes a man honest;
regeneration imparts an abhorrence to dishonesty, while
entire sanctification eliminates all dishonest bias from
the heart.

They are obedient converts.   Jesus said: "If a man
love me, he will keep my word: and my Father will love
him, and we will come unto him" (John xiv. 23).
Thousands of deceived professors have the audacity to
declare that "no one can live without sin."   Why say
they so?   Evidently because they are guilty.   By this
they confess that they are entire strangers to the new
birth.   One becomes and remains a child of God by faith
and obedience, and by unbelief and disobedience ceases
to be, and returns to the "power of sin and Satan."

> "Trust and obey;
>   For there is no other way
>   To be happy in Jesus,
>   But to trust and obey."

A disobedient believer is a condemned believer, and the
condemned believer will be executed, unless a pardon is
secured.   One of the certain marks of an unregenerate
life is a sinning experience, and the disposition to excuse
its existence by claiming its necessity.   Such professors
must be awakened and converted through Pentecostal

preaching now, or else be startled, when too late, by the
stern declaration, "Not every one that saith unto me,
Lord, Lord, shall enter into the kingdom of heaven; but
he that *doeth the will* of my Father which is in heaven"
(Matt. vii. 21). Reader, which shall it be? Take your
choice. True believers who mistakenly regard mistakes
as sins belong to another class.

They are Christ-like converts. They are so much like
Jesus that they were given His name. They were taught
that if any man "have not the mind of Christ, he is
none of his," and so stop short of nothing less than the
Christ-mind. Before being sanctified wholly, then as
now, the seed of carnality remained, and its movings
were sometimes manifest, but the Christ-spirit was im-
planted, and, though hindered by the carnal mind, yet it
was there, and gave character to its possessor. All in
every age who are born of God are like His Son, their
Elder Brother. Conversion implants the Christ-mind;
Pentecost expels all that is contrary to it. The King of
Heaven has emphatically forewarned all that only the
forgiving can be forgiven. Pentecostal converts always
manifest their genuineness by this mark. A professed
experience of regeneration which does not have it is a
delusive foundation on which to build entire sanctification, and needs to be regenerated. Bury your grudges
in the crimson fountain, or they will bury your soul
beneath the billows of hell. All who ignore this funda-
mental principle of the kingdom of God do so against
divine warning, and invite the tragical consequences
which they must suffer throughout eternity. Possession
of an unforgiving spirit is positive proof of a sham
profession. Can he who has been forgiven countless sins
against God refuse pardon to an erring fellow-mortal?

They are loving converts. They know they have

passed from death unto life, because they love the brethren, and they know "they love the children of God because they love God and keep His commandments." They are so conscious of the "love of God shed abroad in their hearts by the Holy Ghost, which was given unto them," that they welcome every test of their Christian character which may be brought to bear upon it, knowing that love stands all tests and comes out of every furnace the brighter for the proving. What a contrast with deceived professors! They love their own social set, but often despise God's humble children. If able, they lavish dollars in gifts on themselves and personal friends to coppers for Christ's suffering poor. They sing,

> "Blest be the tie that binds
> Our hearts in Christian love,"

and sometimes act as if it was a tie of "mutual hate." They have been heard to denounce true believers, seeking or enjoying holiness, as "misguided," "erratic," "fanatic" and "fools." To all such the God of Pentecost propounds this searching question: "He that loveth not his brother whom he hath seen, can not love God whom he hath not seen" (I. John iv. 20). Whited sepulcher, what is thine answer?

They are Spirit-attested converts. God's Spirit witnesses with theirs that they are the children of God. They do not depend for their knowledge on the fact of their repentance, faith, feeling, works, life, or the say-so of other people. The Spirit who worked the change assures them of its completion and reality. Possessed of this God-given assurance, neither wicked men nor devils are able to wrest from them the consciousness of their divine sonship, and in the midst of the world's bitter storms, with confidence they sing and feel:

> " Blessed assurance, Jesus is mine;
>   O what a foretaste of glory divine;
>   Heirs of salvation, purchased of God;
>   Born of His Spirit, washed in His blood."

If one has never received this witness, it is because the work is not complete, for God delights to impart it as instantly as able. The man who would rest without a title to his property or a key to his treasures is a philosopher compared to him who is listless about his soul when uncertified of its regeneration by this witness. Multitudes of churchlings confess their lost condition by the absence of this Pentecostal blessing.

They are fruitful converts. The fruits of the Spirit pictured in Galatians v. 22, 23, are ripening in their hearts. It is true that until the second great change is wrought the carnal mind mars the growth of this celestial fruit, but it grows, and by its presence witnesses to the change. The grapes of true peace and joy and love and kindred graces never grow in unregenerate soil. Their sham substitutes, like painted pictures, may be hung upon the walls of unsaved souls, but meet no tests of real fruit. True converts have their " fruit unto holiness." Regeneration implants them; Pentecost roots out all weeds, and sends celestial showers and sunshine. Glory! Absence of the Spirit's fruitage is a positive proof of absence of the Spirit's regenerating work. Conformity to ordinances and devotion to duty often exists in fruitless formalists, but can not be substituted for the Spirit's work, without which every branch shall be taken away and burned. *Without fruit*, candidates for an eternal bonfire; *with fruit*, for thrones and infinite empire! Which?

They are hungry converts. Spiritual birth always brings spiritual sight, sound, activity and *hunger*. Pen-

tecostal converts are always hungry for holiness.   They
"hunger and thirst after righteousness."   The salvation
experienced in regeneration is so sweet that they thirst
for more of the same kind, and as soon as some impetuous
Peter, practical Paul, or wise Aquila, divinely instructed,
unfolds to them their privilege of baptism with the Holy
Ghost and fire, which will entirely sanctify their souls
and make them fully free, like Cornelius and the Ephesian converts, they eagerly embrace the Blesser and the
blessing.   If any New Testament convert fought holiness, his name, like those of the faithless spies of Canaan,
forgotten, has rotted in merited oblivion.   Critics of
entire sanctification, take warning, for this is a picture
of your coming fate.   The Mudges and the Bolands of
the present day, with their less audacious followers, may
gain a temporary notoriety, but their works, like the
"spark of the wicked," are destined to die in the dark
night of final obscurity.   Hunger for the sanctifying
baptism of the Spirit is the normal appetite of all who
are born of the Spirit.   Hence absence of this appetite
is evidence of the absence of the new birth, and points
with certainty to the fact that the soul is unsaved, and is
resting on a false hope.   Instead of hungering for holiness they hunger for excuses to shield them in rejecting
it, and must repent or perish.   Pentecostal converts, pray
for it, seek for it, wait for it, and, thank God, receive it,
and then spread the good news.   Hallelujah!   All who
have no hunger for Pentecostal Holiness are on the steep
down-grade to hell.   They may be dressed in silks and
satins, in purple and high silk hats, and titled and high
in church or state, but this spiritual law is inexorable.
He who is destitute of spiritual appetite is destitute of
spiritual life.   Corpses never hunger.

They are expectant converts.   They had "turned unto

God from idols, to serve a living and true God, and to wait for his Son from heaven '' (I. Thess. i. 9, 10). They were divinely taught that, as Jesus went away, so he might, at any time, return again, and receive them unto Himself, and that they were to be always ready for His return. Hence, He was the hero of their lives. He reigned in their hearts. If death should come they would at once fly to Him, and at any time He might appear and glorify them. This '' glorious hope of His appearing '' was one of the truths with which the apostles comforted the afflicted. Instead of teaching, as some do to-day, that it would hinder holiness, it was held up as one of its helps. As the mist is being swept from the sky, this Pentecostal star is again appearing to comfort and to cheer.

They are royal converts. They move in high circles. Their names are enrolled among the most honorary in the universe. Fellow-citizens with the saints and of the household of God, kings and priests unto God, they belong to the highest aristocracy of creation, among whom, if true, it is their portion to live and move, and sing and serve, and shout and praise forever.

Reader, these are a few of the New Testament marks which all who are born of the Spirit bear. Satan is luring multitudes to hell who fancy they are saved, though destitute of these clearly expressed New Testament requirements. Church membership, baptism, official position, a past experience, counterfeit happiness and security, or present presumption, will avail naught, if any of these fruits are lacking. If you meet them, you are blessed; if not, whether you think it or no, infinite peril is impending. If sleeping in false security, instead of being awakened, your danger is double. I love your soul. I long for your rescue from the fearful dream that soon will culminate in an awful and eternal nightmare. Fly to Christ. Fast! Pray! Repent! Confess! Restore! Yield! Believe! Take advantage of this moment! Another hour may be eternally too late! Sinai thunders! Calvary pleads! Judgment threatens! Hell warns! Heaven beckons! Eternity is near! The wails of multitudes of deceived souls who were once, as you now, earnestly warned, echo your threatening doom from the caverns of the damned! ''Awake up righteously, and sin not; for some have no knowledge of God: I speak this to move you to shame '' (I. Cor. xv. 34).

> ''I must this moment now begin
> Out of my sin to wake,
> And turn to God, and every sin
> Continually forsake.
>
> ''I must for faith incessant cry,
> And wrestle Lord, with Thee;
> I must be born again, or die
> Through all Eternity.''

CHAPTER V.

Full-orbed Pentecostal revivals are cloud-bursts of salvation, caused by the spiritual atmosphere being so electrified by the Holy Ghost that believers are fully sanctified, sinners converted, opposition confounded, and the devil repulsed.

Pentecost was such a revival. By studying it and other New Testament revivals we can learn the principles which govern these mighty movements. They are the Pentecostal Church, like a mighty army, in motion against a determined and intrenched foe.

The difference between true revivals and the mechanical efforts of Christless clubs to secure members is seen from the following facts:

Pentecostal revivals are conditional revivals. They are cloud-bursts of salvation, caused by the Holy Ghost, yet the precipitation is conditioned upon human compliance with certain spiritual laws. Plural as well as individual Pentecosts are promised, and must be proclaimed. Given one hundred and twenty persons as dead to sin and the world, as absorbed in Christ, as loyal to His instructions, as united, prayerful, obedient, earnest and expectant, as was the first Pentecostal Church, and such revivals would be the rule instead of the exception, varying in quantity of converts with character of surroundings. It is impossible to have Pentecostal revivals without Pentecostal material. A fire can not be built with sea-soaked wood. World-soaked preachers and churches must be kiln-dried before they are fit for revival kindling wood. A box on a street corner is a better site for a Pentecostal revival than a fine cathedral full of spiritual mummies. Prayer, fasting, the baptism of the Holy Ghost upon the church, Holy Ghost preaching, testimony and personal work are all conditions of Pentecostal revivals. Sham revivals are those in which these conditions are either aped or ignored, and result in a fizzle instead of a Pentecostal deluge. A refusal to meet Pentecostal conditions on part of preacher or people, or both, has caused the criminal abortion of many a revival. Perpetrators of the crime are guilty of soul-murder. Meeting the conditions precipitates Pentecost. As they are so simple, reasonable and clearly revealed, all churches may embrace them, and thus share the rich results that follow.

They are Holy Ghost revivals. At Pentecost the Holy Ghost was honored. He was given the place assigned Him by Christ. The church welcomed Him, and yielded to His guidance. Through the Word and fire-baptized workers people were convicted of "Sin, Righteousness, and coming Judgement." Penitents were regenerated, and believers fully sanctified. "Have ye received the Holy Ghost since ye believed?" was the first question propounded by Paul at the great Ephesus revival. A genuine revival is impossible without the supremacy of the Holy Ghost among its promoters as daylight is without the sun. Man-made revivals substitute foxfire for sunlight and human manipulation for the guidance of the Holy Ghost, and compromises in the place of conversions and sanctifications! Possession of the graces and gifts of the Holy Ghost are absolutely indispensible to the highest type of Pentecostal revivals. Where He or any of His offices are ignored He is grieved, and the work stopped or greatly marred. The omission of all mention of Him and His sanctifying work among believers in multitudes of revivals and revival reports do Him great wrong. Out of one hundred, five are seldom found who thus honor Him. Many want the Holy Ghost to help them out of a difficulty, who are not willing to accept Him as their Divine Captain. They are willing to instruct Him what to do and how to do it, but are unwilling to commit all fully to Him and crown Him leader.

They are fruitful revivals. Multitudes were saved and sanctified through them. Thousands were added to the Church. Sins were exposed and forsaken. Sin was confessed and cleansed away. Wrongs were righted and Christless business abandoned. A revival which stops short of such fruits needs reviving. God will not accept a revival of tears, and songs, and sentiment, for righteousness. A revival which does not make men right with God and man is a cloud without water. One whose climax is church-joining instead of salvation is a death trap. Substitution of card-signing for the altar of prayer is one of the marks of an apostate church and hireling ministry. When God unites men to His Church they will not long withhold their names from proper officers where they exist. The time has come for people to discriminate between meetings for stuffing church statistics and those for saving from sin. A revival that a Scriptural sermon on sanctification will spoil is not from the skies. The lightning of Scripture-truth never kills a genuine Scriptural revival, but increases the intensity of its downpour. Pentecostal revivals are characterized by the manifestations and fruits of the Holy Ghost. A reform in reporting revivals is needed. It is customary to report persons joining the church as converts. A diagnosis of an ordinary church membership will find less than one

in four giving evidences of conversion. Some say one
in ten. Where people simply hold up the hand, or rise
for prayers, or unite with the church, instead of passing
through the Bible experiences of pricked-to-the-heart
conviction, tear-blinding, wrong-righting, sin-forsaking
heart-repentance, and assurance-giving, joy - imparting
regeneration, the report would be nearer the truth to
read, "*One hundred dupes deceived*," than "One hundred
souls converted." A lie in the shape of a deceptive
revival may be "ever the blackest of lies."

They are miraculous revivals. Evidently they are
embraced in the "greater works" than His which Jesus
declared His followers should perform. Pentecostal revivals originally were frequently attended by healing of
the body and other miraculous manifestations. "And
the multitudes gave heed with one accord unto the things
that were spoken by Philip, when they heard, and saw
the signs which he did. For from many of those which
had unclean spirits, they came out, crying with a loud
voice: and many that were palsied, and that were lame,
were healed" (Acts viii. 6, 7). "And God wrought
special miracles by the hands of Paul: insomuch that unto
the sick were carried away from his body handkerchiefs
or aprons, and the diseases departed from them" (Acts
xix. 11, 12). Inspired men possessed this power, and used
it for God's glory. The presence of modern fanaticism
and skepticism in regard to divine healing, such as char-
acterizes this period, had not then circumscribed its influence for good. The apostles, divinely led, recognized it
a helpful auxiliary of the "Holiness movement" in its
incipiency, and doubtless, as the movement regains its
Pentecostal purity and power, the exercise of this and
other kindred gifts will shine as then. But gifts all fail
in the presence of graces. The Pentecostal healing and

wonder-working signs which accompanied the revival efforts of the primitive church, compared to the greater works of regeneration and entire sanctification, which were its crowning glory, were like the lightning of a summer shower compared to the falling cloud-burst. Like the lightning bolt they accomplish a God-given work, and, like it, they sometimes cause more comment than the shower, but they can not be substituted for it in time of drought, and there may be mighty spiritual cloud-bursts, as at many Pentecosts, ancient and modern, with no such lightning at all. The absence of any record of it at the first Pentecost proves either that it did not then occur or else that the importance of the shower itself so superlatively transcended it that it was not mentioned.

They are protracted revivals. If the opposition did not yield at once a " Long time therefore they tarried there speaking boldly in the Lord, which bare witness unto the word of his grace " (Acts xiv. 3). Many promising revivals are nipped in the bud because they will not sprout, grow, bud, blossom and ripen in " ten days." A plan which allows an evangelist to adjust his appointments to providential circumstances and leadings seems to have been the apostolic example.

They are opposed revivals. They were mocked, derided, and hindered in every way that Satan and his allies could devise. " But the Jews that were disobedient stirred up the souls of the Gentiles, and made them evil affected against the brethren " (Acts xiv. 2). There is a radical defect in every revival that neither the world nor hypocrites oppose. Satan will not see his kingdom invaded and souls captured without a struggle. Sham professors are among the first and most bitter soldiers to fight true revivals. They declare that they " don't believe in them," "too much excitement," "converts do n't hold out," "extravagance," "magnetism," "hypnotism," etc. In many ways they often oppose, and divert by dances, private parties, lectures, entertainments, social visits, fairs and festivals. Or possibly they will seek to substitute a shallow, sham revival instead. From the many Pentecostal revivals recorded in the New Testament we note the following revival truths which clearly shine from them:

THE REVIVAL AT JERUSALEM shows that the baptism of the Holy Ghost and fire is the mainspring of all true revivals; that revival leaders should tarry until this comes; that Pentecostal revivals are holiness revivals; that genuine revivals cause unity of believers, and benevolence; that they magnify the Word and give God all the glory.

THE REVIVAL AT ICONIUM (Acts xiv.) —This revival immediately followed the great Conference at Antioch. It was conducted by Paul and Barnabas. From it we learn,—

That Spirit-filled men may so speak that multitudes will be saved (ver. 1).

That unconverted church members are among the greatest revival obstructions (ver. 2).

That revival opposition should lead to bold, persevering revival effort (ver. 3).

That Holy Ghost revivals make divisions, the sheep following one Master and the goats the other (ver. 4).

That Jews and Gentiles, *i. e.*, unconverted people, in the churches and out, sometimes unite to stop a genuine Holy Ghost revival (ver. 5).

That God grants marvelous displays of His power to confirm the work of His true ministers (ver. 3).

That opposition sometimes succeeds temporarily, so that workers wisely withdraw to other fields (ver. 6).

That if powerful Paul and eloquent Barnabas, full of the Holy Ghost, working with "signs and wonders," were apparently defeated and driven from the field, and led to take a circuit appointment (ver. 6), sample treatment should not discourage workers to-day.

That removal from one field should stimulate to greater zeal in the new one (vers. 6 and 7).

THE REVIVAL AT LYSTRA (Acts xiv. 8–21).—Paul and Barnabas, fleeing from the persecutions of the Iconium revival, found refuge in Lystra and the surrounding country circuits. Here they preached the Gospel. From their sojourn here we learn,—

That success is attended by the peril of man-worship. Few men can stand success (vers. 11, 12).

That occasion of human flattery and praise should be turned into occasion for preaching repentance and giving all glory to God (vers. 13–18).

That successful Holy Ghost revivals awake the enmity and persecution of pharisaical professors.

That when the enemy stones a Spirit-filled man to death in one place, God enables him to arise and have a greater revival in another (vers. 19–21).

That if the opposition can not hug a Holy Ghost movement to death by the bear of adulation, it will try to tear it to pieces by the tiger of persecution.

That Spirit-filled workers avoid needless controversy; are too busy to needlessly talk back or fight back.

THE REVIVAL AT EPHESUS (Acts xix.).—From this we learn,—

That the children of God have an affinity for each other. Paul in Ephesus drew the believers there around him as a magnet the iron.

That a Pentecostal revivalist unfolds the gift of the Holy Ghost to believers, and leads them to receive it.

That they then become the storm-centers of mighty revival cyclones.

That Holy Ghost testimony is a mighty factor in revivals.

That such revivals stir up great opposition from Satan and his minions.

That Paul persevered and pushed the battle to victory, even though it took two years.

That his bitterest opposition came from unconverted church members.

That it was overwhelmingly defeated.

That repentance was genuine, men publicly burning their false books, though it cost them thousands of dollars.

That God was given all the glory. "The name of the Lord Jesus was magnified."

That the gift of the Holy Ghost in preacher and people was the mainspring of the revival.

That a Holy Ghost revival makes a Holy Ghost church. The church of Ephesus was one of the strongest of apostolic days.

THE REVIVAL AT SAMARIA (Acts viii. 5–13).—*It was a sweeping work*, "the multitudes . . . with one accord" receiving the Word.

It was a genuine work, so that there was "much joy in that city." Spurious revivals and mere church-joining meetings may excite congratulation over numbers, but never beget deep spiritual joy.

It was a Christ-honoring revival. The evangelist did not preach himself or human creeds, but he "proclaimed unto them the Christ"

Healing did not hurt, but helped, the work (vers. 6, 7).

We learn from this that the genuine gift is not a side issue, to be ignored, but a power to be employed, and that its proper use, when really possessed, instead of hindering, is helpful. Philip evidently considered it a power to be utilized, and not fanaticism to be feared, and so utilized it as one of the spokes in the wheel of revival success. However, it is wise for workers to remember that, to have Philip's success in the exercise of this gift, they must possess Philip's possession of it.

THE HOLINESS REVIVAL AT SAMARIA (Acts viii. 14–17).—From this revival we further learn,—

It was customary in the early church to hold special meetings for the promotion of holiness.

That receiving the gift of the Holy Ghost is subsequent to conversion. These people had first been converted in Philip's revival.

That sanctification is not a state to be grown into, but a gift to be received.

God uses human means to lead His *children* to receive this gift.

That early preachers did not allow fears, frowns nor fanaticism to frighten them from pressing this Pentecostal experience.

That young converts should be led at once to receive the baptism with the Holy Ghost, God's remedy for worldly amusements and backsliding.

That religious pretenders are found among professed seekers for the Holy Ghost.

That wrong motives will defeat earnest seeking.

That this kept at least one minister out of the Gift. Simon evidently had been a proud ecclesiastical preacher. Giving out that he "himself was some great one," also a popular preacher who had so bewitched the people that "they all gave heed, from the least to the greatest, saying,

This man is that power of God which is called Great.''
He had affected conviction in Philip's revival, and now
coveted the apostles' power in order to do their deeds.
He was not willing to meet the rightful conditions. "He
offered them money.'' The Simon Maguses of all ages
seek this gift in a similar way. They want it as a gift
of power, or "higher life,'' or "enduement for service,''
or for some selfish motive, and upon their own terms.
They desire it, but not intensely enough to confess the
remaining carnality which its fire would destroy, or to
abandon time, friends, appointments, salary, reputation,
self and all unconditionally and eternally to Jesus. They
desire it, seek it, weep about it and go to the altar, but
offer substitutes for complete abandonment and faith in
Jesus; and instead of being swept into its glorious experiences, they sink deeper into "the gall of bitterness
and bond of iniquity.'' Such preachers should be rebuked and warned of their danger (verses 20–23). Pentecostal revivals bring them to the front, and faithful
Peters should deal with them according to their folly.

They are continuous revivals. Not the scratching of a
match, but the gleaming of an electric light. God never
designed that His army should close the fight until the
war is over. A revival spurt for a few days, and then a
relapse into a restaurant, side-show business, was not
born at Pentecost, and is a burlesque on the true Church
of Christ. There needs to be a great waking and shaking
of God's people at this point. "All at it, and always at
it,'' is the Pentecostal motto.

They are contagious revivals. Their promoters were
magnetic centers of revival power. Full of God and His
gifts they stormed the citadels of sin wherever their conquering Captain led. The fortifications of sins and
superstitions and carnality which defied them, were shat-

tered by the dynamite of divine power. The works of the devil were burned up under the blazing fire of revival truth. Sparks flew from one place to another until the Pentecostal fires spread over the known world, and have been spreading down all the centuries notwithstanding the floods of water with which the devil and his aids have sought to extinguish them.

They are genuine revivals. They come by meeting fixed Pentecostal conditions, and result in leading people into salvation, both initial and uttermost. So-called revivals, which do neither of these, are not worthy of the name. Genuine revivals are beautiful trees, laden with choice, ripe fruit; sham revivals are trees with dead leaves, and full of painted, sham fruit tied to the branches. Genuine revivals alarm the wicked and convince them of their condition; spurious revivals amuse them, or give false comfort, or disgust them. Genuine revivals produce healthy spiritual children; spurious revivals leave the churches barren or crowd them with bastards.

Genuine revivals honor the Holy Ghost and all of His offices. Spurious revivals ignore Him and spurn His fruits. Genuine revivals welcome the sobs of the penitent, shouts of the saved and demonstrations of the fully sanctified; spurious revivals are strangers to all such manifestations. Genuine revivals may utilize the altar, the inquiry-room, rising for prayers, and every other available expedient to awaken and lead into salvation, but it rests in none of these things, and is satisfied with nothing less than clear experiences; spurious revivals rest in the use of means, and leave their victims on the quicksands of a dry profession. As the fog and mist of ecclesiastical darkness clears away, and believers regain primitive Pentecostal simplicity and power, true revivals will doubtless rise to climaxes of power now unknown.

CHAPTER VI.

PENTECOSTAL GIFTS.

"When he ascended on high, he led captivity captive, and gave gifts unto men" (Eph. iv. 8). "But desire earnestly the greater gifts" (I. Cor. xii. 31). God gave His Son to save the world, and His Spirit to sanctify the Church and equip her for warfare here and her reward hereafter. The Gift of the Spirit makes available the gifts of the Spirit which God's people are commanded to "desire earnestly." It is as if a father sent the present of a beautiful, costly box to a large family of children. Touch a secret spring and the lid flies open, and there are many smaller gifts for different members of the family, and a nice, large box which is only for the children who are obedient, loyal, loving, and whose faith will claim it. Touch a secret spring in this box and it opens and reveals other gifts for each obedient child whose faith will grasp them and who will use them to advance the father's interests. This is a faint picture of God's gifts to us. He gives his Son, a priceless box, to the whole world. Within this box is pardon, peace, adoption, and eternal life, which all may have. All who receive these gifts are entitled to the second box, the gift of the Holy Ghost to the Church, and all who receive Him and His sanctifying work become candidates for the third box, which contains His gifts. The first box brings salvation and enrolls as citizens of Christ's kingdom. The second eliminates from the heart every impulse contrary to perfect love and loyalty to Him, and establishes Heaven's rule of perfect love, and light, and victory there, and prepares the heart to receive the coming illuminations, and establishments, and endowments, weapons and ammunition, which will make it a victor on every battlefield. Two great works, but many gifts and blessings.

The Pentecostal graces, concerning which so much is being written, and which can not be too highly magnified, melt the church into glad loyalty and self-sacrifice to God.

The gifts are weapons without which she is unfit for the battlefield. An army may have perfect love for its country, but, unofficered and unarmed, it will be drowned in defeat.

Hence Christ fortifies His forces,—

I. *By a diversity of divinely appointed officers.* "And he gave some to be apostles; and some, prophets; and some, evangelists; and some, pastors and teachers" (Eph. iv. 11). These officers are all designed to work harmoniously together: (*a*) for the perfecting of the saints; (*b*) unto the work of the ministry; (*c*) unto the building up of the body of Christ (Eph. iv. 12). And for the purpose of protecting the church from (*a*) being tossed to and fro; (*b*) and carried about with every wind of doctrine; (*c*) by the sleight of men, in craftiness. The divinity of these appointments is emphasized and most of list repeated, with some additions, in I. Cor. xii. 28: "And God hath set some in the church, first apostles, secondly prophets, thirdly teachers, then miracles, then gifts of healings, helps, governments, divers kinds of tongues." Existence of all of these in the church is essential to its highest success. A church without the apostles would be like a building with no foundation; without prophets, *i. e.*, preachers, like a body with no mouth;

without evangelists, like a wholesale house with no trav-
eling agents; without teachers, like a school without
instructors; without pastors, like sheep without a shepherd; without helps, like a body without hands or feet;
without governments, like a state with no laws or offices.
Deprive the church of these divine appointments, and
you thus cripple her power, and make her like Samson,
when shorn of his locks, the sport of the Philistines.
When she honors these offices, and they all work as God
designs, harmoniously together, then she goes forth, under
her conquering Head, clear as the sun, fair as the moon,
and terrible as some great army.

II. *By a diversity of divinely-bestowed gifts.* Read
I. Cor. xii. In this wonderful chapter we have a photograph of the Pentecostal Church, officered and panoplied and ammunitioned as God designs it to be until
translated. Here is promised the " Nine Gifts" which
the Church may and must possess to be victorious in
her warfare. Many people are sanctified wholly, but in
their zeal for the more excellent way of perfect love,
have evidently neglected the lesser yet vital panoply of
these nine wonderful weapons, which, in the hands of
Spirit - filled believers, are " mighty through God" to
defeat the devil.

(1) " *The word of wisdom.*" God gives wisdom to
do the right thing, and speak the right word in the right
way at the right time. It is not natural sense, but
God-given skill. Without it no one can outwit the devil.
Perfect love always imparts a thirst for this wisdom.
Perfect faith in God's promise will give possession of it.
The possession of this Spirit-imparted gift was one of
the required qualifications of membership in the first
New Testament official board (Acts vi. 3).

(2) *The word of knowledge.* Divinely imparted

knowledge, not studied out, but prayed down, which makes many a man who can not read or write more knowing in things divine than learned schoolmen.

(3) *Faith*. Not saving faith, which regenerates or fully sanctifies the soul, but the "gift of faith," which claims victory and sings and shouts before the walls fall down. Without this "faith," which "laughs at impossibilities and cries: It shall be done," there will be no victory on the battlefield. Every triumph for souls in revivals, and along all lines of advanced spiritual work, must be claimed by faith before it is by sight. God gave the writer the gift of faith for The Revivalist and our Pentecostal publishing work years before the walls of difficulty crumbled.

(4) *Gifts of healing*. This long-neglected, much-derided, frequently-abused gift is catalogued with the nine as a permanent fixture in the Pentecostal church. What God has thus joined together, let not man try to put asunder. If he does not possess it, let him not try to trim God's Church to suit his own experience. This gift embraces the power to claim physical healing for self or others when God reveals such to be His will. It was practiced by the apostles, by Luther, by John Wesley, and beyond doubt is enjoyed by a goodly number in the church to-day. If "earnestly coveted" more it would be criticised less, and doubtless thousands wou'd be blessed by it and the influence of Christianity burst like the sun into many dark corners which have never felt its light.

(5) *Working of miracles*. "Invoking of powers" (*Whedon*); "manipulation of dynamites" (*Godbey*); the possession of miraculous power to do any God-given work when such power is needed, whether it be to heal the sick or do the still greater work of resurrecting the

spiritually dead and healing the spiritual leper. Skepticism as to this gift has well-nigh paralyzed its power to-day, but the fact that the Holy Ghost retains it in the list of available weapons for His work, proves that the day of miracles did not die with the apostles, in tones that a Niagara of human voices, no matter how highly trained, can not drown. There are many evils so strongly intrenched that they can be dislodged only by the explosions caused by the "manipulations of this dynamite."

(6) *Prophecy*. "Inspired preaching" (*Whedon*). Not simply foretelling future events, but heaven-born, God-sent messages from Spirit-filled hearts. "But if all prophesy, and there come in one unbelieving or unlearned, he is reproved by all, he is judged by all; the secrets of his heart are made manifest; and so he will fall down on his face and worship God, declaring that God is among you indeed" (I. Cor. xiv. 24, 25).

(7) *Discerning of spirits*. "The power of detecting the hypocrite, of distinguishing true and false gifts, of recognizing genuine inspiration" (*Whedon*). God does not leave the church at the mercy of false doctrines, false brethren, false preachers and false Christs to be duped by them, but provides a gift able to detect every sham and discern the truth.

(8) *Divers kinds of tongues*. Power of conveying any God-given message to the persons to whom God sends it, in language which they can understand.

(9) *Interpretation of tongues*. Power to interpret God-sent messages so as to convey their intended meaning.

These nine gifts await the appropriating faith of the church as really as do the graces of the Spirit. God designs that they shall all shine in His church to the joy of heaven and dismay of hell.

A young lady came to our office recently. She was baptized with the Holy Spirit and longing to be useful. She definitely sought and claimed the gift of "wisdom" to win souls. She went away with the assurance that it was hers; within six weeks she had won five persons to Christ. Each of these gifts is just as fruitful in its own field.

A sham church is a total stranger to them, and any church is effective in proportion as she claims them and the greater grace that will enable her to possess and use them humbly for man's good and God's glory.

Reader, it is your privilege not only to "follow after love," but to "desire" and possess "spiritual gifts." Let not the adversary by any cunning frighten you from them. Some have vainly taught that all outside of love is fanaticism. Then Paul was a fanatic, for he unfolded these glorious gifts and commanded to seek them. They neither can nor should be substituted for perfect love any more than loyalty in a soldier for a sword and musket, yet like the latter weapons they are to be possessed and used.

See W. B. Godbey's book on "Spiritual Gifts and Graces," for a full and masterly presentation of this subject.

CHAPTER VII.

PENTECOSTAL GIVING.

"And ye are not your own; for ye were bought with a price " (I. Cor. vi. 20).

This grace is one of the stars of the first magnitude which adorned the firmament of the Pentecostal Church, but which, like many of its other lights, has been obscured by clouds. In order to view it in its beauty, the following facts must be kept in mind:

1. Pentecostal giving is not spasmodic giving, prompted by appeals or extreme cases of need.

2. It is not ostentatious giving, to be seen of men, blazoned in the papers or inscribed on temples or costly windows.

3. It is not competitive giving, to outvie a rival in business or religious circles.

4. It is not selfish giving, hoping to receive again.

5. It is not indiscriminate giving, sowing with a reckless hand whenever and wherever caprice or pressure may dictate.

6. It is not Jewish giving, bestowing a tenth of receipts, as a matter of duty, and no more. Lest any should be encouraged by this statement to diminish giving, let it be remembered that one-tenth for God's work is the *very least* that any one can give and not *rob* Him.

The Jews were required to pay one-tenth as a tithe tax and another tenth as offerings, so they really paid *two-tenths*. Therefore he who pays but one-tenth is only *half a Jew*, and he who withholds that is as actually a thief as if convicted and behind prison bars; yea, even more criminal, for he has robbed the Lord God Almighty and His Son Jesus Christ. Tempted by Satan, who is ever active to lead men to this crime, and thus lessen the resources of God's kingdom, men have long sought to shield themselves in this sin under the plea of inability to give so much. If that be true, then God is unjust, for He certainly did require it of the Jews, and more than that, they prospered as no other nation when they obeyed, and perished when they withheld. (See "God's Financial Plan," by Shaw.)

While the above is true, yet it is evident that one-tenth is not the limit of Pentecostal giving, for the following reasons:

1. It was not under the Old Testament. Another tenth was required for offerings, and promises and precepts were continually extended to those who, in addition, would give to the poor: "The liberal soul shall be made fat"; "He that giveth to the poor shall not lack," and kindred instructions lured all who had means above the payment of required offerings to thus invest them.

2. Men are clearly commanded not to lay up treasures for themselves on earth. If they gave only one-tenth, many persons would violate this commandment.

3. Because it is impossible to even enter the kingdom of God without giving more than one-tenth. "He that forsaketh not all that he hath can not be my disciple."

4. Because neither Christ nor His apostles ever even hinted that a tenth was the rule under the Gospel dispensation, but taught that all was to be dedicated to God, and that every man should give "according to his ability."

5. The young man that came to Jesus was commanded to sell all that he had, and the rich were instructed to

"be ready to distribute," and under the influence of Pentecost men sold their possessions and distributed as every man had need, their own ability and the needs of the case being the standard.

That the Christian's duty and privilege, under the light of the new dispensation, is confined to the giving of one-tenth, there is not a shadow of proof from the Word. It is true that in response to the claim of the Pharisees that they paid tithes, Jesus said, "This ought ye to have done," but it must be remembered that He addressed them as Jews under the old dispensation, not as Christians, and even if He had spoken to them as such, it would be no proof that no greater privilege and requirement had not been included, as the greater always includes the less.

Thus the New Testament teaching on the subject of giving, as the gospel the law, supersedes and excels it, as the full-blown rose does the opening bud. In this chapter we can not do the subject justice, but will call attention to the following facts:

NEW TESTAMENT GIVING IS BASED ON STEWARDSHIP, NOT ON OWNERSHIP.—The parable of the talents (Matt. xxv. 14–30) is not a lesson of the results of accepting and rejecting salvation, but a graphic picture of two classes of people, *i. e.*, believers who practice the principle of Pentecostal stewardship, and those who decline to. It shows that we are not masters, but servants. The King does not charge them in regard to their own possessions, but intrusts them with "his goods." They were to invest them in His name, and for His glory, in the bank of heaven, as they believed He would have done if present. Not one-tenth for Him and the balance for themselves, but all for Him. The increase and inexpressibly glorious reward of those that were faithful was because of their loyalty to this principle. The depriva‧ tion and doom of the other was because of failure to thus invest. All who do as he did, like him are guilty of hiding God's talent in the earth. He confessed that the property belonged to God, and not to himself, a striking picture of hosts of professors who admit God's proprie-torship but refuse to deliver His goods, and of whom it will soon be said, as in this warning example, "Thou oughtest therefore to have put my money to the bankers, and at my coming I should have received back [not my tenth but] *mine own* with interest. . . . Cast ye out the unprofitable servant into the outer darkness: there shall be the weeping and gnashing of teeth " (Matt. **xxv. 27–30**).

New Testament stewardship is not like renting a farm or store and paying the owner a per cent. of rent and doing the work in our own way and under our own name, and expending the profits for ourselves, but just the opposite. It acknowledges the proprietorship of Jesus Christ, labors solely under His instructions, and renders all to Him who owns it, with the explicit understanding that all profits above actual economical expenses of food, raiment, shelter, needful stock, etc., shall be given "in His name," as near as can be estimated, as Christ, the Proprietor Himself, would give it were He personally present. What an honor to be thus associated with the King of Heaven in the distribu-tion of His goods! What perfidy to betray this sacred trust and expend them on ourselves or friends, or to "lock them up " for selfish purposes in banks, or stocks, or lands! Such riches is robbery, and every dollar thus devoted will prove a weight to sink some soul to hell unless it be restored. This crime has paralyzed gospel efforts and deferred the millennium centuries. The New Testament standard of stewardship which supersedes all others will remedy this wrong, and should be warmly welcomed.

It involves great personal responsibility. God trusts us and throws us upon our honesty and honor. Do we deal with Him as conscientiously as we require our servants to deal with us? Can we consistently chide them for mis-appropriation of time or money with which we trust them while we are thus robbing God? If they would be answerable for making investments of our funds in ways contrary to our written instructions, how much more are we if we thus use any of the means with which He may have intrusted us contrary to His word, in any way which we know to be displeasing to Him? Can any one invest money for liquor or tobacco in His name and for His glory, or in worldly orders, or for gewgaws with which to feed the pride of a carnal heart? In the face of His commands to give to the poor, and to disciple all nations, and plain instructions to refrain from every-thing questionable, or injurious to soul, mind or body, such investments are a criminal betrayal of sacred trusts which will sink the soul to a hotter hell than the negative crime of hiding the talent in the earth. The worse than wasting time or money at theaters, races, worldly fraternities, or in unprofitable conversation and employments, invites kindred guilt and punishment. Bible conversion with proper enlightenment brings one to acknowledge this stewardship; entire sanctification unfolds its privileges and imparts grace which enables the soul to delight in it.

Such stewardship secures the benefit of Divine wisdom in its investments. God is the Proprietor, and His will as revealed in His Word may be learned and done in everything. His infinite wisdom is available where otherwise there would be human plans. An all-wise

Father knows so much better what investments would be profitable than His little finite children that they love to trust in Him with all their hearts, and lean not to their own understanding. Glorious privilege to be members of a firm whose Manager is none other than Almighty God.

It secures God's blessing and co-operation. We become co-workers with Him. Like Jesus, we go about our Father's business. Whatsoever we do in word or deed, we do all in His name. It is to His interest to prosper His own work. So whether He may lead to plant potatoes or make soap or train children or preach the gospel, God will give " good success." If visible prosperity is sometimes withheld, it is that some greater spiritual good may be bestowed. All who thus " water others " as the servants of God in Jesus' name, shall themselves " be watered."

Accumulation of property for self is absolutely prohibited. " Lay not up for yourselves treasures upon the earth, where moth and rust doth consume, and where thieves break through and steal " (Matt. vi. 19). Every great fortune that is not consecrated to God and used for His glory is a standing monument of the sin of its possessor. While great enterprises require capital, if they are legitimate they should be dedicated to God and run for His glory. If they can not be they should be at once abandoned. All selfish gain is proof of covetousness, which is a violation of God's law, and will sink a church-goer to hell as speedily as grosser sins will damn his fellow-mortals of the slums. The wisdom of God's law against selfish accumulation of wealth is seen from the following results which flow from its violation:

(*a*) Thieves rob, fire consumes, and floods destroy.

(*b*) When property is left to children it usually enervates and dissipates them, and leads to contentions, and often is exhausted in legal contests.

(*c*) The care and love of accumulated property draws the heart worldward instead of Christward.

(*d*) A life devoted to gain is certain to end in ruin. "They that desire to be rich fall into a temptation and a snare and many foolish and hurtful lusts, such as drown men in destruction and perdition" (I. Tim. vi. 9). If this be true of those who desire to be rich, much more does it apply to those who hold wealth for themselves instead of using it for God. Such neglect will certainly condemn its possessor at the Judgment. "Go to, now, ye rich, weep and howl for your miseries that are coming upon you. Your riches are corrupted, and your garments are moth-eaten. Your gold and your silver are rusted; and their rust shall be for a testimony against you, and shall eat your flesh as fire" (James v. 1-3). If I hoard gold for myself, the use of which would save men, then I, by such neglect, become guilty of their murder, and God declares that the rust of that gold will be a swift and sure witness against me.

(*e*) It is a great barrier to salvation. "He that is faithful in a very little is faithful also in much: and he that is unrighteous in a very little is unrighteous also in much. If therefore ye have not been faithful in the unrighteous mammon, who will commit to your trust the true riches? And if ye have not been faithful in that which is another's, who will give you that which is your own? No servant can serve two masters: for either he will hate the one, and love the other; or else he will hold to one, and despise the other. Ye can not serve God and mammon" (Luke xvi. 10-13). Few rich men have ever given evidence of Scriptural salvation. They often cling to a mere profession, but seldom so experience salvation that it makes them glad and free.   "The rich he hath sent empty away" (Luke i. 53).

(*f*)   Riches are unsatisfying.   A little wealth, like a little liquor, simply creates a thirst for more.   Fortune drunkards are more frequent than any other kind.   He who hoards treasures for himself alone is as really drunk with covetousness as the slaves of other vices with lust and liquor.   The soul was created to be satisfied with God, and nothing else will hush its cries.

(*g*)   It leads to fraud and oppression.   "Behold, the hire of the labourers who mowed your fields, which is of you kept back by fraud, crieth out: and the cries of them that reaped have entered into the ears of the Lord of Sabaoth" (James v. 4).   It holds the faces of the poor on the grindstone of want, and frequently practices frauds, under the cloak of shrewd bargains, such as would send a poor man to the penitentiary.

Neglect to use it for God and His cause will bring hopeless condemnation at the judgment.   "Then shall he say also unto them on the left hand, Depart from me, ye cursed, into the eternal fire which is prepared for the devil and his angels: for I was an hungered, and ye gave me no meat: I was thirsty, and ye gave me no drink: I was a stranger, and ye took me not in; naked, and ye clothed me not; sick, and in prison, and ye visited me not.   Then shall they also answer, saying, Lord, when saw we thee an hungered, or athirst, or a stranger, or naked, or sick, or in prison, and did not minister unto thee" (Matt. xxv. 41-44).?

(*h*)   Withholding from God is a source of temporal poverty.   It led Haggai to exclaim: "Ye have sown much, and bring in little; ye eat, but ye have not enough; ye drink, but ye are not filled with drink; ye clothe you, but there is none warm; and he that earneth wages earneth wages to put it into a bag with holes. . . . Ye looked for much, and, lo, it came to little; and when ye brought it home, I did blow upon it. Why? saith the Lord of hosts. Because of mine house that lieth waste, while ye run every man to his own house." The "hard times" which blights earth is doubtless due to this cause.

Wealth hoarded inevitably damns the soul. "And he said unto them, Take heed, and keep yourselves from all covetousness: for a man's life consisteth not in the abundance of the things which he possesseth. And he spake a parable unto them, saying, The ground of a certain rich man brought forth plentifully; and he reasoned within himself, saying, What shall I do, because I have not where to bestow my fruits? And he said, This will I do: I will pull down my barns, and build greater; and there will I bestow all my corn and my goods. And I will say to my soul, Soul, thou hast much goods laid up for many years; take thine ease, eat, drink, be merry. But God said unto him, Thou foolish one, this night is thy soul required of thee; and the things which thou hast prepared, whose shall they be? So is he that layeth up treasure for himself, and is not rich toward God" (Luke xii. 15–21). The sin of this man was that he neglected to honor God with his substance, and laid up treasure for himself. Keep in mind that these words were Christ's answer to a money-seeking man. Christ clearly shows that he, and all who follow in his steps, are fools—busy fools! prosperous fools! troubled fools! shortsighted fools! perplexed fools! summoned fools! surprised fools! deceived fools! and, finally, eternally-damned fools! See story of Dives, in Luke xvi. 19–31, which is a part of Christ's answer to the rich churchmen, who scoffed at His claims of stewardship. "So is he that layeth up treasure for himself, and is not rich toward God."

Christ's law of giving is derided by the rich. "And the Pharisees, who were lovers of money, heard all these things; and they scoffed at him. And he said unto them, Ye are they that justify yourselves in the sight of men; but God knoweth your hearts: for that which is exalted among men is an abomination in the sight of God" (Luke xvi. 14, 15). Satan is prolific with excuses, with which he persuades the rich to "justify themselves" in this betrayal of stewardship. But the standard of the rich worldling and of God are as diverse as the two poles, and theirs is an abomination to Him for the following reasons: It is wrong; it is selfish; it is unscriptural; it is soul-destroying; it cheats its victims out of real joy here and out of heaven, and it damns their souls forever.

PENTECOSTAL GIVING

Is cheerful giving. "God loveth a cheerful giver." Such giving is one of the special marks of Divine son-ship with which God is peculiarly pleased. It does not say He loves a large giver, for large gifts are not always glad ones, but the cheerful or "hilarious" giver. The "upper-room" experience transforms the "I must" of legalism into the "I love" of delight. It makes giving as spon-taneous as the shining of the sun. Sighing over the duty is changed into shouting over the privilege. A Pentecostal sanctification that is below this mark should examine itself, and undergo repairs or replacement.

It is commanded giving. "Give to him that asketh thee" (Matt. v. 42). "Freely ye received, freely give" (Matt. x. 8). "Upon the first day of the week let each one of you lay by him in store, as he may prosper." Whatever the nature of New Testament giving is, this declaration proves it to be divinely required, and, if thus commanded, no more to be neglected than any other duty.

It is systematic giving. "On the first day of the week." The time to stop, consider the matter, settle the sum to be laid aside for specific purposes is divinely specified as definitely as the pay-day of a business house. If a merchant puts a man in charge of his goods, with the understanding that he is to remit profits at certain dates, and he finds that he is neglecting to observe them, how quickly he would discharge him. He who is less honest with God than he would demand his servants to be with himself, should blush, repent, restore and amend.

It should be universal giving. "Each one of you." Not one in ten. Not one for another. Your wife or children can no more do your giving than your eating or praying. Children should be taught this early, and every believer practice it. Men who do all the giving for the family, and thus deprive others of this luxury and spiritual exercise, should be labored with for robbery. All can give something, if it is only part of a meal.

It is rewarded giving. "Give, and it shall be given unto you" (Luke vi. 38). Thus Christ Himself declares that all who so give shall be rewarded.

Reward is proportionate to giving. "Good measure, pressed down, shaken together, running over, shall they give into your bosom. For with what measure ye mete it shall be measured to you again" (Luke vi. 38). If you would receive abundantly and freely, then give in this spirit. God will flood your soul with spiritual blessings worth more than gold, and this promise also declares that men will give in the same spirit to you. The writer has often verified this promise. God laid it on his heart to announce that he would give The Revivalist without charge to all destitute persons who would apply for it. He did so, and then the promise, "He that giveth unto the poor shall not lack" (Prov.

xxviii. 27), was sweetly applied to his soul.   Since then
The Revivalist has prospered as never before, and all its
financial needs been bountifully supplied without any
questionable advertisements.   To God be all the praise.
In II. Cor. viii. 9, Paul paints a beautiful picture of Pentecostal liberality.   Get your revised New Testament and
read it.   Like a kaleidoscope, it surprises with new
beauty at every turn.   He emphasizes the following
among other of its beauties:

It is of God's grace.   "Moreover, brethren, we
make known to you the grace of God which hath been
given in the churches of Macedonia" (II. Cor. viii. 1).
This kind of giving does not characterize heathen lands,
nor worldly minds, but is the result of the impartation
of God's nature.   It is only when the dross of selfishness has been destroyed by celestial fire that it shines
undimmed.

Its exercise is prized by the poor and afflicted.   "In
much proof of affliction the abundance of their joy and
their deep poverty abounded unto the riches of their
liberality" (II. Cor. viii. 2).   Often down in the deep,
dark mines of affliction and poverty, this fair flower
blooms with more than earthly fragrance.

It is spontaneous.   "For according to their power, I
bear witness, yea and beyond their power " (II. Cor. viii.
3).   They realized that such giving was simply investing
in a gold mine that would yield infinite returns, and so
were willing to bankrupt themselves for stock in such
an enterprise.   A burning rebuke to the spirit of this
age, which banks its thousands and millions instead of
investing them in the interests of Christ's kingdom.
What folly to lock money up in worldly schemes for the
meagre interest they return, when God can give greater
interest in this world and eternal dividends hereafter.

It is glad giving.   "Of their own accord, beseeching us with much intreaty in regard of this grace" (II. Cor. viii. 4).   It coaxes to give instead of being coaxed.   Instead of having to be locked in like some modern crowds, to be kept from running away from the collection, they press Paul lest he should leave without taking it.   What a contrast to dainty believers who get nervous because of the "collection," and to the spiritual traitors who disgrace church records with their names, yet stay away from public services because they are too stingy to give, and too proud to publicly decline.

It is co-operative giving.   "The fellowship in the ministering to the saints" (II. Cor. viii. 4).   It anoints one's eyes to see that the communion honors of such fellowship is worth more than that of all the worldly fraternities that Satan has ever tried to substitute in its stead.   It pleads for a place in such select company, and prizes it above human expression.   It abhors the crime, so often perpetrated, of substituting lodgianity for Christianity, and thus wasting time and money, for which the cause of Christ is suffering.

It is consecrated giving.   "But first they gave their own selves to the Lord, and to us by the will of God" (II. Cor. viii. 5).   Pentecostal giving is from givers who are fully consecrated to God.   No others can enjoy its complete blessedness nor share its full rewards.   Under God they also honored the ministers whom He sent to take the offering.

Ministers should teach and preach it.   "That we exhorted Titus, that as he had made a beginning before, so he would also complete in you this grace also" (II. Cor. viii. 6).   Possibly Titus had preached on this subject once, and had desisted because of criticism that he preached from sordid motives.   Hence Paul exhorted him to persist until the saints were perfected in this grace.

It is abounding giving. "But as ye abound in everything, in faith, and utterance, and knowledge, and in all earnestness, and in your love to us, see that ye abound in this grace also" (II. Cor. viii. 7). It is ranked with faith, utterance, knowledge, earnestness, brotherly love, and like graces, whose mighty overflowing streams are to water the earth and fill it with spiritual fertility. The streams of Pentecostal giving are fed from the exhaustless fountain of abounding and overflowing liberality. A so-called Pentecostal experience which is defective here should, for the sake of Christ, have its name or nature changed.

It is proof of love. "Shew ye therefore unto them in the face of the churches the proof of your love, and of our glorying on your behalf" (II. Cor. viii. 24). It is not only a proof of the sincerity of love (see verses 5–8), but of its very existence. It is the first-born child of love. Its absence is positive proof of the absence of its mother. Penuriousness is a positive proof of the absence of perfect love. Coppers in the collection are often an index to covetousness in the soul and brass in the testimony.

It is proof of sincerity. "I speak not by way of commandment, but as proving through the earnestness of others the sincerity also of your love" (II. Cor. viii. 8). Talk is cheap. Men who say and do not are condemned. People invest in what they believe in. Superficial investments in God's cause are positive proof of superficial faith and sincerity. If you give a dime where you could give a dollar, when it strikes God's counter it rings out the size of your faith.

It is available giving. "And he looked up, and saw

the rich men that were casting their gifts into the treas-
ury. And he saw a certain poor widow casting in thither
two mites. And he said, Of a truth I say unto you,
This poor widow cast in more than they all: for all these
did of their superfluity cast in unto the gifts: but she of
her want did cast in all the living that she had "
(Luke xxi. 1–4). From this we learn that a poor widow
may give what is more in God's sight than the legacies
of the luxurious. Her mite may be more than their millions.

It insures freedom from corroding care. " But seek ye
first his kingdom, and his righteousness; and all these
things shall be added unto you " (Matt. vi. 33). This
does not promise the supply of all temporal needs on
condition of idleness or slackness, or half-hearted service,
or even tithing, but upon " *seeking first His kingdom.*"
Who does this will find a never-ending chain of duties in
the service of the King. If the soul be adjusted to
them, and to the whole will of God, like birds to their
spheres and like lilies to earth and air, then like them
all, food and raiment will be provided without " anxiety."
The writer wishes to witness here that under what would,
from a worldly view, have been peculiarly pressing circumstances, he has proved, and is proving, the truth of
this promise.

It is exemplified by God. God gives us light, life,
air, food, raiment, friends, protection, His Son, His
Word, His Spirit, salvation, pardon, sonship, sanctification, the gifts of the Spirit, power over the enemy, kingship and an eternal home in heaven. Indeed, He is the
Giver of every good and perfect gift. There are no
limits to the overflow of His infinite love. One-tenth of
what He has bestowed would be infinitely above all
human merits, yet His love can not thus be bound. We

are to be the "followers of God." Then we must be like our Father, and our liberality like the light.

It is exemplified by Jesus. "For ye know the grace of our Lord Jesus Christ, that, though he was rich, yet for our sakes he became poor, that ye through his poverty might become rich" (II. Cor. viii. 9). "As he is, so are we in this world." "If any man have not the spirit of Christ, he is none of his." Paul, divinely inspired, writing on the subject of giving, points to Jesus as our example. Jesus laid up no money for Himself. He renounced a crown and kingdom for others. As His Father sent Him into the world, so sends He us. He gave not one-tenth, or two-tenths merely, but all for others. He gave till He felt, and died feeling it. If we "suffer with him we shall reign with him." How contemptible unwilling offerings of paltry pennies and compromise tithes appear as we sit at the feet of Him who, though "Lord of all," had nowhere to lay His head, and whose dying couch was a rugged cross. For the "joy set before him" Jesus did this, and offers scepters, crowns and kingdoms to all who choose to tread in His steps.

It glorifies God. "Appointed by the churches to travel with us in the matter of this grace, which is ministered by us to the glory of the Lord" (II. Cor. viii. 19). Pentecostal giving glorifies God as really as praying, testifying or shouting; in fact, they all go together. The minister who has not learned to take a collection to the "glory of God," should tarry longer at the feet of Paul.

It is an artesian well, not a force-pump. "For as touching the ministering to the saints, it is superfluous for me to write to you : for I know your readiness, of which I glory on your behalf" (II. Cor. ix. 1, 2). Instead of

tugging away at the pump handle as ministers so frequently do with congregations beneath the Pentecostal
line, Paul had but to place the pail under the flowing
current and it was quickly overflowing. While Pentecostal giving is so free, yet it is not indiscriminate giving,
at the beck of every passer-by, but, as dispenser of trust
funds, the giver bestows his benefactions when and where
he feels will bring the largest returns for God.

It is adjustible giving. "For if the readiness is
there, it is acceptable according as a man hath, not
according as he hath not" (II. Cor. viii. 12). God can
not be deceived. He reads the heart, and its beats
register the character and worth of the gift in His sight.
A newsboy's copper may be more acceptable than the
wealth of a baron.

It is contagious. "And your zeal hath stirred up very
many of them" (II. Cor. ix. 2). The large and enthusiastic contributions at Pentecost and at modern Pentecostal gatherings, in which the people unite like the
drops of a resistless river, are examples of this contagion.
Prompted by the same Spirit, with kindred motives and
desires, Pentecostal people are one in heart and one in
this celestial grace.

Meager giving insures a meager harvest. "But this
I say, He that soweth sparingly shall reap also sparingly;
and he that soweth bountifully shall reap also bountifully" (II. Cor. ix. 6). The writer, when a farmer boy,
delighted to sow largely, in prospect of an abundant
harvest. Thus all who liberally sow for God are insured a
spiritual harvest of abundant blessing. The man who sows
his means on the rocks of worldly gain, burning sands of
self-indulgence or black bogs of worldly pleasure, will
reap a harvest of death, both here and in hell. He who
hoards them in the granary of greed will reap no harvest

of blessing, and be punished forever for his crime. He who sows sparingly, as most unsanctified believers and mere lip professors of sanctification do, will reap a meager harvest; but all who possess the Pentecostal baptism, which electrocutes stinginess and leaps over the old Jewish mill-dam of only a tenth, and sow bountifully, shall reap bountifully. In them Omnipotence has wrought a work that has transformed the old "how can I afford to give?" into "how can I afford to withhold?" A lost world, a crucified Redeemer, the promised harvest, and, above all, the pure, burning love of God within their hearts, prompts them to invest with joy their all.

Pentecostal giving is from the heart. "Let each man do according as he hath purposed in his heart; not grudgingly, or of necessity" (II. Cor. ix. 7). "Let" him, not make him; "each man," not a select few; as he "purposeth in his heart," not as some one else constrains him; "not grudgingly," wishing he could evade it or get it back; "or of necessity," because of a tithe law or any other pressure but that of love compels it.

God provides for the Pentecostal giver. "And God is able to make all grace abound unto you; that ye, having always all sufficiency in everything, may abound unto every good work" (II. Cor. ix. 8). Here mountain-peak above mountain-peak of Divine provision rises one above the other, until the tops are lost in the infinite height. "*God — all grace — abound — all sufficiency — in everything — may abound — unto every good work.*" Bear in mind that this is a special text on Pentecostal giving, and only to Pentecostal givers. The reason many fail to get much out of it is that they do not meet the conditions. This promise is God's guarantee for support in every work to which He calls His people.

God multiplies the ability to give. "And he that supplieth seed to the sower and bread for food, shall supply and multiply your seed for sowing, and increase the fruits of your righteousness'' (II. Cor. ix. 10). Thus He guarantees to those who abandon all to Him that all their needs, temporal and spiritual, shall be supplied '' according to his riches in glory,'' and that He not only will supply means for giving, but ''MULTIPLY'' them, and intensify spirituality and fruitage—''increase the fruits of your righteousness.''

Pentecostal giving enriches the giver. ''Ye being enriched in everything unto all liberality, which worketh through us thanksgiving to God'' (II. Cor. ix. 11). Banks of England and Klondike gold mines are straws compared to the wealth here bequeathed to Pentecostal givers. They can enrich only with metal and what it will buy; but can not save the soul or bestow a single spiritual comfort, and usually wreck instead of bless, while this legacy, available to all who will abandon everything to God, will ''ENRICH IN EVERYTHING,'' spiritually, temporally and eternally. ''Unto ALL LIBERALITY,'' a climacteric grace; and thus invests its recipient with a wealth that is infinite.

It awakens thanksgiving to God. ''For the ministration of this service not only filleth up the measure of the wants of the saints, but aboundeth also through many thanksgivings unto God; seeing that through the proving of you by this ministration they glorify God for the obedience of your confession unto the gospel of Christ, and for the liberality of your contribution unto them and unto all'' (II. Cor. ix. 12, 13). It inspires joy among believers that people are thus being true to the spirit of the Gospel, and this awakens concerts of praise from many hearts, which in gratitude offer thanksgiving unto God. In proportion as we sink below the Pentecostal standard of giving, in just that proportion we rob God of this thanksgiving.

It secures the prayers and love of those blessed by it. "While they themselves also, with supplication on your behalf, long after you by the exceeding grace of God in you" (II. Cor. ix. 14). Are not the prayers and love which are thus secured big interest on such investments?

It is the "exceeding grace" (verse 14). It may be that it is thus divinely named because it brings such exceeding blessings, or because of its exceeding cost, or because it bursts the bounds and barriers of tithing and cuts a mighty channel of its own, or because it is the glorious river of perfect love overflowing its banks, exceeding its limits and watering and refreshing the world,

God counsels his children to put their capital in the bank of heaven. While He forbids its accumulation for self, He counsels its investment for the interests of His kingdom. His counsel should be sufficient warrant, but this is enforced by the following additional reasons:

It is safe. No one can steal it, and heaven's bank will never break.

It brings big interest. God can get larger returns on money invested for souls than any bank or insurance company. One thousand dollars invested in them may bring six per cent. interest. Put in His kingdom, it will save scores of souls who will shout and shine in glory forever. "My diamonds are restored to me," exclaimed a Christian lady, as she saw the tears of gratitude roll down the cheeks of one who had been redeemed through her benefactions.

It guarantees the divine supply of every need. Paul, thanking the Philippians for their bountiful benefactions declares, "And my God shall fulfil every need of yours according to his riches in glory in Christ Jesus." This covers every possible exigency of the whole being. All who abandon themselves and possessions utterly to the will of God are given this draft on the bank of heaven. What folly to withhold anything when giving so enriches!

It draws heavenward. If our interests are invested in celestial stock, our minds and hearts will be drawn that way. Any investment which thus throws the soul under the influence of heavenly gravitation is to be coveted. Where men's treasure is, there their hearts are. If they invest in insurance, they talk insurance more fluently than anything else; if in wheat, then they will talk wheat; if in railroad stock, they will talk that. They think, talk and live what and where they largely invest. Hence, if their investments are in the world and for it, then their affections will be there, but if in the interests of the kingdom, then that will engage them. Celestial investments transform material gifts into spiritual realities. The money, for instance, which has been invested in the Holiness movement of this city has been transformed, under the touch of consecrated prayer and labor and divine blessing, into fire-baptized souls, that are helping to girdle the globe with salvation, and which will shine as gems in the crown of Jesus.

It is to be openly recognized and rewarded. "Then shall the King say unto them on his right hand, Come, ye blessed of my Father, inherit the kingdom prepared for you from the foundation of the world: for I was an hungered, and ye gave me meat: I was thirsty, and ye gave me drink: I was a stranger, and ye took me in; naked, and ye clothed me: I was sick, and ye visited me: I was in prison, and ye came unto me. Then shall the righteous answer him, saying, Lord, when saw we thee an hungered, and fed thee? or athirst, and gave thee drink? And when saw we thee a stranger, and took thee in? or naked, and clothed thee? And when saw we thee sick, or in prison, and came unto thee? And the King shall answer and say unto them, Verily I say unto you, Inasmuch as ye did it unto one of these my brethren, *even* these least, ye did it unto me. Then shall he say also unto them on the left hand, Depart from me, ye cursed, into the eternal fire which is prepared for the devil and his angels" (Matt. xxv. 34–41). This declares future installments of the rewards of Pentecostal giving that, like those already received, are transcendently glorious. (1) Its public recognition by Him in whose name and by whose grace it is done. Amazing grace that makes a duty delightful and then rewards for doing it! (2) We give a loaf and get an eternal kingdom; we donate our little self and get a King and all of His possessions. (3) Giving for Christ's cause, in His name and for His glory, is a personal gift directly to Him, and is so received and rewarded. (4) Only those who thus give are promised the above reward. Others may be saved, as by fire, but will miss this public reception and gift. Then people will see and lament the shortsighted stupidity which led them to so lock their purses as to lock themselves out of an eternal fortune. Weaklings who doled out their dimes and tithes, instead of "giving according to ability," will lament their littleness. Ananiases who "kept back a part of the price" which belonged to God will weep and wail. Judases who, for money, betrayed the Master by neglecting his interests, will sink in eternal despair. In the light of the final judgment it is a fearful calamity to fall short of the New Testament standard of Pentecostal giving, and high treason to rob God of gifts which should be placed upon His altars.

During the civil war the government issued bonds to help subdue the seceding states. Some said they would not be worth the paper on which they were written, and derided them; others advanced their gold for them and thus helped sustain the government. Finally the Union was preserved, the bonds were at a premium, their enemies chagrined and their holders rewarded. God has issued similar bonds to suppress sin on earth, which is the most unholy civil war that ever shocked the universe. Pentecostal giving is investing in these bonds. Soon the war will be over, the last enemy conquered, earth restored and celestialized, and the flag of Prince Immanuel wave triumphantly over it. Then these bonds will be at a premium, and all who have failed to invest in them too late will regret their stupidity and sin.

May each reader of these pages be not an Achan, hiding God's gold; or an Ananias, "keeping back part of the price," but a "faithful steward of the manifold grace of God," and prove the preciousness of the promise which declares that such "shall be like a tree planted by the streams of water, that bringeth forth its fruit in its season, whose leaf also doth not wither; and whatsoever he doeth shall prosper" (Ps. i. 3).

CHAPTER VIII.

One of the sweetest pictures of Pentecostal life is a family moulded by its influence. Such were the families of New Testament mention, and such are all families which are molded by Pentecostal influences.

They were faithful to the marriage relation. Freelove-ism had no place under the Pentecostal dispensation. The union of two hearts and lives as exemplified at creation in Eden, and enforced by Jesus and His disciples, is the divine foundation of the Pentecostal family. Whatever influence tends to weaken or destroy this foundation is not of God. "Therefore shall a man leave his father and his mother, and shall cleave unto his wife: and they shall be one flesh" (Gen. ii. 24). Shrinking from the burdens of family life, inability to move in certain social circles and live in style, a desire to avoid family restraints, and similar sordid motives, deter many marriages and thus invite many of the ills which follow ignoring this divine provision for human betterment and happiness. The divine design of marriage is fourfold: (*a*) Companionship. "It is not good that the man should be alone" (Gen. ii. 18). (*b*) Helpfulness. "I will make him an helpmeet for him" (Gen. ii. 18). (*c*) Purity. (See I. Cor. vii. 2.) (*d*) Children. "Be fruitful, and multiply, and replenish the earth, and subdue it" (Gen. i. 28). It is divinely declared to be lawful in all. "Let marriage be had in honour among all, and let the bed be undefiled: for fornicators and adulterers God will judge"

(Heb. xiii. 4). Sin deranged it and turned Eden into thorns. Redemption restores it and turns thorns into Eden. The Edenic design of marriage condemns all union for lust, or money, or social position, or any other selfish motive. Pentecostal marriages are those in which God's will is sought and done, and lay the foundation of families that will honor Him.

They are loving homes. "Husbands, love your wives, even as Christ also loved the church, and gave himself up for it" (Eph. v. 25). Christ demonstrated His love for the church by laying down His life for her, by His patience with her faults, by providing for her needs, by sweet and constant companionship, by exemplifying the spirit which she should possess, and by every needed sacrifice and self-denial for her good, suffering the most cruel and shameful death for her deliverance and future glory. This is a Bible picture of a Pentecostal husband. God's grace so sways him in his home that his wife can say of him, as the companion of S. A. Keen, author of "The Pentecostal Library," wrote of him: "We who knew him best could say, 'He lived at home just what he taught in public.'" Scripture is very explicit and imperative as to this love on the part of the "head of the house." "Even so ought husbands also to love their own wives as their own bodies" (Eph. v. 28). "Nevertheless do ye also severally love each one his own wife even as himself" (Eph. v. 33). This commandment is so very important that God emphasizes it by *frequent repetition;* yet how it is disregarded! Husband, you can no more break this and retain God's favor than you can any other commandment. You can not slight your wife, give attentions due her to other women, and censure and scold her, and be guiltless. You can not insist on any selfish indulgence which pains her simply for

your own pleasure, and please God.   A Pentecostal blessing which does not bring to a husband this love is defective.   A home in which it does not exist is not a Pentecostal
home.   Without it no one has a divine right to marry,
and in so doing he invites the divisions and divorces and
home-hell which so frequently is found.   In our holiness
meeting recently a man witnessed that salvation had
prevented his divorce and had led to the conversion
of his wife, and made them, with their six children, a
happy family.   A husband without this love for his wife
is like a stove without fire, a lamp without oil, and must
not complain if she does not respond with the love and
service which would naturally flow if he were what God
commands him to be.   Hence, when husband and wife
are right with God, their home, no matter how humble,
is a heavenly paradise, but when wrong, thorns and this-
tles choke the roses out.   The reason why some men do
not get right in religion is because they refuse to apply its
principles to this relation.   The Holy Ghost will not
abide in the heart of a domineering husband.   Lust can
not be successfully substituted for love, nor bossing for
blessing.   Thousands of unhappy homes would be speedily transformed if the husband, instead of perpetually
quoting "wives, obey your husbands," would give practical and constant demonstration of "husbands, love your
wives."

They are harmonious homes.   "But as the church is
subject to Christ, so let the wives also be to their husbands in everything" (Eph. v. 24).   The husband's
headship in the family is acknowledged by the wife.   He,
being obedient in loving her, she modestly and Scripturally "obeys him," but it is the obedience of love and
trust, and not of fear.   She realizes that this duty is as
divinely hers as his to love and provide, and in it she

feels a sweet and keen delight, a figure used of God to picture the gladness with which His bride, the Church, learns and does His will. Many professed Christians laugh at this clearly-revealed obligation of wives to their husbands, but it is just as much the Word of God as any other Bible truth, and its disobedience is the cause of the wreckage of what might be happy homes. He who tinkers with God's laws dares His lightnings. Trees must be set with roots instead of tops in the soil, or they will die. When the trustful submission of a true wife is planted in the soil of a husband's Christlike love, the tree of a Pentecostal home will bloom. No such husband will knowingly require of his wife anything unreasonable or wrong, nor will such a wife take advantage of his love to her to do him any injustice. Each other's rights, and likes and dislikes, are held sacred, and where both can not see alike the widest freedom of conscience will be freely given, and they will thus keep "the unity of the Spirit in the bond of peace." What a contrast to the strife and discord of many so-called Christian homes.

They are believing homes. "Be not unequally yoked with unbelievers" (II. Cor. vi. 14). God can not build a Pentecostal home with any other material than a Pentecostal experience in both the husband and the wife. All who ignore this reject such a home. For the following reasons God's children can not marry unbelievers and be clear: God forbids it. It is as really a violation of His law as any other sin. There is no spiritual fellowship between a child of God and a rebel against Him, such as all unconverted persons are. Mental and physical affinity does not suffice for spiritual communion. God's blessing never rests upon a marriage which He forbids; hence who marries an unconverted person forfeits God's blessing. Each has different aims in life, one living for Christ and the other not. An unconverted companion often becomes jealous because God is loved more than himself. A goat and a sheep never make a good team. Their sources of enjoyment are opposite. One who will not promise to be true to God you can not trust to be true as a companion. Such marriages are usually unhappy. The Christian who is thus ensnared usually repents when it is too late. The writer refused to marry a friend to an unconverted man. They lived together in misery until two children were born and then separated. The unconverted are frequently regardless of observance of the laws of marital self-control and purity, without which marriage is degraded, and both suffer in mind, soul and body. The children of such marriages are robbed of the sacred prenatal influences to which they have a right, and which largely affect their destiny. The unconverted often insist upon ruinous sexual indulgence and prenatal murder, debasing the sacred bond of marriage into a license for lust. You have no right to choose for the father or mother of your children a godless person. Both husband and wife need all of God's grace that is for them in order to exercise the forbearance and self-denial which marriage demands. There are always matters arising upon which there will be a division. One wants to go to church, the other on a stroll or visit; one wants to give for the Gospel, the other is opposed to it; one welcomes God's ministers, the other dreads them; one wishes to rear the children for God and the Church, the other for the world. How many mothers have aching hearts because the father leads the children to the dance, the theater, the horse-race and the circus.

The fact that God sometimes overrules, so that the unbelieving companion is converted, is no argument in

favor of such marriages.   More frequently the believer is
lost.   A kind disposition, personal beauty, a mere profession of religion, or church membership and promises
of reformation, should never be accepted as substitutes
for vital experimental piety.   All who have not that are
practical "unbelievers."   If, through infatuation or personal magnetism or natural affection, one becomes engaged
to an unconverted person, the first duty to God, the person and yourself, is to wisely, firmly, tenderly, and
quickly as possible, *break off the engagement, the same as
any other sin*, otherwise it will sooner or later be bitterly
regretted.   Though unconverted people sometimes live
happily together on a worldly plane, yet such instances
are rare, and in no wise effects the law which is to govern
the actions of Christians.   The aims of worldlings are
one; those of Christians and worldlings are opposite.

Never marry a person to reform him.   Why not?
Because you can not reform him that way.   Salvation,
not matrimony, is God's prescription for such persons.
Many have been deceived by this device, and discovered
the mistake only when too late.   A friend of mine married a young man on this plea, though repeatedly warned
of the danger.   In less than six months he threatened to
kill her, and they soon separated, he to go on in sin, she
to a blighted life and to fill an early grave.   If your love
and influence is powerless to win your friend before marriage, much less will it be after, when you have lost the
power of religion by marrying against the will of God.

Never marry an illegally divorced person.   Many
lives have been wrecked on this rock.   All persons who
are divorced for other reasons than the single cause mentioned in Matt v. 32 and xix. 9, are illegally divorced,
and marriage of them or with them is adultery.   And as
no adulterer can enter heaven, all such, unless they break

off the unholy alliance, are lost. Neither time, nor affection, nor children, nor public approval, can atone for this express violation of God's law.

Never marry to please others, nor for money, nor a home, nor social position, nor for any other reason less than pleasing God and doing Him better service. Thousands marry from social motives, and reap a harvest of disappointment. If God's blessing is received, His will must be learned and done. A single state with His favor is Paradise compared to a married life without it. Marriage without true love is like a furnace without fire.

It is no reason you should marry a person because infatuated. Two persons may be of such temperament and so keyed mentally and physically as to become infatuated almost at sight. Many mistake this feeling for true love and the basis of matrimony, and by its balmy breezes are wafted into the harbor of a wedded life, only to discover, when the glamour is gone, that they are mismated and mistaken. The bright morning dewdrops of intense infatuation are soon dissipated by the hot sun of the long day of marriage endurance. (For a fuller treatment of this point, see my work on "Impressions," pages 27–40.)

Be sure and learn God's will as to whom and when to marry. You can afford to make no mistake at this point, and victory here means victory at all other points. He knows just who you need and who needs you, and with whom you can be the most useful and happy; and if you will claim His counsels He will make you sure. (See "Impressions," pages 52–69.) Never marry while there is doubt at this point, and be sure never to mistake your own will, or the will of others, for God's will in this matter. Then all will be well. If you have married against these rules and find yourself the wedded com-

panion of an unconverted person, then seek by penitence
and prayer the fulness of God's favor and strive to win
the wandering one to God.

Be right with God yourself. Be sure that you are
converted, and also that your heart is fully cleansed
from all sin and selfishness and filled with the Holy
Spirit.   Until then you are unfitted for the holy offices
which marriage brings.   ''Take heed to yourselves, lest
your heart be deceived. . . .   Therefore shall ye lay
up these my words in your heart and in your soul,
. . . that your days may be multiplied, and the days of
your children . . . as the days of the heavens above
the earth '' (Deut. xi. 16–21).

They are fruitful homes.   ''I desire therefore that the
younger widows marry, bear children, rule the household,
give none occasion to the adversary for reviling'' (I. Tim.
v. 14).   With the exception of barriers because of health,
or providence, or devotion to some special work they are
blessed with children.   Child-rearing is magnified in the
Bible.   To ignore this one of the great ends of the insti-
tution of marriage, is a blow to its being and an insult to
its divine Founder.   People who are not willing to accept
this obligation should remain single.   God promises the
righteous man that his wife '' shall be as a fruitful vine, in
the innermost parts of thine house: thy children like olive
plants, round about thy table.   Behold, that· thus shall
the man be blessed that feareth the Lord'' (Ps. cxxviii.
3, 4).   Families who selfishly evade this responsibility give
occasion to the adversary for reviling in the following
ways: By violating a Scripture duty and privilege.   By
taking the responsibility of defeating all the good which
would have been done by children rightly reared.   By
preventing the existence of immortal spirits which might
have filled earth with blessing, and heaven with shouts of

joy forever.   By robbing earth of the existence, blessing
and example of what might have been a Pentecostal family.
By depriving themselves of those whom God designed to
be a comfort and support in old age.   By giving others
reason to think that the deadly drugs of the world may
have been employed to aid in defeating God's purpose.
By depriving home of what God designs shall be among
its greatest blessings, sweet, bright, young faces.   By
refusing to furnish others to take the places of those who
are falling in Christ's Church.   These are a few of the
fearful responsibilities that parents must take if they will-
fully destroy this natural fruit of the marriage relation.
The hands of multitudes are red with the murder of
millions of the innocent unborn.   Prenatal murder is one
of the most horrible crimes which curses earth.   Its victims are utterly defenseless, and its perpetrators outrage
the laws both of nature and of grace.   Pentecostal families abhor it with all of its accessories, while sham Christian homes reveal their spuriousness by this connubial
crime, as, "without natural affection," and "lovers of
pleasures more than lovers of God," they sink into the
quicksands of this awful crime.

They are obedient homes. "Children, obey your parents
in the Lord: for this is right.   Honour thy father and
mother (which is the first commandment with promise),
that it may be well with thee, and thou mayest live long
on the earth" (Eph. vi. 1-3).   Disobedience and distrust
of parents is family anarchy.   Obedience to home government is the corner-stone of Christian character.   Righteousness, prosperity and long life are promised to those
who heed it.   The opposite threatens all who reject it.
Servants, neighbors or relatives who are invited into the
sacred family circle, and by word or act or look encour-
age a child to distrust or disobey a parent, should be

banished as messengers of hell. The child who disobeys is guilty of home treason, and the person who helps or harbors them in it is a party to the crime. Pentecostal families are obedient families. When children are otherwise it can usually be traced to some Pentecostal lack in one or both of the parents.

They are kind homes. "And be ye kind, one to another, tender-hearted, forgiving one another, even as also God in Christ forgave you." All unkind words and acts are banished from Pentecostal homes to the Siberia of eternal exile. Regeneration enthrones kindness. The baptism by the Holy Ghost expels every unkind impulse. An experience which does not make one kind at home is a stupendous humbug. People who profess to be saved or sanctified "up to date," but who are unkind in church, business, or home relations, should go to the mourner's bench for lying. Those who make no professions, but are guilty, should go for harboring vipers. Much which is labeled religion advertises its counterfeit character by a break at this point.

They are hospitable homes. "Addicted to hospitality." We have no record of the conferences of that day, big or little, having to beg for entertainment or to resort to public boarding-houses. It would be vain to knock at the doors of a dead family for entertainment. Many families of professed Christians have this symptom of death. True Christian families always feel like reserving the best they have for others who may knock at their doors in His nâme. "Forget not to shew love unto strangers: for thereby some have entertained angels unawares" (Heb. xiii. 2). A revival of Pentecostal conversion always enthrones this grace, and its lack in many churches is good proof of spiritual destitution. "We need only reflect on the narrative of the Acts of the Apostles,'' says Professor Lumby of Cambridge, ''to realize how large a part hospitality must have played in the early church as soon as the preachers extended their labors beyond Jerusalem. The house of Simon the tanner, where Peter was entertained many days (ix. 43); the friends who at Antioch received Paul and Barnabas and kept them for a whole year (xi. 26); the petition of Lydia, ' Come unto my house, and abide there ' (xvi. 15); and Jason's reception of Paul and Silas at Thessalonica (xvii. 7), are but illustrations of what must have been the custom.'' Another says: '' Nor is it God's purpose that the grace of hospitality should ever disappear from the Christian Church. We are exhorted in Scripture to use ' hospitality one to another, without murmuring ' (I. Pet. iv. 9). To be ' given to hospitality ' (Rom. xii. 13) is one of the marks by which Christians are ever to indicate that they, ' being many, are one body in Christ.' Jesus regards its exercise toward His disciples as though it were a service rendered to Himself — ' I was a stranger, and ye took me in '—and will count it as one proof of that love whose crowning joy shall be the invitation, ' Come, ye blessed of my Father,' etc. (Matt. xxv. 34). There is, in many instances, a great lack of this grace among Christian people of to-day. Too often ' the prophet's room ' is forgotten in building, buying or renting our dwelling houses. Too often we let little inconveniences that might readily be overcome hinder us from entertaining some of the Master's beloved disciples whose presence in the homes would bring blessings immeasurably greater than the trouble and expense it would make us to take them in. Too often the lack of hospitality in our churches makes it impossible to entertain revival workers and general religious gatherings which would do much to quicken and build up the work of God among us, and so the work declines — largely on account of our self-ishness. My brethren, these things ought not so to be. If we have erred in these respects in the past, let the future witness our reform; and henceforth, in the true gospel sense, let us use ' hospitality one to another, without murmuring.' '' They are celestial oases in the Saharas of earth's Great Desert of Inhospitality. A mark of the spuriousness of many so-called Christian homes is their deadness to this Pentecostal grace. A family that is a stranger to Pentecostal hospitality has not stepped even into the vestibule of a Pentecostal experience.

Such is a brief outline of such homes as God wishes to fill this earth. They have existed from Pentecost until the present day, and are multiplying. They are verdant islands in the great ocean of humanity, full of pleasant harbors safe and restful, and their fragrance is borne by celestial breezes very far. God Himself protects them, and delights and abides in them. They are among His brightest stars in the dark night of human woe.

> Blessed homes and happy people,
> Where the Saviour loves to dwell;
> Where, uniting in His praises,
> All redemption's story tell.
>
> Where the Pentecostal fire
> Leaps and shines and burns and glows,
> Melting every selfish purpose,
> Till each heart with love o'erflows.
>
> Blessed homes and happy people,
> Live the world to bless and cheer;
> Witnesses of Jesus' power
> Heaven itself to bring so near.

Such homes are surrounded by the marble walls of God's protecting providences. They are roofed by His mercy, and from their beautiful windows of faith they can always see the King in His beauty and the land that is far off. They are heated by love, lighted with the electric radiance of divine truth, and watered by the celestial artesian fountain which continually springs up within. They are sections of the kingdom of God on earth. All who belong to them are already " in heaven." To die or welcome Christ and His coming will simply be moving up to more celestial shores. There is a hint that the King's purpose is, that there will be such removals frequently from one degree of glory to another for ever and ever!

What a contrast to the cold homes where selfishness and sin united reign. No prayer, no praise, no heavenly Christian love, no hope of a future home above, and no Christ to share life's joys or sorrows. Such a place is the object of God's curses and His judgments. Such are the families who reject God and who add to their rebellion, allegiance to the god of this world. Professing to be homes, they are pits of quicksand whose inmates are sinking down to doom. Such places are roofed by rebellion, windowed by unbelief, floored by doubt and foundationed by deception. Within lurks fear and wrong. God's lightnings are restrained from them only by infinite mercy, but soon will leap upon and destroy them. Professed Christian homes they may be, yet really feeders of the eternal flames.

CHAPTER IX.

PENTECOSTAL HEALING.

"The prayer of faith shall save him that is sick, and the Lord shall raise him up" (Jas. v. 15).

Redemption embraces three great and definite works for fallen man. First, Justification, through which he is forgiven and becomes a child of God. Second, the Baptism with the Holy Ghost, which sanctifies him wholly, destroying the "old man" of inbred sin, and enduing with "power from on high." Third, Final Glorification, which will totally eliminate disease and infirmities and all the effects of sin upon our minds and bodies, making them like that of our glorified Lord. Even now they become the "temples" of the Holy Ghost, and as usefulness here depends largely upon their condition, it is important to know the relation of redemption to them, even in this stage of their being. If they conform to all the laws of nature and of grace, and are temples of God, and are indwelt by Him who has all power in heaven and on earth, this certainly will lead us to expect that such a change will be salutary.

1. *It recognizes them.* Scripture frequently mentions them, and is explicit in its instructions for their well-being. Pentecostal consecration presents them a living sacrifice, holy and acceptable, and the God of peace who "sanctifies wholly" is able to preserve body, soul and spirit (I. Thess. v. 23).

2. *It conduces to health* by forbidding all over-indulgence of their lawful functions. Overeating and

sexual excesses are sapping the health and shortening the lives of many. A Pentecostal experience saves from these and all other excesses, and thus dries up a murderous torrent which is sweeping thousands upon its fatal flood.

3. *It demands cleanliness.* "Filthiness of the flesh" put away and "bodies washed with pure water" are conditions of closest communion with God. The Holy Ghost will not permanently abide in a filthy temple. Dirt must be washed from body as well as soul. It often is an index to the blacker filth within. A frequent bathing of the whole body is essential to the highest type of Christian vigor, and its practice would prevent many diseases. Clean hearts, clean spirits, clean habits, clean bodies, clean clothes, clean food and clean homes are all requisites of a Pentecostal experience, yet people persist in professing it who seldom take a thorough bath, and when dirt begets disease, wonder at the appearance of the dreaded child, and invoke a miracle to kill it. If such persons would more frequently call for "Elders," Soap, Water and Diet, there would be less need for other "Elders" to pray for Pentecostal healing.

It saves from all injurious habits. Tobacco, opium, candy, pork, tea and coffee are all authoritatively declared to be injurious to the health. Hence Pentecostal people, when convinced of this, drop them, and conserve health where others imperil it. Regeneration retained involves this question, but Pentecost brings intense light.

It makes happy homes. It makes every home where its principles are adopted an Eden. Instead of ghostly skeletons in its closets, its tables are surrounded by glad believers whose very presence banishes care and brings sunshine. He who has a happy Pentecostal home possesses a constant elixir worth more than all medicines besides. It banishes care and anxiety. Worry kills more than work. Anxiety breeds fever and insanity. A Pentecostal experience sepulchers worry and banishes anxiety, crowning contentment and perfect peace instead. It smoothes the wrinkles from the care-worn brow and brings roses to cheeks that were paling for the grave. It lengthens life by giving guidance from danger. Under its blessed reign the Holy Spirit warns, directly and indirectly, of imminent exposures, over-eating, injurious foods, accidents, dangerous companion-ships and places, or in the midst of these, divinely opens a way of escape. To avail one's self of these safeguards one must be very still and attentive. (See my book on "Impressions.") In all these ways possession of a Pentecostal experience and conformity to the laws which govern the Pentecostal life, conduce to the maintenance of health and to recovery from disease. This alone is worth more than all the insurance policies and **patent** medicines ever made. Were more attention paid to these laws of Pentecostal health there would be a smaller field for drugs and for divine healing. The healing promised to God's people under the Old Covenant was conditioned on observance of the most stringent sanitary regulations. Certainly the New does not lower the standard of the Old. It is presumption to knowingly break God's laws in nature and then ask Him to perform a miracle of grace to mend them.

But apart from all these beneficial accompaniments of salvation, there is a special healing of the body, as experienced in New Testament times and bequeathed to the Christian Church. That it is not a dangerous super-stition to be shunned or a fatal fallacy to be feared, is found from the following facts:

1. *It is Scriptural healing*. It was practiced by

Christ and His apostles, declared to be one of the "signs" which "follow them that believe," catalogued in the glorious list of "Nine Gifts" of the Spirit to the Pentecostal Church (I. Cor. xii. 7–11), and all who are sick are exhorted to call the church to the exercise of it (James iv. 14, 15).

What it is and some of its beneficent results are beautifully pictured in the healing of the lame man at the temple through Peter and John. This instance, with others, proves that it was not confined to Jesus; and its exercise by Philip, its enumeration among the gifts of the Pentecostal Church by Paul, and proclamation by Peter, prove that it is not designed to be confined to the Apostolic Church.

It is actual healing. The lame man did not think, guess or even believe he was healed. "And he, leaping up stood and walked, and entered with them into the temple, walking, leaping and praising God." It not only claims healing by faith, but possesses it in fact; a sad comment on the haggard ranks of professors of faith-cure who are constantly fading into skeletons. The writer has personally known persons to drop into their graves declaring they were healed, and seen many others, thus professing, who looked as if a breath might blow them there. This does not disprove Pentecostal healing, but simply the failure of these persons to grasp it, like many people who profess salvation but live destitute of its power. The error that healing of the body is like healing for the soul, available instantly to all, instead of being a special sovereign gift, has doubtless misled many sincere believers at this point. That some are deceived by counterfeit coin will not keep a sensible man from taking the genuine. The subjects of Pentecostal healing are not a line of emaciated shadows limping

towards the grave under the delusion that they are well
because they try to imagine it or believe it, "but are
made every whit whole, so that they see clearly," though
it takes the second touch to do it.   Presence of all the
disease symptoms is positive proof of the presence of
disease.   Such symptoms disappear when Jesus heals.

It is divine healing.   "But Peter said, . . .   In the
name of Jesus Christ of Nazareth, walk" (Acts iii. 6).
This was persistently repeated by Peter in his report
both in the presence of the multitude and to the Sanhedrin when he was on trial.   It is healing in response to
an appeal from one or more of God's true children to Him
in the name of Jesus Christ.   Healings have been effected
by mind cure and by false teachers, who have, like the
magicians who withstood Moses and Paul, "done many
wonderful works"; but all of these lack one of the above
marks, and are in no sense Pentecostal healings, and
none but mistaken men will urge their existence as an
argument against this Scriptural gift.

It is demonstrated healing.   Peter's patient is but one
of a great host who have experienced it and testify to its
power.   Scripture teems with examples of it, and there
are many such remarkable witnesses of it in the world
to-day.   The writer has experienced it, and has known a
number of such instances where, without any remedies,
saved people have been led of the Spirit of God to
commit themselves to Him for healing, with the assurance that He would give it, and have not been disappointed.   To affirm that all those thus healed were simply
deceived or would have recovered anyway, is a simple
way for people who oppose Pentecostal healing to seek to
subvert facts.

It is instantaneous healing.   "Immediately his feet and
his ankle-bones received strength" (Acts iii. 7).   There is

not a single record of apostolic healing where the subject
was exhorted to ''believe he was healed, whether he felt
any better or not,'' but all were actually healed, and
healed as soon as their faith touched the battery. That
God heals with means and without means, gradually, as
well as in an instant, is certain, but that is not the kind
of healing which Jesus did and the apostles dispensed, and
which we here examine under the head of Pentecostal
Healing. That kind is like light, this like lightning;
that is effectual through known natural laws, but this
by a superhuman act.

It is limited healing. So far as the record shows, the
lame man of Acts iii. was the only case of healing
among the multitudes at Pentecost or on this occasion.
This omission strongly indicates the precedence which
spiritual healing and saving held in the mind of the
Spirit and of His Pentecostal ministers, but the emphasis
that is given shows the divine endorsement, and that
it is a part of the work of the Pentecostal dispensation.
It was limited both in Christ and the apostles. In one
place, because of their unbelief, '' Jesus did not many
works,'' healing but '' few,'' while the apostles failed
completely in the case of the unclean spirit which '' came
out only by prayer and fasting.'' So that in the days
of its pristine power we see that there were at least
two limitations even with divinely-inspired men, *i. e.*,
unbelief and lack of prayer. The fact that the temper-
ature of the modern churches has fallen clear below
zero on both of these limitations accounts largely for
the frozen condition in regard to this Scripture truth.
Whoever heard of a person writing a book against it
fresh from a Pentecostal fast, or prayer chamber, or
revival victory? Only the prayer of *faith* is promised
to prevail, and when the gift of faith for healing is

not possessed, this prayer can not be offered, and healing must be sought by other means or give way to
submissive acquiescence in providential discipline. That
Jesus "bore our infirmities and carried our sicknesses"
will be known in its fulness only when clad in resurrection robes at His appearing, though scintillations of it
reach us here subject to the limitations mentioned. That
"He is just the same to-day" as when He healed
on earth proves that the limitations which bound Him
have not yet been broken, and indicate that they may
greatly circumscribe the triumphs of this gracious gift.
And we know of no guarantee in the Word, or in common
sense, that God will heal a man who will use that health
to live on in rebellion, or one who will persist in breaking the laws of nature. The candidate for Pentecostal
healing is required to so surrender to God as to be converted. "And the prayer of faith shall save him that is
sick, and the Lord shall raise him up; and if he have
committed sins, it shall be forgiven him" (James v. 15).
The bodily healing train is on the track and will enter
Resurrection depot on schedule time, but stops to take on
passengers only at the pleasure of the Conductor, and the
meeting of fixed conditions. Faith for this purpose is a
special gift,* bestowed when these conditions are met, and
the healing is in harmony with God's will, but is withheld
in other cases. Blindness to this fact has brought defeat,
disappointment, shame and perplexity. Prayer-meetings
for healing were customary in the early Church, and are
Scriptural, sensible, and helpful to Pentecostal holiness,
a gun which God will not allow the devil or His own
children to spike.

It is healing without medicine. Peter did not administer one patent pill. Not that medicine never should be

---

*See Godbey's "Gifts and Graces."

used, or that God never directs to it. Someone has said that "medicine is God's remedy for those who have not the gift to be healed without it." Such healing may be in answer to prayer, but is not Pentecostal healing as practiced by the early Church, imparted by the "gift of healing." That modern Peters should boldly claim that God never heals without the use of drugs, is open advertisement that they need the post-graduate course of some "sheet let down from heaven," and that the time has come for some Paul to withstand such error. God heals through means, but often does without them.

It is God-glorifying healing. "And they, when they had further threatened them, let them go, finding nothing how they might punish them, because of the people; for all men glorified God for that which was done" (Acts iv. 21). Whoever makes God's power known, glorifies Him. Pentecostal healing does this. As of old, it makes men know that Jesus is almighty and divine, and is a striking type of the higher, greater healing of the sin-sick soul. It shows His tender interests in the concerns of His children. He declares that not a hair of their heads can fall without His notice, and invites them, in everything, by prayer and supplication, to make their requests known unto Him. When He comes and heals, it is a token of His continued love and solicitude for His own.

It is a benediction to humanity. "And all the people saw him walking and praising God" (Acts iii. 9). Whatever blesses man, glorifies God. Sickness and pain flee before the command of the Galilean Conqueror, and death himself, startled, turns pale and knows that his crown soon must fall before His power. Doubtless there are priceless boons for suffering humanity stored away in this long-locked treasure-house. Even if it does no more than its enemies are compelled to admit, it is a blessing that should

be hailed as a benediction rather derided as a super-
stition.

It draws people to Christ.　If some come for the
"loaves and fishes" they may be constrained to remain
for the "treasure" and the "pearl."　The people "run
hither, greatly wondering" where such power and mercy
are displayed.

It exalts Jesus.　Any kind of professed superhuman
healing which does not exalt Jesus and give Him all the
glory is not Pentecostal healing.　"In the name of Jesus
Christ of Nazareth, whom ye crucified, whom God raised
from the dead, even in him doth this man stand here before you whole" (Acts iv. 10).

It is a revival power.　"But many of them that heard
the word believed; and the number of the men came to be
about five thousand" (Acts iv. 4)).　Instead of hindering the revival or detracting from holiness, it added an
impetus to both.　Though the multitudes marveled, and
sanctimonious ecclesiastics shook their heads and threatened Peter, yet thousands of people were saved, the enemies of Christ confounded, God glorified and the apostles
recommissioned to press the battle.

It confounds infidelity.　"And seeing the man which
was healed standing with them, they could say nothing
against it" (Acts iv. 14).　Wiser than when they arrested
the blind man whom Jesus had healed, and than some
modern opposers of divine healing, they did not deny the
fact, belittle it, or try to attribute it to other sources,
but admitted it and kept still.　Always and everywhere
Pentecostal healing confounds opposers, until they have
nothing to say or say something more silly than nothing.　Scripturally taught and claimed it always proves a
power instead of an embarrassment, as some have vainly
taught.

It helps develop a trustful Christian character. It culti-vates reliance directly upon God for healing, thus opening a new avenue of communion with Him, and of dependence on Him, which is a pleasing contrast to the self-sufficient conceit which scorns such reliance. It thus helps to develop a sturdy faith in God, like that magnified in Hebrews xi., and which will shine with celestial lustre when the names of its opposers shall have rotted in ob-livion.

It awakens opposition. "And they laid hands on them, and put them in ward unto the morrow: for it was now eventide" (Acts iv. 3). Satan will not see God thus honored and Jesus magnified and be quiet. It stirs up the high priests and Caiaphases and Alexanders and the "kindred of the high priest," who, "moved by envy," and jealous over the exercise of a power beyond their possession, tremble for the prestige of themselves and party. These men always try to kick up such a dust as to hide the truth, and blind the eyes of all who see it, but God defeats them by facts they can not dis-prove, and which it is folly for them to ascribe to Beelze-bub, and He emboldens His true servants to still claim such victory that with all boldness they speak His word so that, by the stretching out of His hand to heal, "signs and wonders may be done through the name of thy holy Servant Jesus" (Acts iv. 29, 30). To all oppo-sition from such voices the Peters and Johns of all ages have the ready answer: "We must obey God rather than men."

It is divinely indorsed healing. "And when they had prayed, the place was shaken wherein they were gathered together; and they were all filled with the Holy Ghost, and they spake the word of God with boldness" (Acts iv. 31). God attested its divinity by effecting the cure, defeating its foes, defending His ministers, and baptizing them afresh with the Holy Ghost for new victories.

It is miraculous healing. Pentecostal healing is a miracle, and the age of miracles has not passed. Men claim it has, but none can prove it. The power to work them is well nigh a lost art, but who shall say that it will not be restored? If you have not learned to appropriate this healing lightning, do not reason that therefore all who have are the victims of a sickening "superstition." If you are too tall to reach down and touch the button that brings it from the skies, do not call the children names that are little enough to reach it. If the fog and darkness of the black centuries have been so dense that but few have found it, and that those finding have not yet learned to manipulate it with the force and freedom of Jesus and the apostles, do not conclude them fools and fanatics, but give them your patience and your prayers. If many have mistaken a nailhole in the wall for this button, and their own fancies for the healing touch, do not be so foolish as to ransack history and heathendom, Scripture and superstition, to prove that therefore the currents have ceased and lightning falls no more. Remember that some secrets are hidden from the "wise and prudent" and revealed only to "babes." "Even so, Father, for so it seemeth good in thy sight."

It is available healing. "Silver and gold have I none; but such as I have, that give I thee." Like salvation, it is a free bestowment. Money can not buy it. "Is any among you sick? let him call for the elders of the church; and let them pray over him, anointing him with oil in the name of the Lord: and the prayer of faith shall save him that is sick, and the Lord shall raise him up: and if he have committed sins, it shall be forgiven him '' (James v. 14, 15). Scripture infers and facts show that where this course is taken, faith for healing, at least in some instances, will be given and cure effected. A close walk with God, sensitiveness to the teachings of His Word and leadings of the Holy Spirit, will enable each 'to detect God's will in the matter. '' Beloved, I wish above all things '' that you may be filled with all the fulness of God, and also that you may '' prosper and be in health even as thy soul prospereth.''

> In His promises confiding,
>   Let us learn His perfect will;
> In His secret place abiding,
>   Let us trust Him and be still.
> When He granteth "gifts of healings,"
>   Let us praise Him and believe;
> Thank Him for His gracious dealing,
>   And with joy the gift receive.
>
> When the gifts His love withholdeth,
>   Greater good to thus bestow;
> Let us kiss the hand that mouldeth,
>   Kindly caring for us so.
> Saviour, work this very hour,
>   Whatso'er Thy will may be;
> Thine the honor, glory, power,
>   Now and evermore shall be.

DIAGRAM OF THE RETURN OF JESUS.

V.
ASCENT OF CHRIST

PARADISAL PERIOD I

II PRE-CHRIST PERIOD. 4000 Yrs.

OLD TESTAMENT CHURCH

III COMING OF CHRIST
IV ATONEMENT PERIOD

VI DESCENT OF HOLY SPIRIT

VII.
PENTECOSTAL PERIOD
2000 YRS.

NEW TESTAMENT CHURCH

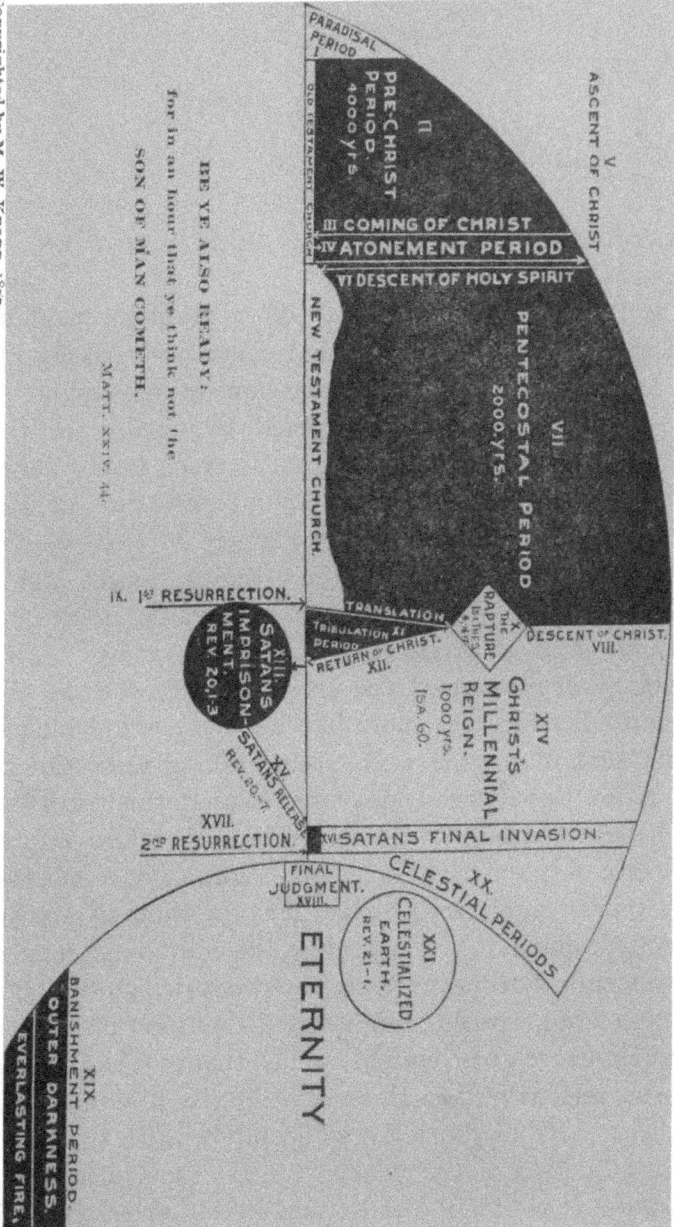

BE YE ALSO READY:
for in an hour that ye think not the
SON OF MAN COMETH.

MATT. XXIV. 44.

IX. 1st RESURRECTION.

TRANSLATION

X.
THE RAPTURE
1 THESS. 4. 17.

Tribulation XI Period

RETURN OF CHRIST. XII.

DESCENT OF CHRIST. VIII.

XIII.
SATANS IMPRISON-MENT. REV. 20, 1-3

XV.
SATANS RELEASE
REV. 20, 7

XIV
CHRIST'S MILLENNIAL REIGN.
1000 Yrs.
ISA. 60.

XVII.
2nd RESURRECTION.

XVI. SATANS FINAL INVASION.

FINAL JUDGMENT. XVIII.

XX.
CELESTIAL PERIODS.

XXI
CELESTIALIZED EARTH.
REV. 21-1.

ETERNITY

XIX.
BANISHMENT PERIOD.
OUTER DARKNESS.
EVERLASTING FIRE.

CHAPTER X.

The Pentecostal Church was like a beautiful maiden, robed in spotless bridal attire, and constantly looking for the promised return of the Bridegroom, who, having redeemed and won her, had departed to prepare for the wedding. This expectancy was not so much from a sense of duty as pain at the separation and pleasure in His presence. The true bride does not say of her beloved "must I expect him" nor even "may I expect him," but finds herself at the door and window a dozen times a day if there is a probability of his appearing. This expectancy characterized the early Church, and as the Church to-day becomes more like her Pentecostal model, we find similar longing and looking taking possession of her. Satan has always endeavored to keep this truth hid from believers, who, if unsanctified and therefore unprepared, are only too loth to listen. He has succeeded in filling men's minds with vague, misty notions of a post-millennial coming, which magnifies the church and human achievements, attributing to it the work which only our returning Lord can do, and wrested many prophecies of His millennial reign below and applied them to the Church, or to the celestialized earth as it will exist after the final judgment. He has buried it so deeply beneath the errors of "annihilation of the wicked" and "soul sleeping," setting the very day of the Return and other errors, that he has actually scared many good men from accepting and teaching this great Bible truth of Pentecostal signifi-

cance and power. Under the specious plea that its preaching would divert from holiness, he has prevented others
from its enjoyment and the comfort which its possession
and proclamation brings. The cause of holiness has nothing to fear from the preaching of this glorious truth,
but may well beware of being deprived of liberty by the
lasso of human prohibitions in regard to it. Instead of
hindering holiness, if rightly preached and received, like
the doctrine of the final judgment, it is one of the greatest
incentives thereto, as it represents holiness victorious and
eternally triumphant. Who constantly expects the coming of the Bridegroom will see that no sin-stains be found
on bridal robes, and that slumbering souls be awakened
and prepared. Others have been frightened from it
because of mistakes which some of its advocates have
made, and also because of the fog in which Satan has
sought to envelop it. And others, because learned schoolmen have derided it. But all doctrines have suffered in
the hands of their professed friends, and all have mysteries yet unfolded for us to learn, so that none of these
excuses should turn the truth lover from its consideration.
The vital place it occupies in Pentecostal doctrine and
experience should impel us to brush these cobwebs all
aside, and view it and review it as it really is. Thus
did the Pentecostal Church in early days, and if we
would possess its full-orbed privileges we must learn
the secret of the possession of this, as well as correlated
truths. Briefly we will bring its view, as well as able,
before our readers, for each of whom we covet the comfort
which it brings.

That tremendous emphasis is placed upon it by Scrip-
ture is seen in the expectant attitude of the entire
Church, in its mighty emphasis by our Saviour in
His charge to His people to be constantly watching and

ready for it, in the parables by which He vividly pictured it, by the uniform teaching of the apostles, and by the fact that it was the first message which God sent back to earth after our Saviour's ascension, and that He delegated two angels to proclaim it and charge the Church not to stand idly repining because of His absence, but assured of His personal return "in like manner" as He went away.

The fact that the possession of this truth is a source of peculiar comfort to the believer and inspiration to holiness, an incentive to soul - winning work, and its preaching is a mighty gospel power to strengthen, convert, sanctify and edify, further increases our interest in it.

What are the teachings of Scripture on this absorbing theme? In one brief chapter it is impossible for us to give them in full, but we will aim to give a clear outline, referring our readers to books named at close of chapter for fuller treatment of the subject. The accompanying diagram is designed to represent the Pentecostal view of this subject and its relation to preceding and following events, so that, by a little attention, it can be easily grasped.

1. *The Paradisiacal Period*, embracing the time from Creation to the fall of our first parents. It opens with man created in the image of his Maker, in "righteousness and true holiness," having "dominion" over "every living thing," and reigning with God in His Paradisiacal home; and closes with his rebellion against God, league with the devil, curse, and fatal fall. However, with the promise of the coming Christ, who should save from sin and "bruise the serpent's head."

2. *The Patriarchal and Mosaic Periods*, extending from Eden to the first fulfillment of the promise given

there of the coming of the Christ, a babe in Bethlehem's manger. This embraces repeated types and promises of the Messiah, who, as a helpless Lamb, "slain from the foundation of the world," would come and bleed and die upon the cross, and then as "Mighty God" and Israel's Shiloh King, should come again, "vex the nations in His sore displeasure, dash them to pieces like a potter's vessel," and with His white-robed Bride, upon the ruins of all creeds and kingdoms, establish an everlasting government of truth, in which all His people should be holy, and His will be done in earth as it is done in Heaven. During this period the Law was given and multitudes of flaming fingers in prophecy and type pointed ever onward to the coming of the Son of God to His Pentecostal Church and everlasting Kingdom.

3. *The Incarnation of Christ.* "Therefore the Lord himself shall give you a sign; behold, a virgin shall conceive, and bear a son, and shall call his name Immanuel" (Isa. vii. 14, also Matt. i. 21–25). The Jews confounded Christ's first coming with His Return. That they understood that a part of His mission was to restore the kingdom of Israel is evident from their question in Acts i. 6, and that such evidently is a part of His plan is inferred from the fact that He did not deny it, but simply withheld knowledge of the time. His first coming prepares the way for His promised Return. On Calvary the serpent bruises His "heel"; when He returns it will be to crush the serpent's head, and thus effect the Edenic prophecy in a sense which still lacks fulfillment.

4. *The Atonement Period.* This embraces the life of Jesus from the cradle to the cross and ascension; His life, His teachings, His Gospels, the call of His followers, His miracles, His crucifixion, Resurrection, Commission

to the Church, until He returned to the right hand of the Father. This period witnessed the fulfillment of all the prophecies foretelling His coming, and gave mighty emphasis and addition to those which heralded His Return. (See the Gospels and their references.) At this period, Christ, on the cross, redeemed the world and purchased the robe of entire sanctification, in which His Bride is to reign with Him forever.

5. *The Ascension.* Jesus had declared that He must " go to the Father " and prepare a place for His people. This He did. "So then the Lord Jesus, after he had spoken unto them, was received up into heaven, and sat down at the right hand of God" (Mark xvi. 19). "And if I go and prepare a place for you, I will come again, and will receive you unto myself: that where I am, there ye may be also" (John xiv. 3). "And when he had said these things, as they were looking, he was taken up; and a cloud received him out of their sight" (Acts i. 9).

6. *The Descent of the Holy Ghost.* The promise of the Holy Ghost is a white thread of many strands running through the prophecies of the Old Testament and the Gospels. "For I will pour water upon him that is thirsty, and streams upon the dry ground; I will pour my Spirit upon thy seed, and my blessing upon thine offspring" (Isa. xliv. 3; also Ezek. xi. 19; Joel ii. 28.) Their glorious fulfillment is found in Acts ii. 1–4, when, on schedule time, He descended, forming the Pentecostal Church, and taking the superintendency of the same on earth.

7. *The Pentecostal Period.* This embraces the Pentecostal Church, from the advent of the Holy Ghost at Pentecost until it is "caught up" at the Rapture. Escaping the fearful judgments of the Tribulation period,

she celebrates the nuptials with the Bridegroom and then returns with Him to the earth. This is the dispensation of the Holy Ghost, whose office it is to prepare the bride for the wedding. Under His leadership the Gospel is preached to all the world, and the Church prepared and perfected for the Rapture, Reception and Return.

8. *The Descent of Jesus* to receive the Bride. "But at midnight there is a cry, Behold, the bridegroom! Come ye forth to meet him" (Matt. xxv. 6; Rev xix. 7).

9. *The Translation* of living saints and *resurrection* of those who are dead, and their triumphant ascent to meet the Bridegroom in the skies. This is the first resurrection (Rev. xx. 5, 6). "For the Lord himself shall descend from heaven, with a shout, with the voice of the archangel, and with the trump of God: and the dead in Christ shall rise first: then we that are alive, that are left, shall together with them be caught up in the clouds, to meet the Lord in the air: and so shall we ever be with the Lord" (I. Thess. iv. 16, 17).

10. *The Rapture.* This represents the meeting and greeting of the Bride and Bridegroom, the marriage feast and preparation for the triumphant Return to earth. The length of time which the Rapture will continue is not given, but will doubtless not be long. In the nature of the case it can not be, if it is embraced in the time intervening between now and the close of the two thousand years of the present period. This meeting of the rescued and raptured bride with her beloved, the wedding, the greetings, and the glory, are too sweet for words to paint. Who would miss it for a million worlds like this! It will doubtless be a theme of song and story through all the bright millennial years, perhaps forever.

11. *The Tribulation.* While the Rapture is trans-
piring above, the time of Tribulation, such as never was
before or ever shall again be known, is taking place on
earth. "For then shall be great tribulation, such
as hath not been from the beginning of the world
until now, no, nor ever shall be" (Matt. xxiv. 21).
During the time between when Christ comes for His
bride and the time that He returns with her, the climax
of wretchedness will be reached on earth. Above the
earth the bridal gathering, upon it Satan's carnival of
crime and cruelty, compared to which the dark ages
were glorious day. During this period the following
events are all to transpire. Some of them seem to be a
continuation and intensification of the "vials of wrath"
mentioned in Revelation, and already being poured out
upon the earth. (See Godbey's Commentary on Rev.
xvi.)

From all these Judgments God's holy people will be
delivered, except those who may be saved through this
period, who will doubtless suffer martyrdom. The recent butchery of Armenian Christians may be the first
fruits of this bloody harvest, which will probably move
on until in the Tribulation it will be an awful cyclone.

People will be given up to revelling, gluttony and
drunkenness. "For as in those days which were before
the flood they were eating and drinking, marrying and
giving in marriage, until the day that Noah entered into the ark, and they knew not until the flood came, and
took them all away; so shall be the coming of the Son
of man" (Matt. xxiv. 38).

There will be a climax of skepticism in regard to
Christ's Return. "In the last days mockers shall come
with mockery, walking after their own lusts, and saying,
Where is the promise of his coming?" "For from the

day that the fathers fell asleep, all things continue as they were from the beginning of the creation " (II. Peter iii. 3, 4). "But if that evil servant say in his heart, My lord tarrieth; and shall begin to beat his fellow-servants, and shall eat and drink with the drunken; the lord of that servant shall come in a day when he expecteth not, and in an hour when he knoweth not, and shall cut him asunder, and appoint his portion with the hypocrites " (Matt. xxiv. 48–51).

Then will occur the fearful conflict of Har-Magedon. "And they gathered them together into the place which is called in Hebrew Har-Magedon " (Rev. xvi. 16). "And I saw the beast, and the kings of the earth, and their armies, gathered together to make war against him that sat upon the horse, and against his army " (Rev. xix. 19).

There will be fearful physical convulsions. "And there were lightnings, and voices, and thunders; and there was a great earthquake, such as was not since there were men upon the earth, so great an earthquake, so mighty. And the great city was divided into three parts, and the cities of the nations fell: and Babylon the great was remembered in the sight of God, to give unto her the cup of wine of the fierceness of his wrath. And every island fled away, and the mountains were not found " (Rev. xvi. 18–20).

There will be great national wars and distresses. "Then said he unto them, Nation shall rise against nation, and kingdom against kingdom; and there shall be great earthquakes, and in divers places famines and pestilences; and there shall be terrors and great signs from heaven. . . . And there shall be signs in sun and moon and stars; and upon the earth distress of nations, in perplexity for the roaring of the sea and the billows " (Luke xxi. 10, 11, 25).

There will be awful forebodings of coming catastrophies. "Men fainting for fear, and for expectation of the things which are coming on the world" (Luke xxi. 26).

Fearful and frequent earthquakes will convulse the earth, topple and crush like egg-shells its noblest structures, famines and pestilences shall decimate, and fearful sights and great signs from the Ancient of days who administers these merited judgments shall astound. "And there shall be great earthquakes, and in divers places famines and pestilences; and there shall be terrors and great signs from heaven" (Luke xxi. 11).

The false Christs and false preachers which abound now will multiply when the Pentecostal Church is withdrawn, and wax confident and increase in power to deceive. "For there shall arise false Christs, and false prophets, and shall shew great signs and wonders; so as to lead astray, if possible, even the elect" (Matt. xxiv. 24).

Antichrist will be revealed. "And then shall be revealed the lawless one, whom the Lord Jesus shall slay with the breath of his mouth, and bring to nought by the manifestation of his coming" (II. Thess. ii. 8).

Papacy will flourish and fall during this period. (See Rev. xviii.)

Antichrist will arise and combine all the forces of earth against the coming kingdom of God (II. Thess. ii. 8–10; Rev. xix. 20).

These and many more portentious events will find fearful fulfillment during the short but awful judgment-falling period preceding the final Return of Christ. Many of the events are already in the air. We can see the black cloud, and hear the awful mutterings of the thunder of this awful cyclone. There have been more earthquakes during the past century than in the eighteen which preceded it. Marvelous signs in the sun, moon and earth are being recorded by scientific men. Nations, as never before, are preparing for the great Har-Magedon conflicts of the Tribulation period. More whisky is made and drank now than ever before, and there are more suicides, murders, rapes, and lynchings. Saloons, gambling dens and brothels, like huge boa constrictors, are tightening their murderous folds. Ecclesiasticism, even among Protestants, seeks to lord it over spirituality, and Popery to grasp the reins of church and state. False prophets multiply, and the "people love to have it so." These are earthquake rumblings greater than even those which yet shall shake the physical world. They proclaim the nearness of the collapse of sin and Satan's power, and of the coming of the victorious blood-washed Rider of the white horse for the rescue of His saints, and the establishment of His everlasting kingdom.

"But when these things begin to come to pass, look up, and lift up your heads; because your redemption draweth nigh. . . . But take heed to yourselves, lest haply your hearts be overcharged with surfeiting, and drunkenness, and cares of this life, and that day come on you suddenly as a snare. . . . But watch ye at every season, making supplication, that ye may prevail to escape all these things that shall come to pass, and to stand before the Son of man" (Luke xxi. 28, 34, 36).

The Return. As the awful judgments of the Tribulation increase in fury, the hosts of hell grow more bitter, determined, defiant and united in their rage against the Son of God. When this period *is ripe* for the event Christ as He has promised will suddenly return. "And then shall they see the Son of man coming in a cloud with power and great glory" (Luke xxi. 27; also Acts i. 2; Rev. i. 7, and Rev. xiv. 14). The King and His shining, victorious hosts in triumph now come down. "And I saw the heaven opened; and behold, a white horse, and he that sat thereon, called Faithful and True; and in righteousness he doth judge and make war. . . . And he hath on his garment and on his thigh a name written, KING OF KINGS, AND LORD OF LORDS" (Rev. xix. 11, 16). Earth's armies arise to destroy Him as of old, but are defeated. "And I saw the beast, and the kings of the earth, and their armies, gathered together to make war against him that sat upon the horse, and against his army. And the beast was taken, and with him the false prophet that wrought the signs in his sight, wherewith he deceived them that had received the mark of the beast, and them that worshipped his image: they twain were cast alive into the lake of fire that burneth with brimstone" (Rev. xix. 19, 20). At this time the following events are scheduled to occur:

Sham political governments and counterfeit ecclesiasticisms, with all their leaders, will be destroyed (Rev. xix. 20).

Satan will be arrested, bound and banished to the bottomless pit for one thousand years. "And I saw an angel coming down out of heaven, having the key of the abyss and a great chain in his hand. And he laid hold on the dragon, the old serpent, which is the Devil and Satan, and bound him for a thousand years, and cast him into the abyss, and shut it, and sealed it over him, that he should deceive the nations no more, until the thousand years should be finished" (Rev. xx. 1-3).

Martyrs will be resurrected, and will share in the millennial reign. "And I saw thrones, and they sat upon them, and judgement was given unto them: and I saw the souls of them that had been beheaded for the testimony of Jesus, and for the word of God, and such as worshipped not the beast, neither his image, and received not the mark upon their forehead and upon their hand; and they lived, and reigned with Christ a thousand years'' (Rev. xx. 4). Christ will personally replace all governments of church and state with His own kingdom, and fill every position with holy persons, and Daniel's prophecy that the government shall be given into the ''hands of the most high,'' shall find glad fulfillment.

The Millennial Reign. This extends from the Return to the final judgment. The following events are evidently scheduled for this period:

1. It is in the kingdom period in which Christ Himself shall reign over all the earth. ''And there was given him dominion, and glory, and a kingdom, that all the peoples, nations, and languages should serve him: his dominion is an everlasting dominion, which shall not pass away, and his kingdom that which shall not be destroyed'' (Dan. vii. 14. Also Ps. lxxii. 8; Zech. xiv. 9; Rev. xi. 15).

2. His bride, the church, crowned as kings and priests with resurrection bodies, shall with Him share the government over all the teeming millions of earth. '' But the saints of the Most High shall receive the kingdom, and possess the kingdom for ever, even for ever and ever '' (Dan. vii. 18). ''And the kingdom and the dominion, and the greatness of the kingdoms under the whole heaven, shall be given to the people of the saints of the Most High: his kingdom is an everlasting kingdom, and all dominions shall serve and obey him'' (Dan. vii. 27). ''Blessed and holy is he that hath part in the first resurrection: over these the second death hath no power; but they shall be priests of God and of Christ, and shall reign with him a thousand years'' (Rev. xx. 6. Also Rev. v. 9, 10, and I. Cor. vi. 2).

3. God's people will have bodies like the Saviour's after His resurrection. "Celestial flight alternating with terrestrial travel." "But they that wait upon the Lord shall renew their strength; they shall mount up with wings as eagles; they shall run, and not be weary; they shall walk, and not faint" (Isa. xl. 31).

4. The twelve apostles will be prime ministers of Christ's kingdom, to the twelve tribes of Israel. "And Jesus said unto them, Verily I say unto you, that ye which have followed me, in the regeneration when the Son of man shall sit on the throne of his glory, ye also shall sit upon twelve thrones, judging the twelve tribes of Israel" (Matt. xix. 28).

5. Inanimate creation will rejoice as now she sighs. "For the creation was subjected to vanity, not of its own will, but by reason of him who subjected it, in hope that the creation itself also shall be delivered from the bondage of corruption into the liberty of the glory of the children of God" (Rom. viii. 20, 21).

6. Animal nature will lose its ferocity, and the earth, singing instead of groaning, will bring forth roses instead of thorns and briars (Isa. lv. 13).

Wars will be no more. "And he shall judge between the nations, and shall reprove many peoples: and they shall beat their swords into plowshares, and their spears into pruning-hooks: nation shall not lift up sword against nation, neither shall they learn war any more" (Isa. ii. 4).

All who before this time forsook all for Christ, now receive an hundredfold. "Verily I say unto you, that ye which have followed me, in the regeneration when the Son of man shall sit on the throne of his glory, ye also shall sit upon twelve thrones, judging the twelve tribes of Israel. And everyone that hath left houses, or brethren, or sisters, or father, or mother, or children, or lands for my name's sake, shall receive a hundredfold, and shall inherit eternal life '' (Matt. xix. 28, 29).

Unprecedented revivals will sweep the multitudes into the kingdom of God. ''Then thou shalt see and be lightened, and thine heart shall tremble and be enlarged: because the abundance of the sea shall be turned unto thee, and the wealth of the nations shall come unto thee '' (Isa. lx. 5). With the devil chained, and godless governments and ecclesiasticisms destroyed, the saints in power in both church and state, and the Holy Ghost co-operating with a holy people, revivals of religion will flood the earth with their mighty Niagaras of saving grace until it is inundated.

Holiness will be characteristic of the age. ''And they shall call them The holy people '' (Isa. lxii. 12). Holy churches, governments, preachers and people shall be the rule instead of, as now, the sad exception.

God's people will be made rulers over many things and enter into the joy of their Lord. '' His lord said unto him, Well done, good and faithful servant: thou hast been faithful over a few things, I will set thee over many things: enter thou into the joy of thy lord '' (Matt. xxv. 21).

The Release. At the close of the one thousand years of more than Paradisiacal glory on earth, Satan is loosed for a little season out of his prison. ''And when the thousand years are finished, Satan shall be loosed out of his prison '' (Rev. xx. 7). True to his diabolical instinct, he flies back to reattempt the conquest of earth. He yet will show the Son of God that earth is not invulnerable nor sanctification a proof against his wiles. Multitudes, '' the number of whom is like the sands of the sea,'' listen to him. They rally round the beautiful capital of earth,

Jerusalem, where peace has reigned for one whole thousand years, and threaten the destruction of the unarmed King and people, but, as the prize so greedily grasped for seems to be right in their hands, the heavens open, as upon the fated cities of the plain, and fire comes down from God out of heaven ''and consumes them.'' ''And they went up over the breadth of the earth, and compassed the camp of the saints about, and the beloved city: and fire came down out of heaven and devoured them '' (Rev. **xx.** 9).

Thus ends Satan's final invasion of earth, in total and inglorious defeat and eternal banishment, with his two lieutenants of political and ecclesiastical intrigue, to burning and eternal torments.

The Final Judgment. This is represented as following the execution of the devil. As Christ is already on His throne there is at this time no mention made of His coming. The judgment of the wicked began at Christ's Return, falling in fearful fury upon the living and holding the wicked dead awaiting this, their final, execution.

The righteous, who shared the first resurrection, ''shall not come into condemnation '' (judgment, Gr.), but have received rewards according to the deeds done in the body, doubtless to be blessed with unfolding capacities and installments of glory forever. At this point the following named events occur:

The dead, small and great, are summoned before the Judge, this including the good who have died during the millennium, and the wicked of all the ages. ''And I saw the dead, the great and the small, standing before the throne: and books were opened: and another book was opened, which is the Book of Life: and the dead were judged out of the things which were written in the books, according to their works '' (Rev. **xx.** 12). ''All that are in the tombs shall hear his voice, and shall come forth; they that have done good, unto the resurrection of life; and they that have done ill, unto the resurrection of judgement" (John v. 28). The parable of the sheep and goats evidently has application both to the preliminary judgments and rewards which are given at the close of the Tribulation period, and also to those at the final invasion and defeat of Satan. The same principle applies in both cases, and both are administered "when the Son of man comes and sits upon the throne of his glory." When we remember that the "then" mentioned in this parable is from the lips of Him with whom "one day is as a thousand years," and that the penalty at His appearing imprisons the wicked until the sentence is passed upon all at the final judgment, apparent difficulties dissolve. The parables of the talents and of the sheep and goats recorded in Matt. xxv. evidently embrace events which begin to transpire at the inaugural of Christ's millennial reign, but find their completion in the rewards and penalties at the last resurrection and final judgment at the end of time. The popular conception that they all occur at one time is doubtless incorrect. If we say that when a President takes the chair such events will transpire, we do not necessarily mean that they will all take place the day or year of his inauguration, but during his administration. This view of the meaning of these parables shows their harmony with other teachings of Scripture on this point. How strange that men who interpret the word "then" to cover years, when applied to the administration of a President or King, insist upon it meaning an instant when applied to God!

The good are rewarded according to their works, and the wicked all banished to hell to be punished according to theirs; the righteous differing from each other as stars in glory, the wicked receiving "few stripes or many," in eternal doom according to light rejected and opportunity abused.

"And if any was not found written in the book of life, he was cast into the lake of fire" (Rev. xx. 15). The crime of opportunity neglected, is here branded with awful condemnation. "And cast ye out the unprofitable servant into the outer darkness; there shall be the weeping and gnashing of teeth" (Matt. xxv. 30). "Then shall he answer them, saying, Verily I say unto you, Inasmuch as ye did it not unto one of these least, ye did it not unto me. And these shall go away into eternal punishment: but the righteous into eternal life" (Matt. xxv. 45, 46).

Angels are judged. "And angels which kept not their own principality, but left their proper habitation, he hath kept in everlasting bonds under darkness unto the judgement of the great day" (Jude 6).

The Banishment Period. This embraces the never-ending doom of Satan, devils, and wicked spirits from earth. "But for the fearful, and unbelieving, and abominable, and murderers, and fornicators, and sorcerers, and idolaters, and all liars, their part shall be in the lake that burneth with fire and brimstone; which is the second death" (Rev. xxi. 8). "Without are the dogs, and the sorcerers, and the fornicators, and the murderers, and the idolaters, and everyone that loveth and maketh a lie" (Rev. xxii. 15; also Matt. xxv. 46, and Mark ix. 43–48).

The Celestial Periods. These cover the infinite ages of the kingdom of God, in which His redeemed blood-washed people, as co-heirs with Jesus, have free access to that great city, the holy Jerusalem (Rev. xxi. 10), and to the purified, celestialized earth, which will be divinely fitted for their eternal inheritance (Rev. xxi. 1). "He that overcometh shall inherit these things; and I will be his God, and he shall be my son " (Rev. xxi. 7). "And there shall be night no more; and they need no light of lamp, neither light of sun; for the Lord God shall give them light: and they shall reign for ever and ever" (Rev. xxii. 5).

"He that testifieth these things saith, YEA: I COME QUICKLY." May each reader, like the prophet of Patmos, say and feel, "AMEN: COME, LORD JESUS."

Blessed are all who are ready for these great events. Fearful will be the fate of those who are found without the wedding garment of holiness, and whose lamps are not filled with the oil of the Spirit.

This, the Pentecostal view of Christ's Return and related events, is a mighty incentive to holy living, and brings blessings to all who welcome it. The following are its advantages over the idea that defers Christ's coming to the misty, indefinite future:

It reminds that the King may come at any moment, thereby presenting a double need of watchfulness, compared to the view that removes His return beyond the millennium, and is a constant incentive to keeping arrayed in the wedding robe of entire sanctification, "holy in all manner of conversation" and inciting others to be thus prepared.

It harmonizes with Scripture and facts; the postmillennial view with neither.

It eliminates neither the Tribulation nor the millennium.

It naturally and beautifully points to the fulfillment of both Old and New Testament prophecies.

It explains the first and second resurrections.

It locates harmoniously Satan's imprisonment, his

final invasion, and eternal banishment from God's celestial worlds.

It does not depend on creeds or members, but Scripture for its support.

It reveals man's "golden age," as the product of human achievement, but through the power of Christ, that in "all things He might have the pre-eminence." Instead of treating Christ's return as a dry doctrine outside of the range of experience, it begets the "glorious hope" and anticipation of His coming. Is not this an "experience" worth possessing?

It begets a longing to meet the Saviour, instead of a disposition to dispute about His return.

It avoids the error which teaches that the mission of the Spirit and the Church is a failure unless they convert the earth in this dispensation, and the pessimism which relegates the advent of the millennium to a slow process of human endeavor, instead of according it, as Scripture does, to the return of Him upon whose shoulders the government shall be.

It saves from the blunder that expects the world to "grow better and better" until Jesus comes, in the face of facts and Scriptures, which clearly declare that that time shall be "as the days of Noah," and that then "one shall be taken, and the other left." (See Matt. xxiv.). Would Christ have said, "Nevertheless, when the Son of man cometh, shall he find faith on the earth?" if He taught that the earth was to be in full millennial bloom at His Return. A correspondent of the Western Christian Advocate recently and truly writes: "The condition of the modern world is not much better than was the condition of the ancient world. The decay of faith which has been going on for the last three hundred years has left a vast body of men and women without God in the world.''

It is a bond of union between Pentecostal people, who have largely stampeded from the ranks of post-millennialism into the bright day of New Testament sunshine on this subject. Such princely commentators as Alford, Godbey and their associates, and such soul-winners as Spurgeon, Moody, Gordon and many more, have led the way along this shining Pentecostal path, and prove this position impregnable without resort to creeds, church history, wresting Scripture, or trying to belittle the work of men of different views, upon whom God has unmistakably set His seal.

It blows away the dust in regard to Christ's coming, which has been raised by post-millennial theorists, and in which many honest souls have been befogged. Knowing that the Word of God is on its side, its possessors welcome the odium of Chiliasts, etc., with which speculators in lieu of Scripture arguments, have sometimes ridiculed them.

It avoids the unscriptural assumption that there is but one resurrection, and plants itself upon the Gibraltar of the Word, which clearly declares two. (Rev. xx. 5, 6, and references.) When God thus clearly speaks, let every human voice be hushed.

It rejects the unwarranted assumption that the Holy Ghost will be withdrawn during the millennial reign, but believes that He will, as now, lead a holy people in the great revivals that will then flood the earth.

It repudiates the charge that it teaches a future probation, unless by that is meant probation during the millennium, which all views of Christ's return admit.

It is saved from the necessity of trying to build an argument on an exception instead of a rule. All the

parables and other teachings of the New Testament like
a rolling river, declare that the righteous are to be resurrected and rewarded before the wicked.   See parable of
the net (Matt. xiii. 47, 48); the virgins, the talents, and the sheep and goats (Matt. xxv. and references).   The only seeming exception we find is the
parable of the tares (Matt. xiii. 36-43).   This single
exception has been quoted by the adherents of post-
millennialism as a *rule*, while the fact is that it is an
exception, and is explained from the fact that it evidently
refers to the final banishment of all the wicked before
the saints possess, not the millennial but the celestialized
earth, which time follows the final judgment.   Truth
needs no such perversion of Scripture to sustain it, and
error thus advertises its own defeat.

It gives men a chance to develop the highest character both on probation here, and in the exercise of all
their powers as kings and priests unto God and the
Father in the future.

It does not depend on mere reformatory movements,
but seeks to convert men, and teach them "all things
whatsoever" Jesus has commanded, and sympathizes
with all efforts that are for the good of man and glory of
God.

It acknowledges the failure of the world and of sin
and Satan's kingdom, and magnifies grace and Heaven's
Kingdom.

It is in harmony with the goodness of God.   He
warns the sinner of his doom, yet respecting His free
agency allows him to take his choice and "eat the fruit
of his own doings," while He rescues and rewards all
who heed His voice.

It explains many of the prophecies which declare the
Return, but does not, as some mistaken people have

done, presume to set the day or the hour, which God has clearly declared that "no man knoweth."

It avoids the unscriptural position which foists upon us the sacrilegious conclusion that the work of the Holy Ghost up to this time is largely a failure, and shows that He has done, and is doing, the work designed by God, though greatly hindered by human slowness and stupidity.

"Christ and the apostles preached it." "Be ye also ready: for in an hour that ye think not the Son of man cometh" (Matt. xxiv. 44, and preceding references.) It is mentioned hundreds of times in both the Old and New Testaments. In the light of this, how glaring is the mistake of those who deride it, or who would muzzle ministers proclaiming it. Either burn the Bible or believe it.

Its proclamation leads to salvation. "How ye turned unto God from idols to serve a living and true God, and to wait for his Son from heaven" (I. Thess. i. 9, 10). It was one of the motives which led early converts to forsake their sins. The first time the writer preached it, two penitents came weeping to the altar. It has awakened and blessed multitudes.

It heralds the highest elevation of the human race, a progress unparalleled, in which a holy, kingly Christ shall lead a holy people, with the co-operation of the Holy Spirit, up summits of victory more glorious than it has ever entered into the heart of man to conceive.

It teaches that it is always better farther on. If, as a post-millennial philosopher claims, "we are now in a far better school of faith than we would be by gazing on the visible Christ enthroned on earth," then by the same kind of reasoning we are better off now than we will be hereafter, and heaven itself is a step backward! We prefer to be excused from a belief which compels such a conclusion. In God's curriculum the ever-advancing student reaches a course where faith is lost in sight and prayer in praise.

It harmonizes with the facts of Scripture and history. Men are being born much faster than they are being saved, and hence the wicked, in that proportion, are and ever have been increasing. A parade of bloated religious statistics in which mere church-joiners are counted as converts, is no argument, for even if they were really converted, the above fact remains.

It is guiltless of the false charge that it preaches the Gospel "for a witness only," but proclaims it in its primitive purity, power and effectiveness. (See preceding chapters of this book.)

It is in harmony with God's government in all ages. In the antediluvian world, sin brought castigatory judgments, and only a favored few were saved. So with Lot in Sodom. So with Jerusalem, and so it is declared to be at the coming of the Son of man. "Narrow is the way and few there be that find it."

It is winning its way on every side, in face of the fanaticism and mistakes of some of its friends and the opposition of its foes, who use the same sophistries to defeat it that others use to defeat holiness.

It is a foe to pessimism. It vividly pictures the final abolishment of sin, the defeat and banishment of the devil, the failure of his diabolical campaign to capture earth, and the full, final and overwhelming triumph of grace through our Lord Jesus Christ. It is pessimistic only in its view of sin and its consequences, but of Christianity it is superlatively optimistic.

It fixes the eyes of the soul on the Return of Jesus rather than the advent of death as a crowning motive to repentance and holiness. Scripture seldom warns of death, but frequently of the coming of the King.

The possibility of Christ's sudden appearing and the certainty that all who are not ready, if they live, must suffer the awful woes of the tribulation period, are mighty awakening truths which Scripture bequeaths to the Church, and of which post millennialism robs it.

It is a mighty incentive to unworldliness. He who anticipates early removal to fairer climes will be less likely to set the affections on things below. Worldliness is spiritual treason. This Pentecostal view of Christ's return, thus lessens temptation to it, and impels to lay up treasures in the skies.

It fosters a missionary spirit. The movements and people who hold it are among the most aggressive in mission work. If some of them, as it is claimed, preach the gospel for a "witness only," let us rejoice instead of complaining, that Christ is even thus preached, and send on others to perfect the work thus begun. The effect of this truth in inspiring to missionary effort, is illustrated in the last message of the sainted Gordon, who said: "He who is not a missionary Christian will be a missing Christian when the great day comes for bestowing the rewards of service. Therefore ask yourself daily what the Lord would have you do in connection with the work of carrying the news of salvation to the perishing millions. Search carefully whether He would have you go yourself to the heathen if you have the youth and fitness required for the work. Or, if you can not go in person inquire diligently what blood mortgage there is upon your property in the interest of foreign missions — how much you owe to the heathen, because of what you owe to Christ for redeeming you with His precious blood. I warn you that it will go hard with you when your Lord comes to

reckon with you if he finds your wealth invested in superfluous luxuries or hoarded up in needless accumulations
instead of being sacredly devoted to giving the gospel to
the lost.''

It represents Holiness universally and eternally
triumphant, and gives all the glory to the Father, Son
and Holy Ghost. No marvel that Satan has long sought
to bury such a truth in oblivion, piling upon it unscriptural errors and mountains of ecclesiastical rubbish like
that with which he hid the precious doctrine of entire sanctification. The opposition of its enemies, the
errors of some of its friends, and criticisms of good people from whose eyes the scales concerning it have not
yet fallen, should impel all upon whose hearts, like a
star of hope, it has sweetly dawned, by pen and voice to
proclaim its facts as a vital part of the glad tidings of
the Gospel to every creature.

''Who then is the faithful and wise servant, whom
his lord hath set over his household, to give them their food
in due season? Blessed is that servant, whom his lord
when he cometh shall find so doing. Verily I say unto
you, that he will set him over all that he hath. But if
that evil servant shall say in his heart, My lord tarrieth;
and shall begin to beat his fellow-servants, and shall
eat and drink with the drunken; the lord of that servant
shall come in a day when he expecteth not, and in an
hour when he knoweth not, and shall cut him asunder,
and appoint his portion with the hypocrites: there shall
be the weeping and gnashing of teeth'' (Matt. xxiv.
45–51). ''Watch therefore, for ye know not the day nor
the hour'' (Matt. xxv. 13). ''Be patient therefore,
brethren, until the coming of the Lord. Behold, the husbandman waiteth for the precious fruit of the earth, being
patient over it, until it receive the early and latter rain.

Be ye also patient; stablish your hearts: for the coming of the Lord is at hand. Murmur not, brethren, one against another, that ye be not judged: behold, the judge standeth before the doors '' (James v. 7-9).

> Christ is coming! Let creation
> Bid her groans and travail cease;
> Let the glorious proclamation
> Hope restore and faith increase;
> Christ is coming!
> Come, thou blessed Prince of Peace!
>
> Earth can now but tell the story
> Of thy bitter cross and pain;
> She shall yet behold thy glory
> When thou comest back to reign;
> Christ is coming!
> Let each heart repeat the strain.
>
> Long thy exiles have been pining,
> Far from rest, and home, and Thee;
> But in heavenly vesture shining,
> Soon they shall thy glory see.
> Christ is coming!
> Haste the joyous jubilee.
>
> With that '' blessed hope '' before us,
> Let no harp remain unstrung;
> Let the mighty advent chorus
> Onward roll from tongue to tongue;
> Christ is coming!
> Come, Lord Jesus, quickly come!—J. R. Macduff.

For further treatment on this subject see Gordon's '' Ecce Venit,'' $1.25; Godbey on '' Revelation,'' $1.00; Pickett's '' Behold, He Cometh,'' 25 cents.

CHAPTER XI.

THE PENTECOSTAL CHURCH.

There are few subjects concerning which there has been more confusion than that of the Church. Satan has taken advantage of this fact, and made the most of it. In order to help dispel the fog which settles down upon the subject, the following truths must be borne in mind:

1. That no body of unconverted persons, no matter by what name called, ever was, or ever can be, the Church of Christ or any part of it.

2. That the fact that a body of such persons may have the names of a few regenerate or sanctified people upon its rolls, does not constitute it a New Testament church, any more than a few sweet apple trees in a thorn thicket would constitute that field a sweet apple orchard.

3. That a body which was once a branch of the Church, but whose ministers and members have back-slidden, is not the Church, even though it bears its name, any more than the bed of a river is still a river, when its waters are dried up.

4. That observance of baptism, the Lord's Supper and other forms of public worship, do not in themselves constitute a church, any more than boys playing at war constitute an army.

5. That religious activity and deeds of benevolence, fairs and festivals, mission contributions, etc., fail to constitute a church, for all of these things, and many like things, may be done by people destitute of salvation (I. Cor. xiii.).

THE RAPTURE.

6. That fine places of worship, and elegant furniture, and eloquent religious orators and artistic music do not constitute a church, for it exists with none of these things, and these things often exist under its name, but totally destitute of its nature.

7. A body of converted and even sanctified persons, if officered and controlled by unconverted men and manipulated in the interest of the world, is not the Church of Christ any more than the State of Ohio would be a Union State, even though many of her sons were loyal, if her offices and government were controlled by traitors. The Jewish Church, betrayed by its leaders, forfeited divine recognition as a Church, though many devout persons were within its fold.

8. A building with a steeple, and pulpit and pipe organ, does not constitute a Christian church, for all of these might be the accompaniments of even unbaptized infidelity and worldliness.

9. That a society of "nice people" does not constitute a church. If so, many secular societies would be churches, as they are full of "nice people," as the world measures. The Greek word translated "church" is indicative of its true nature, meaning "the called out." People who have come out from the world and worldly ties and associations, been regenerated by the power of the Holy Ghost and accepted God as their Father, Jesus as their Saviour, and have received or are ready to welcome the Holy Ghost as their Sanctifier, are the only material out of which Christ's Church can be built. Any body of persons which claims to be a Scriptural church, without meeting this primal condition, is a fraud, and guilty of the spiritual crime of sorcery, the punishment of which is declared in Rev. xxi. 8.

A common dodge of the enemy is to organize a worldly

club, or to transform a body of God's people into one, engaging in all sorts of worldly deeds, and then if any individual with spiritual sight protests and warns, upbraid him with being "disloyal to the Church" and if one has love and courage enough to unmask the fraud, to impale him on the sharp spikes of cutting criticism. The lightning bolts of God's truth, which leap from Pentecostal skies of Scripture revelation upon these hypocritical shams, will doubtless be considered "sacrilegious" by the class of sanctimonious Pharisees who accused Christ of blasphemy and of devil possession, because of kindred lightning leaping from Him upon their heads. But modern hypocrites are just as snugly housed behind their mock religions, as were the ancient, and only bolts of lightning will break their influence upon souls they have deceived.

One of Satan's shrewdest tricks is to mask his generals as ministers and his army as churches, and thus by his "sorceries" seek to deceive the whole earth. However, the Scripture marks of Christ's true Church are such that the simplest saint, with open Bible and open eyes, may see the difference between the genuine and the counterfeit. The following are some of the characteristics of a genuine New Testament Church:

It is an unworldly Church. It has renounced the world and all its ways and works, and is free from all complicity in worldly schemes. Its buildings, furniture, singing, ministry, finances, mission work and members conform to God and not to the world. A church controlled by worldly men and a worldly policy, given up to carnivals, concerts and carnality, has ceased to be a church of Christ. If it will not repent and be converted, the true believers in it should transfer their presence and support from the apostate harlot to some living branch of the true Vine. Upon such sham churches and people the Pentecostal declaration, "Ye adulterers and adulteresses, know ye not that the friendship of the world is enmity to God?" leaped with death-dealing fury. The following clipping from a secular paper is a sample from multitudes which might be cited illustrating the apostasy of so called churches, and the reproach which their treason foists upon the cause of Christ: "A pious fraud. Ladies beat the world in getting up attractive church entertainments. They held one a few nights ago, and advertised as a feature of it a 'Swimming Match' between two young ladies. The house was crowded of course. When the 'Swimming Match' was reached on the programme and the curtain raised, two ladies were seen on the stage with a stand between them. On the stand was a wash bowl of water; and on the surface of the water was a lucifer match floating or swimming. The audience was hit in the center of its risibilities, and screamed and roared with laughter." Thus Samson shorn of his locks grinds corn for the Philistines, while some of them laugh, others mock, hell rejoices and angels weep.

It is a converted Church. The Epistles addressed the churches as being "in Christ" and in God the Father, and the members as "sanctified" and "saints," terms that millions of worldlings in the churches to-day actually despise, and which can no more be applied to their character than gold to rust. That Ananiases and Simons crept in can not be doubted, but they were shot off like water from a redhot stove. The first Pentecostal Church was composed of the one hundred and twenty who gathered at the upper chamber for the express purpose of receiving the Holy Ghost as their Sanctifier. They were not disappointed, but received Him, were fully sanctified, and transformed into such enthusiastic, demonstrative, world - forsaking, sin - destroying dynamite for God, as would be unwelcome in the proud, aristocratic churches of our day. These, and the multitudes converted under their ministry, constituted the first Pentecostal Church. What a rebuke to apostate preachers who substitute church-joining and rites for regeneration, and pack the so-called church with poor deluded worldlings who have not given up their sins. A practice which leads ministers to omit the call for penitents and the altar of prayer, and substitutes the uplifted hand, the signing of a card, or joining of the church, for the experiences of salvation, in the light of Pentecost, is as black treason as the fall of Lucifer, yet practiced on every side.   True churches are composed of genuinely converted members.

Its membership is enrolled in heaven. '' But ye are come unto Mount Zion, and unto the city of the living God, the heavenly Jerusalem, and to innumerable hosts of angels, to the general assembly and church of the first-born who are enrolled in heaven, and to God the Judge of all, and to the spirits of just men made perfect, and to Jesus the mediator of a new covenant, and to the blood of sprinkling that speaketh better than that of Abel'' (Heb. xii. 22–25).   Its records are kept on high, and its attendants are angel hosts and departed saints.

It is a sanctified Church.   '' Wherefore Jesus also, that he might sanctify the people through his own blood, suffered without the gate '' (Heb. xiii. 12).   Sanctification is the daily attire of Christ's Bride.   In regeneration she puts on this robe, in entire sanctification it is cleansed from every stain.   Hence, the apostle addresses the churches as the sanctified, and at the same time prays that they may be sanctified wholly.   All true church members are sanctified in part, and either long for or possess entire sanctification. The howl and the growl which rises from some sources against sanctification prove the crowd from whence they come to be a pack of wolves that fear the fire, instead of Christ's true Church, of which that fire is the very source of light, life, love, victory and power.

It is a faithful Church. The oft-repeated definition that the "Church is a body of faithful men in which the Word of God is preached and sacraments duly administered," is a good one, and between the lines declares in type of vivid lightning that a body of *unfaithful* men, where the Word is *not* faithfully preached, aping as a church, is a sacrilegious humbug.

It is an obedient Church. Christ commanded it to tarry at Jerusalem until entirely sanctified, and though on the very ground where human hyenas were still howling against them and their Leader, yet its members tarried, men, women, and children, until the promised power came, and it became the storm-center of a salvation cyclone which transforms sinners into saints, and sweeps them up to be with Him forever, and whose sin-exposing, fraud-detecting lightnings have been the terror of the Judases, Caiaphases and Ananiases of all the ages.

It belongs to God. "That thou mayest know how men ought to behave themselves in the house of God, which is the church of the living God, the pillar and ground of the truth" (I. Tim. iii. 15). Some people speak of "*my* church," as if they were the owners; others of "*our* church," as if they were its possessors. God owns His Church as really as He does His throne in heaven; in fact, it is His throne on earth. By the threefold right of creation, redemption and preservation, it belongs to Him, and His lightning falls upon all who seek to rob Him of His rights.

It is subject to Christ. "And he put all things in subjection under his feet, and gave him to be head over all things to the church, which is his body, the fulness of him that filleth all in all" (Eph. i. 22, 23). As the head He plans for the body, and as the body it is directed by His will. Hence, ecclesiastical organizations which defy His will, whether Popery or dead Protestantism, are no part of His true body. She must be loyal to Him. When cliques, and committees, and counsels seek to come between her and Him, she must resist them as Peter and John did the Sanhedrin, loyal Luther the Papal Diet, and as a true bride would the approach of a treacherous seducer. Loyalty to organization or doctrine must not be substituted for loyalty to Christ. He who allows doctrine, or organization and ministers to usurp the headship of Christ in the Church, desecrates the temple of God by idolatry more inexcusable than that of pagan lands, because in the presence of greater light. In God's true Church His headship is recognized and obeyed.

Its officers should be baptized with the Spirit. "Look ye out therefore, brethren, from among you seven men of good report, full of the Spirit and of wisdom, whom ye may appoint over this business" (Acts vi. 3). Here we get a hint that the temporalities of the Church should be in the hands of laymen whom God especially qualifies for the work, and that they should be holy men. A holy ministry and officiary is God's design for the Church. If men must graduate at West Point to officer an army, how much more must they graduate at the Pentecostal chamber for the more arduous work of officering Christ's Church? As well put traitors at the head of an army, as worldly officials in the Church. God prefers no church in a place, to one manned by holiness-fighting preachers and worldly officials. When you place an unsaved man on your Board because he is shrewd or influential or wealthy, and set aside men and women full of the Spirit, you insult the Holy Ghost, and advertise to all worlds that you think yourself wiser than God. Better a million fold to fast, pray, preach, and plead with God, until He shall convert and fit such men for these sacred offices as He can use, and whose ministrations He can bless. President Finney began a great revival by disbanding a worldly church, converting the disbanded members, and re-organizing. Men who would denounce a builder for putting decayed timber in a material building, will persist in putting crumbling clay in God's temple, where He has clearly indicated that there should be blocks of gold. Such churches prosper! How can they?

It is a Spirit-led Church. When Stephen was made deacon, and also when Paul and Barnabas were "separated" to their work, the mind of the Spirit was learned, and His will was done. Thus counsels and conferences of the Pentecostal Church seek the Spirit's mind, and learn and do His will, while sham churches are swayed from other sources and by lower motives.

It is a divinely-defended Church. "For the Lord is our defence; and the Holy One of Israel is our king" (Ps. lxxxix. 18, A. V.).

> "Zion stands by hills surrounded,
>   Zion kept by power divine,"

is a sickening burlesque when applied to the dead, worldly ecclesiasticisms, which parade under the name of the Church; but when applied to God's true people, it is full of beauty, comfort and truth. Hid in the pavil-

lion of God's power and providences, the Bride is kept
from "strife of tongues," and no one can touch a hair of
her head without divine permission, for her good and
God's glory.

It is a holy Church.   By its conformity to the will of
God, its nonconformity to the world, its freedom from
compromise measures, its fire-baptized testimonies, its
pointed, loving, inspired rebukes, its passion for Jesus,
its love for souls, its self-denial and liberality, and by its
judgments upon shams and dishonesty it proves its possession not simply of a theoretical belief in holiness, but
that it is in full possession of this priceless jewel.

It is a divinely-provisioned Church.   God provides.
for all her spiritual needs.   Apostles, prophets, evangelists and teachers are given for her regeneration,
her edifying, her unity, her protection from false doctrines and crafty impostors, her illumination, her edifica-
tion, her growth and her perfection in love.   "And he
gave some to be apostles; and some, prophets; and some,
evangelists; and some, pastors and teachers, for the
perfecting of the saints, unto the work of ministering,
unto the building up of the body of Christ: till we all
attain unto the unity of the faith, and of the knowledge
of the Son of God, unto a full grown man, unto the
measure of the stature of the fulness of Christ'' (Eph.
iv. 11–13).   The above named classes of ministers are
designed to work together unitedly to this end, and the
Pentecostal Church recognizes and welcomes all whom
God thus commissions.   The objection to Pentecostal
evangelism and evangelists which is in the air, was not
born nor is it fostered in the real Church of Christ, which
is too humble to dictate to her divine Head as to the
agencies He shall employ, and too grateful for the bless-

ings thus bestowed to harbor such a spirit of censorious criticism.

It is a hospitable Church. It used "hospitality without murmuring." A great Christian paper says: "One of the most deplorable features is the way in which the laity have ceased to entertain their members; it has a widespread habit of sending deputations to public hotels." Churches which conform to the New Testament model, love the society of their ministers too well to thus banish them from their homes.

It is a united Church. "There can be neither Jew nor Greek, there can be neither bond nor free, there can be no male and female: for ye all are one man in Christ Jesus" (Gal. iii. 28). Baptized into one body by the Spirit of God, there is a divinely imparted unity of faith, of love, and of expectancy of His return and endless reign. Branches of the true Vine, they derive their life and strength from one Centre, and unitedly bear fruit for His glory. A clique of divided, jangling, jealous, self-seeking, place-grasping churchlings is no more God's Church than heaven is hell. Such may creep into it, but its heat will soon melt them or make them move out. Barriers of race, and color, and social position have no true place in Christ's Church. Black faces may have hearts whiter than snow, while many a white face has a heart as black as the "outer darkness." High-toned social clubs, claiming to be churches, but throwing stones of criticism and ostracism at saints of God because of caste or color, are among the most stupendous of Satan's frauds which curse the earth to-day. Respecters and selecters of persons, they are drifting into the merciless whirlpool of divine retribution to certain and fearful doom. What a contrast to the "Body of Christ," in which there "worketh the one and the same Spirit, dividing to each one severally even as he will. For as the body is one, and hath many members, and all the members of the body, being many, are one body: so also is Christ" (I. Cor. xii. 11, 12).

It is a fruitful Church. Like the tree by the rivers of waters, it brings forth its fruit in its season. Beautiful blossoms of bright and ripened fruit of holy lives perennially abound upon its boughs. Like the banyan tree, it spread, until its converts were found from the tents of the desert to the courts of the Cæsars. Pentecostal churches are always fruitful churches.

It is a righteous Church. Unrighteousness is the dirty, ragged uniform in which Satan clothes the members of his sham churches. He who is knowingly wrong in public or in private life, has not upon him the righteous robe which covers every member of Christ's real church. Tricks in trade, neglect of church, business and home obligations, refusal or criminal neglect to right wrongs, all debar from membership in the Church of God, where "judgement must run down as waters, and righteousness as a mighty stream." Much of the wrong in the world to-day can doubtless be traced to the lack of discipline in regard to righteousness in the dead and dying churches of the land.

It is a Word-honoring Church. It searches the Scriptures whether these things are so. It does not look to a worldly pastor to see how easily it can live, but to the Word of God to learn how right it can be. It seeks, obeys and rejoices in the Word of His grace which is "able to build up," and "give an inheritance among the sanctified." Hence it is saved from censorious wildfire, fanaticism and kindred perils, which subvert people who ignore God's Word, and substitute dreams, visions, impressions, desires, carnal counsel and fancies instead.

It is a divinely-made Church. "And the Lord added to them day by day those that were being saved" (Acts ii. 47). Only God can unite a person to His church, and He unites only saved persons—positive proof that church-named crowds of unsaved people are no part of the Church of Christ, and that the farce of substituting baptism or church-joining for coming to Christ is a delusion and a snare. Sham churches coax people to unite with them. True churches point them to Christ, who alone can initiate into His body.

It is a universal Church. "From whom every family in heaven and on earth is named" (Eph. iii. 15). It consists of the regenerated in all climes and conditions above and below, living and dead. Its members are found in many diverse communions, but all have the marks of celestial birth and citizenship. They all love each other, and will soon be gathered in a grand, final, inseparable family reunion with their Father and their Elder Brother in the mansions being made ready for their eternal habitations.

It is a persecuted Church. "For ye, brethren, became imitators of the churches of God which are in Judæa in Christ Jesus: for ye also suffered the same things of your own countrymen, even as they did of the Jews; who both killed the Lord Jesus and the prophets, and drave out us, and please not God, and are contrary to all men; forbidding us to speak to the Gentiles that they may be saved" (I. Thess. ii. 14–16). The devil hates true Christians and true churches full of Pentecostal power and activity. Hence if he can not silence them he always marshals all his hosts against them. He is too wise a general to waste his ammunition on paper men. The reason sham churches do not draw his fire is that they are his allies, and he has nothing to fear from them. But in every age Pentecostal churches have been persecuted churches. If you think this is not true get the baptism with the Holy Ghost and fire, sanctified wholly, and lead an aggressive campaign in which sinners are genuinely regenerated and believers entirely sanctified. Hold after-services persistently and definitely for these purposes. Persevere until upon the Church the Holy Ghost comes down and the people weep, and laugh, and shout with Pentecostal joy. All who are doing this know by experience the truthfulness of this paragraph.

They are rejoicing Churches. They "took joyfully the spoiling of their goods," and counted it all joy that they were permitted to be co-sufferers with the heavenly Bridegroom. Defective and spurious churches can not do this, but shirk duty and repine at censure and opposition.

It is a praying Church. When opposed, perplexed and persecuted, it prayed until the powers of darkness were shaken; until prison doors burst asunder, enemies were conquered, chains broken and Satan defeated. This is the mightiest weapon in God's true Church. It knows how to fly to its knees and "lift up holy hands without wrath and doubting," and bring down Omnipotence to fight its battles. Its prayer-meetings are places of power, and it has no need of church kitchens except to feed the poor. Its prayer of faith heals the sick, delivers the tempted, converts the sinner, sanctifies and edifies believers, removes mountains of financial embarrassment and divides Red Seas of seeming insuperable barriers. Sham churches are destitute of this power of all-conquering prayer. The true church flies to its knees when assailed, a weak church stands still with fright, a sham church resorts to controversy and compromise. Prayerless men are powerless men. Spiritual power comes not so much from a learned pulpit as from a church upon its knees.

They are thoroughly organized Churches. Under the Holy Ghost they were equipped and organized for conquest. Each person had His proper gift utilized for the good of the entire body. Women divinely called, preach, and prophesy, and witness, while the unlearned in human lore are wise in the things divine. God chooses the weak things to confound the mighty, and the things that are not to bring to naught the things that are. The human body and an army are divine types of the Church of Christ—both perfect in their organized capacities, subject to a controlling head, each function or division working in organized unison with all the rest. No organization is a scheme of the devil to prevent the mighty, resistless onset upon His kingdom, which united, organized effort brings.

It is a loyal Church. Loyal both to its divine Leader and to His appointed agents. It welcomed, obeyed and supported them. It was a stranger to the stingy disloyalty which refuses to liberally sustain the Gospel ministry; and gave not grudgingly but from a glad heart and with a willing mind. A professed church which is disloyal to God has no claims on the loyalty of believers. It must be loyal to God and His Word, and disloyal to all that is contrary thereto. If a man can not be loyal to Jesus Christ, the Holy Ghost, the Word of God and the church of which he is a member at the same time, it is proof that something is wrong with his church.

It is an exile Church. It was born from above, and is a pilgrim and stranger in this world. Its home is in heaven; its rest is not here. It is not conformed to the fashions of this world. Like a missionary among bar-

barians, who retains the customs of his own country, expecting to return, so the Pentecostal Church, like its Divine Redeemer, retains the customs, fashions and laws of the royal family of which it is a member, instead of those of the traitorous world, in which it for a little time has its mission.

It is a working Church. It is a total stranger to the dead works of the day which have been so widely substituted for Christian labor. We hear of no hospital being built professedly for the glory of God—really for the praise of some rich man; no aid societies to stitch shoddy garments to be sold to the highest bidder to lessen the assessment on rich members; no lecture-bureaus and musical rehearsals, broom drills and crazy-quilt socials, etc. These shameless bastards were not yet born. Her works were prompted by faith in Jesus and executed out of pure love for Him. This led the Pentecostal Church barefooted to climb thorny steeps, descend into serpent-infested ravines, and brave heat, cold, penury, fire and sword, to become "all things to all men that it might *save some.*" It is just the same to-day.

It is a witnessing Church. A stream of testimony broke forth at Pentecost that, like a mighty Amazon, flooded the entire world. At home, abroad, in private and in public, among friends or foes, the members of that Church ceased not to speak forth the power of Jesus to fully save. There is no record of any Pentecostal preachers attempting to suppress the fire-baptized witnesses. One sure mark of the dead condition of many churches to-day is their dumbness. In backslidden churches there are many substitutes for primitive testimonies. Scripture quotations, commenting on the preceding sermon, political harangues, talking about trials and tribulations, expressing desires and resolutions, exhortations, etc., have been allowed to take the place of witnessing to the power of Jesus to save from sin, and of the Holy Ghost to fully sanctify; but God detects and rejects the cheat, and none are deceived but its perpetrators. A dumb church on the subject of experimental salvation is a dead one, no matter how aggressive she may be on other lines. Spiritual lock-jaw is a certain sign of spiritual death. A Pentecostal experience always brings the blossom and fruit of a Pentecostal testimony.

It is an uncompromising Church. It had no alliances, public nor secret, general or individual, with the world, the flesh or the devil. Its members did not "renounce the vain pomp and glory of this world" with their lips, and then attire themselves in the height of worldly fashion, and thus belie the vow in their lives. Yet just such public religious lying as this is constantly occurring under the cover of the sacred rite of baptism. We read of but one Ananias and Sapphira in the early Church, but their blood seems to be the seed of a fearful harvest. What hollow, hypocritical mockery! Baal thus offers incense to Jesus Christ, where His professed ministers officiate! When some honest soul protests and points to the wrong, his voice is drowned in an uproar of protests and excuses such as rival the commotion which the town clerk at Ephesus was unable to hush. None of its ministers officiated at the secret rites of worldlings. No modern "Diana of the Ephesians" cry of party politics, social influence, or popularity could cause them to veer one iota from their fidelity to the principles of Christ's kingdom. The worldly compromise methods which to-day are a fixture in many churches for raising money and for entertaining and amusing, were then all unknown. Imagine Paul putting a leading pagan upon the Official Board because "he would be a great financial

help," and give the church "social standing." Modern
worldlings who are resisting the light of the Gospel as
it now shines are a millionfold worse than were the
honest pagans of that age; yet modern methods give them
church membership and official position on every hand.
Truly, the Pentecostal constitution is violated and God
displeased, and His curse rests on such a combination.
Imagine Peter joining some worldly society to "extend
his influence" and get help or protection should he or his
family ever "come to want." Yet, would-be modern
Peters are doing the same far and wide. But they differ
widely from Pentecostal Peter, in that they are destitute
of his zeal for God, his spirit of self-sacrifice, his assurance of salvation, his endowment of the Holy Ghost, his
power to heal the sick, and to bring down revivals of
flaming fire in the proud Jerusalems where so many of
them have their appointments. What apostle in the
Pentecostal zone ever announced a "Necktie Social," or
"Singin' Skule," or "Crazy Social" at the opening or
close of one of their discourses, and followed the an-
nouncement with the "hope that it will be liberally
patronized"? Yet how frequently professed apostles of
our sleeping churches do this. How few have the conviction and courage to say "No," and teach their people
the difference between Satan's shams and God's gold.
One must be dead indeed to dare to do such a thing. In
many places it would cause a volcanic eruption which
would land the preacher away in some backwoods Car-
mel, where he would be tempted to feel that he was the
only one not bowing the knee to Baal, and where his
auditors would largely be mosquitoes, ticks, and pine
stumps, unless God should interfere, and, as with Paul
at Iconium, bear His faithful servant to some fairer field
of usefulness. We hear of no members of the Pente-

costal churches who gave more time and money to worldly orders than to the Church, for they were not conformed to the world, but were transformed by the renewing of their mind to prove the perfect and good and acceptable will of God. Hence "No compromise" was stamped by the Spirit on every Pentecostal Christian's brow. That seal is not stamped there in lodges, nor theaters, nor at church frolics, though quickly lost at these places, but at the altar of prayer, in the secret place of the Most High, under the burning seal of the Pentecostal baptism.

The members of the Pentecostal Church were all baptized into one body. They were all bound together with the golden bond of love. Celestial fire had burned out the dross of carnality so that there was no foundation within their hearts upon which to build sectarian walls. The Paulites and Johnites and Peterites were too insignificant a minority of unsanctified members to start a new denomination, so no iron walls of separating creeds had yet been reared. Faults and individual differences were all buried deep beneath the flowery sod of perfect love. This was the Church as launched from the Pentecostal harbor. It soon was corrupted so that even in apostolic times, divisions, such as have led to the sects of this and preceding centuries, appeared. All were exhorted to be "of one mind," and at Pentecost this mighty miracle was wrought, a token of God's will and power to His people in His Church forever. What a sad comment on this privilege and requirement is the jangling factions into which Satan has split the churches of the present day.

It is an expectant Church. "For our citizenship is in heaven; from whence also we wait for a Saviour, the Lord Jesus Christ" (Phil. iii. 20). "When Christ, who is our life, shall be manifested, then shall ye also with him be manifested in glory" (Col. iii. 4). "And when the chief Shepherd shall be manifested, ye shall receive the crown of glory that fadeth not away" (I. Pet. v. 4). As an enraptured bride anticipates her wedding day and the constant presence and communion of the bridegroom, so she looks forward to a like joyful consummation. Now He dwells in her heart by faith, but then both heart and eyes shall behold Him. Now her love for and sympathy with Him is limited by infirmities, but then with perfect mind, soul and body she shall be like Him, and able to love Him, and serve and delight in Him as never before. So, while she "occupies until He comes," preparing herself and others for His appearing, she, as He commanded, is constantly looking for His return. Satan has made a desperate effort to steal this robe from the Church, but is being defeated. Sham churches dread to meet Him in their ragged, dirty robes, and so deride His coming. Pentecostal churches rejoice in the "glorious hope of His appearing."

It is a victorious Church. "Upon this rock I will build my church: and the gates of Hades shall not prevail against it" (Matt. xvi. 18). Triumphantly overcoming opposition from traitors within and earth and hell without, it is destined to sweep on from victory to victory, until "every foe is vanquished, and Christ is Lord indeed."

It is a blood-bought Church. "Which he purchased with His own blood" (Acts xx. 28). At an infinite price He purchased its freedom by shedding His own blood upon the cross, and thus demonstrated His love for it, and by His glorious resurrection His power to make it like Himself.

It is built on a firm foundation. "Behold, I lay in Zion for a foundation a stone, a tried stone, a precious corner stone of sure foundation: he that believeth shall not make haste" (Isa. xxviii. 16). The Church of Christ is built upon Himself. Hence no storms can shake it, and no earthquakes can cause it to move. Every lie forged against it by the devil and his false preachers shall be "swept away," and all its foes, like so many drowning rats, shall be flooded out of their hiding places. During the coming "overflowing scourges" of the Tribulation, when the wicked shall be trodden down under its awful castigatory judgments, it, divinely delivered, shall rest unmoved upon its divine foundation.

It shall be blessed with inspiring revivals. "The Lord shall arise upon thee, and his glory shall be seen upon thee. And nations shall come to thy light, and kings to the brightness of thy rising. Lift up thine eyes round about, and see: they all gather themselves together, they come to thee: thy sons shall come from far, and thy daughters shall be carried in the arms. Then thou shalt see and be lightened, and thine heart shall tremble and be enlarged: because the abundance of the sea shall be turned unto thee, the wealth of the nations shall come unto thee" (Isa. lx. 2–6, also balance of chapter lx.) The Pentecostal Church is a revival Church. The revivals of this period will doubtless continue to multiply until the Rapture, and sweep over the earth in cyclones of converting, sanctifying power all through the millennium.

It shall have universal dominion. "For that nation and kingdom that will not serve thee shall perish: yea, those nations shall be utterly wasted" (Isa. lx. 12). This prophecy is not yet fulfilled. There is not a nation on earth that serves Christ's Church, nor even recognizes

His Kingship. Such are doomed, and must make room for those which shall delight in righteousness.

It is a comforted Church. "To appoint unto them that mourn in Zion, to give unto them a garland for ashes, the oil of joy for mourning, the garment of praise for the spirit of heaviness; that they might be called trees of righteousness, the planting of the Lord, that he might be glorified" (Isa. lxi. 3). Thus God comforts it with His abiding presence and protection, and with the promise of glorious victory over all its foes, culminating in the participation in the coming millennial kingdom, and eternal possession and joint ownership with Christ of the celestialized earth, and administration of the universe.

From the foregoing facts it is evident that there is a great chasm between the Church as pictured in the New Testament, and many organizations which go by that name to-day. The following are some of the differences:

Every church may have unworldly members, but they do not control it. Sham churches are controlled by them. True branches of the visible Church acknowledge Christ as the supreme Head, the Holy Ghost as His Executive, and the Word of God as their Guide. Sham churches substitute committees, conferences, cardinals or popes in the place of Christ, ignore the Holy Ghost, twist Scripture to suit creeds and substitute the opinions of men for the Word of God. The first is a conservator of Holiness and Bible truth, the latter a cage of "unclean birds," whose stench pollutes the air, and who fly with its errors to the uttermost parts of the earth. The first is born from above; the second, from below. One is a life-boat to save men; the other, a death-trap to decoy and destroy men. The first arrayed in white will reign with Christ forever; the second, whether in the form of popery or of her fallen Protestant daughters, He will consume with the "Word of His mouth, and by the brightness of His coming." Sham churches are open for fairs, festivals and frolics, but closed to Pentecostal Revivals! They seek and support man-pleasing servants instead of God-pleasing ministers. They prefer essays and lectures to sermons on sanctification. They glory in their social position, rather than in Jesus Christ, and magnify culture and a college curriculum above experimental salvation. Such are a stench in the nostrils of God, and snares through which Satan is peopling hell with victims. The Pentecostal Church, unlike much that is called church to-day, was not a social club, or dress parade, or amusement bureau, or a restaurant, or a literary association, but God working through His people to save and edify. So called churches which do not this are dead, while they profess to live. Their hypocritical pretension will be unmasked at the judgment, where their faithless officers and members must meet the God whose trust they have betrayed, and the lost souls they have deceived.

The following duties and privileges fall to all who are true members of the Church of Christ:

Do not despise it. "What? have ye not houses to eat and to drink in? or despise ye the church of God, and put them to shame that have not? What shall I say to you? shall I praise you in this?" (I. Cor. xi. 22). Men who despise it by spurning all organization, or by foisting upon it their ungodly lives, or by feeding it upon poison doctrine, or seeking to fill it with unsaved people or disgracing it by worldly amusements and comic entertainments, are guilty of a gross insult both to the King of kings and His espoused bride. Its enemies are warned. "If any man defile [margin, destroy] the temple of God, him will God destroy." The temple of God here indicates souls both in individual and Church capacities, and people who by neglect, or false doctrine, or persecution thus "destroy," thereby invite the lightning bolts of divine retribution.

The believer's privilege and duty in regard to Church relations is plain. God will show His own what to do under all circumstances if His will be earnestly sought. If you belong to any branch of Christ's true Church, serve Him faithfully there. If you belong to some sham combination that is professing to be His Church, but is not, if you can not effect a change, then identify yourself with some true branch of the living Vine. God wants His people to waste no time nor money in support-ing Satan's shams. Pray, counsel with wise, experi-enced, faithful children of God, who know all the facts, and if your way is completely committed to God, "He will direct your steps." Beware, however, lest Satan, because of carnality and counterfeit coin identified with His true people, should on that account cause you to dis-card it. A vessel with traitors on board, yet manned by true men, is vastly different from one owned and con-trolled by them. The crowd which decries all organiza-tion and ostracizes all who will not join it, lacks at least one of the main marks of the true Bride. Each member under God must decide his own course of action. If he is not to judge, who then is to do it? The hireling pastor? The worldly official members who guard the spurious church? Such judgment is one of the preroga-tives of every free moral agent, which neither church nor state has a right to wrest from him. Men apply this principle individually to political parties, and on the same principle they should to churches. He who would rob of this right is a self-constituted pope.

Magnify it. "If I forget thee, O Jerusalem, let my right hand forget her cunning. Let my tongue cleave to the roof of my mouth, if I remember thee not; if I prefer not Jerusalem above my chief joy'' (Ps. cxxxvii. 5, 6). True church members thus pray for and plan for and prefer the prosperity of the Church above their ''chief joy,'' gladly sacrificing their own personal preferences for her good. Sham members selfishly sacrifice her interests for personal profit or promotion.

Appeal to it. ''And if thy brother sin against thee, go, shew him his fault between thee and him alone: if he hear thee, thou hast gained thy brother. But if he hear thee not, take with thee one or two more, that at the mouth of two witnesses or three every word may be established. And if he refuse to hear them, tell it unto the church: and if he refuse to hear the church also, let him be unto thee as the Gentile and the publican'' (Matt. xviii. 15–17). It is the duty of the Church to thus settle differences among its members which they can not adjust in the manner described above. To ignore this commandment and fly to worldly courts is wrong.

Feed it. '' Feed the church of God '' (Acts xx. 28). Ministers are thus intrusted with its sustenance. He who feeds it poisoned or diluted food, or starves it, does so at both its peril and his own.

Pray for it. '' Pray for the peace of Jerusalem '' (Ps. cxxii. 6). True Church members pray for the highest prosperity of the Church, not simply for its material prosperity, but that, ''without spot or wrinkle, or any such thing,'' its ''salvation may go forth as a lamp that burneth.''

> ''For her my tears shall fall,
>   For her my prayers ascend;
>   To her my cares and toils be given,
>   Till cares and toils shall end.''

Love it. "They shall prosper that love thee" (Ps. cxxii. 6). Christ so loved the Church that He gave Himself for it, and its members possess a kindred love. As His Father sent Him into the world, so sends He them.

> "With stately towers and bulwarks strong,
>   Unrivaled and alone,
>   Loved theme of many a sacred song,
>   God's holy city shone.
>
> "Thus fair was Zion's chosen seat,
>   The glory of all lands;
>   But fairer, and in strength complete,
>   The Christian temple stands.
>
> "The faithful of each clime and age
>   This glorious Church compose;
>   Built on a rock, with idle rage
>   The threatening tempest blows.
>
> "Fear not; though hostile bands alarm,
>   Thy God is thy defense:
>   And weak and powerless every arm
>   Against Omnipotence."   —Harriet Auber.

For a fuller treatment of the subject of this chapter, see "The Ideal Pentecostal Church," by Seth C. Rees. 50 cents.

ON THE ROCK AND ON THE SAND.

PENTECOSTAL PREACHERS.

Hear they the King's command,—
Though foes on every hand
Rise up through all the land
      Him to defy.

        Though fiery fagots burn
        Their feet from Him to turn,
        All pain they nobly spurn,
            Victory, their cry.

Theirs not the craven cry,
Theirs but to do or die,
Loyal to God on high,
      Onward they move.

        Though men and devils rage,
        All hell its powers engage,
        Yet still from age to age
            They faithful prove.

When on the field they fall,
Hear they the Saviour's call,
Sounding to one and all:
      "Reign thou with me."

        Soon in His kingdom fair,
        His power they shall share,
        And reign in glory there,
            Eternally.

CHAPTER XII.

The Bible is an album full of pen portraits of Pentecostal Preachers, which are placed there for our study. The object of the following pages is to point to the divine portraits of the privileges, requirements and character of these heroes of the Cross.

The view of them thus seen has been an inspiration to the writer, and he hopes and believes that it will be to every true preacher who reads these pages. It is also believed that it will incite in the hearts of every reader greater love and more intense loyalty for Christ's ministers, and that it will also help to discern between their character and that of the "apostate apostles," whose pictures will be found in subsequent chapters.

God requires that all of His ministers under the Pentecostal dispensation shall possess a Pentecostal experience. Wise commandment ! glorious privilege ! Those who are living in its light bear the marks and share the blessings herein magnified. Their character and qualifications are the same now as when the Pentecostal fire first fell.

They are divinely-called preachers. They do not select the ministry as men do a trade, but God selects them as a workman selects his tools. They are divinely chosen tools—chosen to accomplish a divine work. This they know, and it inspires both their confidence and humility : confidence because they feel that their "sufficiency is of God" ; humility, because they know that of themselves they are utterly unable to accomplish the work. Self-appointed ministers are unprepared, unchosen tools, which seek to thrust themselves into the Master's hands. Pentecostal preachers are God-called men. "No man taketh the honour unto himself, but when he is called of God, even as was Aaron" (Heb. v. 4). "Not from men, neither through man, but through Jesus Christ, and God the Father, who raised him from the dead" (Gal. i. 1). One may be self-called, friend-called, and even church-called, without being God-called. Such are not Pentecostal preachers in the Scriptural sense of that term.

They are Christ-commissioned preachers. Jesus himself gives all his true preachers a personal call to that apostleship as really as He did Peter, John and Paul. Thus the Second Person in the Trinity unites with the First in selecting whom He wishes for these places of sacred trust and responsibility.

They are Spirit-endorsed preachers. The Holy Ghost said: "Separate me Barnabas and Saul for the work whereunto I have called them" (Acts xiii. 2). The Spirit Himself, through the church, voices the call of the Father and Son, so that every true minister has the authority of the Trinity to his call.

They are Church-commissioned preachers. God always leads His Church to recognize those whom He calls to preach His truth. When a dead ecclesiasticism usurps the place of the real Church of Christ, it does not do this, but His real bride always does.

New Testament preachers all had this recognition and worked in harmony with and subject to the visible Church.

Pentecostal preachers, now as then, are thus favored and sustained. If God's true people, with all the facts of the case, are unable to recognize a minister's gift to this sacred office, he may rest assured that he is mistaken or that the time for its exercise has not yet come.

They are divinely qualified preachers. "Who also made us sufficient as ministers of a new covenant; not of the letter, but of the spirit : for the letter killeth, but the spirit giveth life" (II. Cor. iii. 6). A true Pentecostal preacher is dead to self-sufficiency, but glowingly conscious of God's sufficiency. Instead of having the "big head" he has a big heart, and big faith in a great almighty God, who is more than a match for all the Jezebels and Pharisees and Herods and Sanhedrins of the ages. He also knows that this God who made the heavens and earth and all that in them is, has, upon a guilty, hell-doomed rebel, even the chief of sinners, turned His redemptive omnipotence, and pardoned, baptized with the Holy Ghost, endowed with the Spirit's gifts, and "made an able minister " of His spiritual kingdom. Hence every Pentecostal preacher is a divine creation for a special work—a sun created to shine on uncreated spiritual worlds and warm them into being.

Christ promises to *make* all His ministers "fishers of men." Not fishers of their money, or their influence, or their patronage, but of themselves. Neither moral training nor mental culture can effect this divine creation. God must do it, or the minister will fish in vain. His polished pole and glittering bait will scare the fish away if he is not a God-made fisherman, or if he catches any it will be the "bad ones" of unconverted worldlings and formalists, who, no matter how big they may be, are fit only to be "cast away " (Matt. xiii. 47).

They are converted preachers. Christ declared them to be "branches of the true vine," "chose them out of the world," and declared that "their names were written in heaven." They evidenced their regeneration by "forsaking all" to follow Him, by their obedience, by their un-worldliness and by the burning thirst for holiness which led them to tarry in earnest, heart-searching wrestling for ten days and nights at the Pentecost prayer chamber.

What a contrast to the many unconverted, worldly, popularity-seeking, holiness-evading, sanctification-fight-ing preachers. Pentecostal preachers always have a solid foundation of sin-forsaking, world-relinquishing, devil-fighting, soul-winning, holiness-loving, God-attested, sanctification-seeking regeneration. Preachers who have not this experience are houses of straw, painted it may be, but on a foundation of mud and quicksand, not only sinking down to hell themselves, but are dragging deceived victims down with them. Awful spectacle! Fearful fate!

They are Spirit-baptized preachers. Soundly converted before Pentecost, at the upper chamber they received the gift of the Holy Ghost, which "purified their hearts by faith," and filled them with "all the fulness of God," so that "having all sufficiency in all things" they "abound in every good work." All Pentecostal preach-ers have this baptism. A minister without it is an un-tempered, rough-edged sickle who will tangle more grain than he will garner.

They are fully sanctified preachers. Entire sanctifica-tion is the work which Jesus does for a believer when He baptizes him with the Holy Ghost and fire. This work they had received, and this they testified and preached. Jeers and ridicule of sanctification, such as are sometimes heard from professed ministers of Christ, had no place among Apostolic preachers. By it men to-day advertise the spuriousness of their profession and their alliance with hell.

There is no Scripture warrant for ministers to rush into the pulpit before being wholly sanctified. The general standing order from the great Head of the Church to all His followers is to "tarry" until thus endued. So the apostles interpreted it, else Pentecost might have been but a series of lectures from musty manuscripts, or a dress parade, or musical entertainment, like many modern farces which pass for gospel services.

What folly to try to light a lamp with an unlighted match!

How can I warm others if there is no fire in my own grate?

If I do not receive the gospel myself, how can I tell others how to do so?

If I have not tested a medicine, how can I recommend it?

How can I teach others to obey if I am shirking duty?

They waited earnestly, persistently, obediently, and effectually until the *promised power was received*.

What folly it would have been for them, even with their three years' schooling directly from the Master, to have rushed out on the field of battle without waiting for the enduement, which was the only guarantee of their success, and without which they could but hopelessly fail.

They were too wise to be the victims of such folly and sin, yet thousands to-day are doing this very same thing, substituting a college diploma for Pentecostal enduement. A piece of paper for a heaven-forged armory. A painted pop-gun for celestial artillery! Mere human agencies in the place of omnipotent energy!

No wonder that such officers fall under the assaults of the world, the flesh, and the devil, and, defeated, must be borne to a hospital.

Pentecostal preachers were obedient and consistent, and saw that their own furnace was glowing with fire which drew others to its genial warmth.

They are witnessing preachers. The parting words of our Saviour to the twelve apostles was not to preach, but to tarry, and to receive the Holy Spirit, and to do that without which the execution of all other orders would prove useless—*to be "witnesses."* This charge was to His *ministers*, and has *never been revoked*. It was not only to apostolic preachers but to all ministers in all ages, unto the "uttermost part of the earth." In view of this standing order from the supreme Head of the Church, preachers should apologize for *omitting testimony* instead of for giving it, as is too often the case.

Any minister who is not a "witness unto me" in the sense here meant, is living in violation of the supreme command of his supreme Bishop. It is an absolute impossibility to be such a witness without the sanctifying baptism with the Holy Ghost. "But ye shall receive power, when the Holy Ghost is come upon you : and ye shall be my witnesses, both in Jerusalem, and in all Judæa and Samaria, and unto the uttermost part of the earth" (Acts i. 8). First the power, then the testimony, is God's order. Yet ministers guilty of this criminal neglect are sometimes among the foremost to accuse believers who place loyalty to Christ above loyalty to church entertainments and worldly committees of being "disloyal to the church !" Such inconsistency is ridiculous enough to be amusing, yet traitorous enough to make a Judas blush. Such men may soon find themselves arraigned before a higher tribunal on the charge of high treason against the *supreme* charge of the *great Head of the Church.*

Pentecostal preachers heed their Master's word, obtain a Holy Ghost experience, and "*tell it* in spite of the world." They have been converted, and know it. They are fully sanctified, and know that. Not in vain have they "freely received that they might know," and that knowledge is as much a part of their being as their existence. Hence they not only declare the gospel, but witness to its saving power. Paul never, like many now, apologized for turning his pulpit into a witness box. Spirit-baptized testimony in the pulpit is like the rushing stream of which the doctrines of salvation is the exhaustless fountain. Both are essential. There must be a mill-pond to run a water-mill, but unless the water is turned on the mill will never grind. It was when the stream of testimony, under the mighty pressure of the Holy Ghost, poured out upon the people at Pentecost, that the revival mill commenced to grind, not stopping until thousands were pulverized into the glorious experiences of salvation. Satan, through open opposition, broad hints from fireless schoolmen, and in thousands of other ways, is always trying to stop this stream of testimony. Great pressure is brought to bear against proclaiming possession of this gift of a Pentecostal experience.

The blindness of unsanctified believers and the bitterness of unregenerate professors and preachers frequently shows itself in this oft expressed opposition to testimony, until many preachers have drifted so far away from the Pentecostal standard that they almost invariably apologize for alluding to their experience while preaching.

But you might as well try to dam a Niagara or cork a volcano as try to muzzle a minister who has the Pentecostal baptism. Those who attempt it will either get drowned in the current or burned with the fire.

This bolt of lightning may hit some, who, resting in a theory of sanctification instead of abiding in its experience, fancy that they have found the more than Apostolic wisdom of so "living" holiness as to awaken no unkind comment. May it burn up the drapery of a sham profession, electrocute the "old man," and be attended with a cloud-burst of salvation !

With this dynamite of a Spirit-baptized testimony, an ignorant Kru boy, Sammy Morris, accomplished more for God and souls in ten years than a thousand graduated divines can without it in a lifetime. Just one torch ablaze will kindle more fires than a million icebergs or any number of torches unlighted, no matter how tinselled they may be.

Pentecostal preachers, no matter how inexperienced and uneducated, can do something which multitudes of titled schoolmen can not do : *they can tell their experience of regeneration and entire sanctification*—a qualification worth more in a soul winner than all the learning of all the ages, human and angelic, without it.

An alarming symptom of apostasy in the churches is the advancing of men without these experiences to places of control, and the requirement of a college diploma instead of a Pentecostal experience as a condition of ministerial acceptability.

God wants no men for His ministers who can not tell the experiences of salvation as well as proclaim its doctrines, and no one can tell the experience unless he has it, hence all who have it not should take time to get it or else retire.

This fact has driven thousands to their faces before God, where they have sought and found that which made testimony as spontaneous as the whistle of a school-boy.

The lack of this experience in the pulpit increases the lack of it, in the pews, and robs the Church of what God means should be one of its mightiest forces.

The influence of many in high places, who are conspicuous in their failure at this point, is used of Satan to silence others. Some one will have a fearful account to meet and to settle at the Judgment. Thank God, there are notable examples, in places high and low, of ministers who joy to give a Pentecostal testimony from the pulpit. Mighty God, increase this number !

They preach the whole gospel. A fractional gospel, stopping short of the baptism with the Holy Ghost and fire which fully sanctifies, was never designed by God. The Bible definition of the word gospel is : ''The power of God unto salvation.'' Hence he who evades preaching holiness omits the very mainspring of the Saviour's commission to his ministry. Paul, in Acts xvi. 18, in explaining the application of the minister's call to himself, clearly states that it includes proclaiming :

(*a*) The forgiveness of sin.

(*b*) Privilege of receiving the ''inheritance among them which are sanctified by faith'' in Christ.

All of the apostles were true to their commission, preaching and writing the glorious gospel of complete deliverance from inbred sin, through faith in Jesus' blood, by the power of the Holy Ghost. They not only laid a sure foundation, but built upon it the gold and silver and precious stones of a Spirit-baptized, sanctified Church.

Hirelings substitute instead, the quicksand foundation of church-joining, water-baptism, or some other human work for regeneration, and then evade or deride the second work of the sanctifying baptism with the Holy Ghost and fire. Blind leaders of the blind, like their fathers whom Jesus rebuked, with their flocks, unless rescued by divine mercy, they ''fall into the ditch'' of sin and unbelief, to keep on sinking forever. God's Pentecostal preachers, with ''hearts made pure and garments white''; with faces beaming with Heaven's own radiance, and voices ringing with the vibrations of God's truth, attended by their victorious flocks, ascend the Beulah heights of perfect love, and amid its overflowing joys "feast on the milk, and the honey, and the wine" of God-given Pentecostal experiences.

They are Scriptural preachers. Like Jesus, they have an "it is written" for every truth they utter. They are commissioned to preach the Word, not themselves; not to tinker it, nor evade it, nor apologize for it, but to preach it. Living exponents of its power, they both declare and demonstrate its divinity. A man-made ministry reading a man-made gospel in a man-pleasing spirit to a man-worshiping people is as different from the Pentecostal type as the breath of a dying fever patient is from the rush of a cyclone.

A gospel minister is a herald of the government of heaven, not to please and amuse the people, but to proclaim to them their peril, and the only way of escape.

He who substitutes aught for this message deceives men, betrays God and brings upon himself an awful doom.

A mimic ministry study their congregation to learn what will please *them;* a Pentecostal ministry study the Word and tarry before God to learn what will please *Him.* It would dare the wrath of a world in arms rather than depart one hair's breadth from declaring His revealed will. The pressure brought from worldly sources to divert and deaden God's message is tremendous. Deacon Pay-well will frown, Elder Love-the-world will fidget, and their families will protest, if the truth hits them. Many Pentecostal ministers have been compelled to move simply because of their fidelity to the gospel message. Howbeit God cared for them, for their "bread is given and water is sure." Pentecostal preachers are willing to lose their heads rather than their peace of conscience and God's favor by betraying the sacred trust committed to them. When the final conference comes, all who have followed in their steps will receive appointments paying them a million fold for their fidelity.

They are powerful preachers. They have received the power of the Holy Ghost coming upon them, and though weak themselves, declare the gospel in "demonstration of the Spirit and of power," so that they can boldly say: "Our gospel came not unto you in word only, but also in power, and in the Holy Ghost and in much assurance."

Simply proclaiming the truth is not preaching the gospel, any more than filling a stove with coal is building a fire. As a fire is coal ablaze, so the preached gospel is the truth ablaze from human lips aglow with the power of the Holy Ghost. Many ministers spend their lives filling and refilling the gospel stove with the coal of truth, tinkering with the pipes, blaming the chimney, and fancy this is preaching the gospel. No; the coal must be kindled into a blaze. The secret of kindling such a fire is revealed only in the Pentecostal upper chamber.

It is one thing to throw solid chunks of coal at a freezing man, and quite another to kindle a rousing fire and bid him come and warm. Some preachers turn their pulpits into coal-throwing gymnastics, hurling great chunks of cold truth at the heads of the people.

Others paint the coal artistically, and analyze it every Sabbath.

Others prefer handling the cold pearls of science, philosophy, and art.

Others play with the sensational topics of the present hour.

Others apologize for the looks of the coal, and try to fix it up so as to please their congregations.

The Pentecostal preacher sees that it is saturated with the oil of the Spirit ; and kindled by fire from on high, so that it glows, and sparkles, and warms, and draws, and amazes. It burns proud Pharisees, and thaws out ice-bound worldlings and formalists, and kindles fires which are the heralds of the millennium.

The preaching of such ministers frighten the gospel's foes, breaks down whole forts of opposition, and advertises to heaven, earth and hell that the kingdom of God is not a painted picture to please and entertain, but the voice of God to awaken, warn, save, melt, mould and fashion into the image of His Son.

They are holiness preachers. Not of the vague, indefinite, sheet-lightning sort, but in the sense of possessing the experience and urging others to its obtainment. An indefinite marksman is no marksman at all. All who fail to press the life and testimony of Bible holiness are far short of the Bible standard of Pentecostal preachers. All who fight it knowingly are its foes, as loyal citizens never take arms against their own country. Holiness is loyalty to God and His government. He who declares loyalty to his country impossible is a traitor. He who says the same of holiness is a worse one. Beware of such false spirits, who would deceive and fleece God's flock that they may feed themselves, and thus even out-Pharisee the Pharisees of old, for Jesus commanded to hear and heed their preaching, but beware of their example. To heed the preaching of ministers who teach the impossibility of living holy, would be to sink with them into hell. They should neither be listened to nor supported, but protested against and exposed. Their opposition to holiness will always be found to be rooted in some sin, either public or private, like that of an opposer who preached against it at a recent camp-meeting, who was found to be a slave to tobacco.

They are wise preachers. Not in the ordinary sense of worldly wisdom or shrewdness, which schemes to please all at any cost. This is not wisdom, but simply worldly policy under the cloak of religion. This is Jesuitism in another garb.

They possessed the gift of wisdom, one of the nine gifts with which the Spirit panoplies loyal Christian workers for soul-winning work. "For to one is given through the Spirit the word of wisdom; and to another the word of knowledge, according to the same Spirit: to another faith, in the same Spirit; and to another gifts of healings, in the one Spirit; and to another workings of miracles; and to another prophecy; and to another discernings of spirits; to another divers kind of tongues; and to another the interpretation of tongues" (I. Cor. xii. 8-10). Thus Christ is made unto them wisdom, so that they are divinely directed by Him, and given a mouth of wisdom which all their adversaries are not able to gainsay or resist.

The lack of this divine gift, and the substitution of worldly policy in its stead, is the source of much needless confusion in the churches.

This wisdom will enable one to see the folly of depending on carnal plans, when the instructions of infinite wisdom may be possessed.

It detects the absurdity of attempting to build up the Church of God with people who are not born of Him, and saves from much kindred foolishness.

It enables to approach individuals in the wisest possible way, and to circumvent the stratagems of men and devils. This wisdom is not a product of the schools, nor of experience, but is a direct gift of God, illuminating the human faculties, and manipulating them for God. Possessed of it, a converted cow-boy in this city is wiser to win souls than multitudes of educated Christians. Through it the early Pentecostal preachers outwitted the combined wisdom of jealous Jews and intriguing Gentiles, and on the ruins of their kingdoms planted the empire of the humble Carpenter, which shall stand forever. Another illustration of the fact that God never has, nor never will, give the reigns of His government into the hands of conceited schoolmen, who exalt brains above God and the gifts of the Holy Ghost.

Instead of approaching people on points of disagreement, they presented truths mutually embraced, and having thus captured attention, and interest, and confidence, their hearers were better prepared to listen to their message of salvation.

Notice how differently Peter approached his congregation at Pentecost and at the home of Cornelius, Paul's addresses before Agrippa and at Athens, and the tact which he shows with the early converts, in placing the question of entire sanctification before them in the form of the " gift of the Holy Ghost " instead of the set phraseology to which some seem to be slaves.

With a multiplicity of methods, this wisdom is loyal to the truth, and yet continually surprises and defeats both men and devils. Every Pentecostal preacher may have it if humble enough to confess his need and seek its supply.

They are convicting preachers. It is said that Webster declared that he wanted men to preach, so that he would feel that the devil was after him. Thus Pentecostal preachers declare God's message.

Men were drawn to them by the divine battery within them, and then pricked to the heart by the electric currents of divine truth which leaped from them until they " cried out " for salvation, like people still do under Pentecostal preaching and at Pentecostal altars. They preached the crucifixion and resurrection, repentance, forgiveness of sins, and entire sanctification, human responsibility and accountability, Christ's intercession and royal return, heaven and hell, and judgment, until men trembled, and were converted and sanctified by the thousand. They availed themselves of the power hid in every great gospel truth to awaken and bring men to repentance, and succeeded under circumstances most forbidding.

No simpered sermonettes, nor crude orations, nor learned lectures ever fell from their lips. They were not commissioned to paint word-pictures, nor entertain with sky-rockets, which blaze a moment only and then expire, but to hurl electric bolts of Holy Ghost lightning to the destruction of sin, the defeat of the devil, and the triumph of an everlasting kingdom. The minister's mission, and his sources of power, are just the same to-day as then. Satan is no less strongly intrenched, nor the need of such men and ammunition less than then.

In the heat of a spiritual war, like the one we are in, there is no time nor place for preachers to substitute human inventions for divine equipments. Celestial heat and light, bombshells, and dynamite, and electric bolts are the only weapons that will awaken a sleeping church, a dying world, and a compromising ministry, convict of sin, and bring about Holy Ghost conversions and sanctifications. Pentecostal preachers are satisfied with heaven's armor and ammunition, and use it without apologies.

The learned commentator, W. B. Godbey, recently preached ten consecutive sermons on hell, with few, if any, immediate conversions, but shortly after there were two hundred. Jacob Knapp and kindred spirits were on this Pentecostal line. It is impossible to have Pentecostal conversions and sanctifications without this kind of Pentecostal, convictive preaching.

The lack of it accounts for the multitudes of little, shriveled, painted, modern apples, which are tied to the boughs of the gospel tree by the silken cords of church-joining, where there should be luscious, ripening fruit. The process of tying on these apples is even reported as a revival! And the minister who can tie on the most, the greatest revivalist! [See chapters on *Pentecostal Revivals* and *Pentecostal Conversions.*

When the Pentecostal preacher comes, his first sermon will knock these sham apples off, and show that the tree must be purged before it can bear gospel fruit. This is one of the reasons why Holy Ghost evangelists and pastors are distrusted in certain circles. They insist on Scriptural, Pentecostal conviction, and press the truths which promote it regardless of who it hits.

They are devoted preachers. "Separated unto the gospel" (Rom. i. 1). They allow no business, social nor political entanglements to come between them and the exercise of their whole duty as gospel ministers. If temporally they "make tents" or books, it is that they more effectually preach the gospel, reaching in this way some that otherwise might not be saved. Such separation from the world is an absolute necessity, that they may receive God's message and faithfully proclaim it. If a man can not be a good soldier unless separated to military life, much less can one be a good minister unless severed from hindering ties.

They are trusted preachers. "But even as we have been approved of God to be intrusted with the gospel, so we speak; not as pleasing men, but God which proveth our hearts" (I. Thess. ii. 4). Thus are God's true ministers

trusted by Him with infinite interests, treasures of unspeakable value, diadems of unfading splendor, which
they are commissioned to burnish and keep from spiritual
rust and robbers ; their only motive to bless men and to
please God by faithfulness to the trust committed.   God
trusts them to see that no sheep of his, unwarned, shall be
destroyed by the wolf or allured by the world.   The true
preacher feels that his is a privilege "allowed of God,"
an honor conferred upon him.   Away with the sickening
twaddle sometimes heard, of "what I gave up to be a
minister of the gospel!"   He who has no nobler view
of this high calling has surely missed his place.   'T is an
honor allowed to God-chosen persons only, and one that
angels would doubtless gladly leave their posts to fill.

They are God-pleasing preachers.   "Not as pleasing
men but God, which trieth our hearts."   A minister
has only one person to please, and that is God.   A true
bride cares little how the world esteems her if she has
the approval of the bridegroom.   God is the minister's
bridegroom.   In writing this book I would rather offend
my best friends and all the world than to displease Him.
If I have His smile, Satan may rage "and the people
imagine vain things and the rulers take counsel against"
me, it all is like the loss of a copper to one who knows
he is taking possession of a gold mine.   Glory !   It is
impossible to be a God-pleasing preacher and a world-
pleasing preacher at the same time.   One or the other
must be renounced.

They are not flattering preachers.   "For neither at
any time were we found using words of flattery, as ye
know" (I. Thess. ii. 5).   At no time did they resort
to this trick of false preachers and failing of weak ones.
Every true preacher is commissioned of God, who guarantees His protection and support.   Hence he has no

need to be obsequious to either appointing or petitioning powers, for his times are not in their hands, only as God shall permit. A minister is not a puppy to lick the hands of hoped-for patrons, but an electric storm-cloud to send showers and thunderbolts when and where and upon what God shall bid.

They are not glory-seeking preachers. " Nor of men sought we glory." Neither the glory of popular praise, nor newspaper notoriety, nor statistical pre-eminence, nor " first grade" appointment was the object of their care. Pentecostal preachers belong to this class. A " glory "- seeking preacher is a bubble-seeking preacher. He, how-ever, who seeks God's glory will find it a globe of gold. This the true preacher seeks and finds.

They are gentle preachers. " But we were gentle among you, even as a nurse cherished her children." Such ministers have the mind of their Master. Spiritual nurses, they watch over precious ones whom He has intrusted to them. Patient, tender, kind and gentle, they minister to their needs. Though a terror to the spiritual thieves and robbers who would break in and murder and destroy, yet to the children of God they are as tender, kind and gentle as the most solicitous, loving nurse. Like a storm-cloud, they are lightning bolts on one side and sunshine on the other.

They are holy preachers. " Be ye clean, ye that bear the vessels of the Lord" (Isa. lii. 11). " Ye shall be holy; for I am holy " (I. Peter i. 16). If the flock is required to be holy, much more is the shepherd. God never designed an unholy preacher. Even under the old dispensation holiness was required. An unholy minister of the gospel is as great a contradiction as a disloyal patriot. If the teacher is disloyal, what else can be expected of the pupils? If a general would be accounted mad if he appointed disloyal officers, how can God appoint unholy men to lead His armies? Unholiness is disloyalty to God. Pentecostal ministers are holy men and women. Why are some ministers proud to wear a "D. D.," and yet ashamed to wear God's title of "holy"?

They are humble ministers. "Serving the Lord with all lowliness of mind, and with tears, and with trials which befell me by the plots of the Jews" (Acts xx. 19). They realize that they are but weak agents of the great God, that their salvation is all of Him, and that without His Spirit and gifts and protection they can but utterly fail and sink into hell. This view of God and of their own dependence on Him keeps them humble. Humility is a mark of spiritual greatness. Pentecostal ministers are never pompous and haughty. They despise pompous titles and glittering regalia and lofty style and peacock strut, and personally prefer obscurity to notoriety. Their King, by the instinct of His nature, flew to a humble home or the mountain solitude, except when duty bore Him to the field of battle and of conquest. His kingdom "is not of this world," whose fashions and thrones and crowns all quickly crumble and rot; but it shall shine forever above the brightness of the sun, and to its kings and priests the brightest honors of earth are less than sawdust. Humility is one of the stars which their King has placed in their crowns, and it alone is worth more than all the riches and all the glory of all the ages of this tinselled, gaudy, vanishing world. This sparkling jewel adorns every true minister of Christ.

They are plain preachers. The language they used was transparent as light. They are free from cant and set phrases, and circumlocution, and all the tricks of truckling to tone the truth down to the tastes of fastidious critics. They speak plainly of sin and destruction, of hell and lust and judgment.

Like their Master, they so unmask men before them, that they "perceive that they spoke of them." They illustrated the truth by allusions to Scripture and history, and by figures familiar to all, so that none need miss their meaning. They are total strangers to the conceited, gaseous verbosity with which speculative theologians inflate the balloons of their egotistical opinions, as they speak with "great swelling words of vanity."

Their power is independent of mental culture. "Now when they beheld the boldness of Peter and John, and had perceived that they were unlearned and ignorant men, they marvelled" (Acts iv. 13). To the chagrin of the schoolmen, and the perplexity of the Pharisees, the founders of Christianity, with but one exception, were not college-bred men. God might have chosen his representatives from the doctors of that day, but He passed them by and conferred the highest degrees ever known on earth upon unschooled laborers, and chose them to be the foundation of His eternal temple. Only one scholar to eleven unlearned men was the proportion in the first conference organized by Christ Himself. This is a burning rebuke to the spirit that insists on foisting upon the the Church diplomied men, destitute of the baptism with the Holy Ghost. It is not designed to be a premium on ignorance, but shows that neither the foundation or building of heaven's kingdom is dependent upon human lore. God has thus chosen the weak things of this world to confound the mighty. The ingenuous attempt of scholars to show that the mental culture of the Galilee fishermen was such as to be an argument in favor of requiring a college diploma of ministers, is a failure.

Though unschooled, they instructed scholars. While the

"elders and the scribes had been imbibing finite knowledge through the painted straws of their college courses,
out of the tinselled thimbles of human learning, these
unlearned men had been to the great exhaustless Fountain
of living water, and out of His infinite ocean had been
filled with such a fullness that these grieved and empty
doctors were compelled to confess it, taking "knowledge
of them, that they had been with Jesus." Many an
uncouth, unschooled preacher to-day is winning more
souls to God and holiness than a whole city full of
learned scholastics.

They are learned preachers. Not in the knowledge of
this world, but of a wiser world. Not in the mastery of
Greek roots, but in the conquest of the deeper, more perplexing roots of carnality. Not in the philosophy of the
material world, but of the spiritual, of the plan of salvation, and the processes of winning souls; not in the
chemistry of the schools, but in the chemistry that transforms sinners into saints, and changes spiritual darkness
into glorious light; not in the astronomy of the astral
heavens, but in the astronomy whose stars will shine
when all things visible shall pass away; not in the bot-
any of earth's fields, and forests, and flowers, but in that
which possesses and analyzes the "Lily of the Valley,"
and the trees, plants, and flowers of Beulah land; not in the
geology of the schools, but the geology which digs down
to the eternal Rock of Ages, and possesses gold "tried
in the fire"; not versed in modern systems of agricul-
ture, but seed-sowers, preparing the fallow ground of
human hearts for eternal harvests. So, while they may
be "ignorant and unlearned men," as to the bursting bubbles of time, yet in the knowledge that "passeth understanding" they are advanced beyond all degrees named
in the lists of worldly honors.

They were bold preachers. "And when they had prayed, the place was shaken wherein they were gathered together; and they were all filled with the Holy Ghost, and they spake the word of God with boldness" (Acts iv. 31). Love had cast out all slavish fear, and they were "bold as lions." This enabled them to speak boldly before the great Sanhedrin, rebuking and accusing of murder men in the highest places of ecclesiastical honor and authority, when such rebukes might, and finally did, cost them their lives. Continually confronted with the authorities, principalities, and powers of all earth and hell, there is no place for fear in Pentecostal preachers. Neither fear of losing salary, or place, or prestige among the churches, nor reputation will cause them to desert their posts, or tone down their messages to please or appease the wrath or the itching ears of Pharisees and formalists. They fear to offend or displease God a million-fold more than all the potentates of Church and State combined.

They are spontaneous preachers. "We can not but speak the things which we saw and heard" (Acts iv. 20). In the hearts of Pentecostal preachers the gospel is an ever-flowing, overflowing artesian well. They can not curb or stop its flow, nor do they try. Hence the "I must" of duty is transformed into the "I love" of delight. Preaching is no longer a load to be drawn, but an electric motor to propel.

They are flames of fire. "Who maketh his angels winds, and his ministers a flame of fire" (Heb. i. 7). John, the last great preacher of the old dispensation, was divinely named a burning and a "shining light," and Paul is called the "light of the Gentiles."

Every Pentecostal minister is a verification of the

above definition. Not of false fire, nor rhetorical fire, but aflame with God.

One single leaf, saturated with oil and *on fire*, will set a whole forest in flames. The minister is the little leaf. Saturated with the anointing of the Spirit, and enkindled with Him, the fire soon spreads, until there is among the trees of sin a glorious revival conflagration.

God wants millions of preachers who are willing to be nothing but leaves, saturated with God, and ablaze with God, and borne by Holy Ghost gales wheresoever He will.

Pentecostal preachers, like the leaves of Moses' burning bush, thus are aflame, but never are consumed.

They are persecuted preachers. Pentecostal preachers are always subjects of Satanic persecution. Persecution is a name for Satan's efforts to hinder gospel workers, and retaliate for the losses they bring to his kingdom. Preachers who affect no such losses will receive no such discharges of grape and canister from this source. Pentecostal preachers are constantly capturing his soldiers, arming his enemies, and unmasking his plots, and hence awake his special hatred. Men who are on the battle-field will hear the bullets whiz, and are liable to get hit. Pentecostal persecutors camp there, and are never off on a furlough. Persecution is one of the gauges which helps a Pentecostal minister to measure his effectiveness. No persecution, no Pentecostal power, is a rule in the kingdom of God.

Complaint under persecution, or the resenting of it, is a mark of a lack of Pentecostal piety. Those who have the most of the Holy Ghost mention their persecutions the least, and never in a complaining nor retaliatory manner.

They are victorious preachers. God gives them not

only support, but victory. We have no record of a Pentecostal preacher starving ; "their bread is given, their water is sure." Sanhedrins may arrest them, but this is to them simply a divine opportunity to preach the gospel, and ecclesiastical executioners are compelled to admit that they have "been with Jesus," and can find nothing for which they may punish them.

When the apostles were thrust into the "lockup" "many believed,—and the number of the men was about five thousand." What loyal general would not be willing to be confined over night if he could see five thousand prisoners captured, and the enemy defeated and its guns spiked?

Thus they are certainly "more than conquerors" through Him that loved them. Their watchword is "victory," and they shout it in the face of the combined opposition of earth and hell until God gives it, transforming the most untoward circumstances into chariots which bear them triumphantly to certain conquest. Arrest, defeats, prisons, stripes and death all to them are stepping stones to victory.

Though the doors of dead ecclesiasticism may slam back against them, the New Jerusalem, "Christ's Bride," descends, and with gates closed neither night nor day to such ministers and people, takes them in, and gives them positions in which they will serve and shout forever.

Satan is powerless to extinguish the fires which they built.

Imagine a block ablaze in a big city. All the fire engines at command are instantly on the spot, and a deluge of water promises to quickly extinguish the flames. Suddenly, by the touch of some secret spring, the water from every hose is transformed into coal oil! Immediately the flames fly up on wings of triumph, and threaten the whole city !

This is a picture of Holy Ghost fire in human hearts and homes and churches. The devil at once sounds the fire alarm, and runs out every available hose to extinguish the flames. His property is perishing ! Some of his best servants may be lost ! How the pumps work, and the cold water of criticism, and ostracism, and persecution fairly pours in from every side ! But lo ! A secret spring is touched, and the water is converted into oil, which feeds the flames, and God's people become "exceedingly glad," and even "leap for joy." Thus it was when Stephen was translated, when Peter and John were summoned before the Sanhedrin, when James was killed, Peter imprisoned, and Herod smitten of God.

Thus God makes the wrath of man, and of devils, work for His own glory and His people's good. To Him be praise forever !

If He be for them who can be against them ?

They were irregular preachers. When church regulations stood between them and God-revealed duty, they snapped the webs asunder, and, like John Wesley in his answer to the Bishop of Bristol's order designed to restrict his preaching, they "obey God, rather than man," setting an inspired precedent for all preachers under similar circumstances.

Loyalty to a cobweb, no matter from what human brain it may have been spun, or how many or how highly titled the high priests who weave it, is disloyalty to God.

Pentecostal preachers always recognize the supreme authority of the Word of God, the Spirit of God, and the Son of God. If this is religious anarchy, as has been intimated, then Daniel, the Hebrew children, the Apostles, John Wesley, C. G. Finney, William Booth, and many

others, now eulogized as saints, were "anarchists."
Pentecostal preachers prefer that sort of anarchy to the
rule of ritualism, priestcraft, and popery. I rejoice in
the fact that all who suffer opposition and oppression
from any sources, may possess degrees of grace that will
give as joyful victory as it did their brethren in Pentecostal days.

They preach repentance. The great message God
heralds to the lost is repentance. So preached John the
Baptist, though it cost him his head. So preached Jesus
and the apostles, and so preach all ministers who are
true to their commission. The reason of many spurious
conversions is doubtless a lack at this point, causing men
to try and believe themselves into the kingdom of God
over sins of which they do not repent. The minister
who does not preach and insist on genuine repentance of
sin as a condition of regeneration is misrepresenting the
kingdom of God, helping Satan to people hell with deluded victims, and is like a builder who would place
the foundation of his house on sand instead of stone.

This doctrine is not popular on earth, but is in
heaven, where angels always rejoice when sinners accept
of it and repent.

They are divinely-protected preachers. Whenever their
enemies "take counsel to slay them " before their work
is done, God provides some Gamaliel or Felix to interfere in their behalf and deliver them. He commands
forces of earth, and air, and church, and state, and
heaven, and hell to protect His people, when that is His
will ; so that so long as God thus wills no one can pierce
the pavillion in which He hides them. Persecution must
get God's consent before it can enter this inclosure, and
when within it can only do what He may permit, and for
every blow He has healing balms and Pentecostal stimu-

iants that transform the pain into pleasure, so that instead of complaining we find them " rejoicing that they are counted worthy to suffer shame for His name."

They are persistent preachers, "And every day, in the temple and at home, they ceased not to teach and to preach Jesus as the Christ" (Acts v. 42). Pentecostal preachers are as pious and persistent on Monday as as on Sunday. "Blue Monday" is not in the calendar of this line of preachers. With them all days are white, and none blue nor black. While in keeping with the Sabbatic law of rest they may observe Monday for recreation, yet like other days it is full of grace, with nought of gloom.

Spiritual artesian wells, a ceaseless current continually flows from their lives. Spiritual suns, they cease not to flood the world with their light. They flow and shine and glow, and Satan waits in vain for a cessation of their hostilities against his kingdom. Not only are they persistent in their public ministrations, but as opportunity invites they go from house to house. They realize that no amount of pulpit effectiveness can be substituted for house-to-house visitation. Spurious preachers neglect this altogether or substitute mere social calls in its stead ; talk on the topics of the day and eat chicken, instead of preaching Christ !

Christ commands that the gospel be "preached to every creature." As not one in ten come to church, how can the Saviour's orders be executed without this persistent house-to-house work such as the apostles did ?

They preach a personal Christ. Not themselves, nor their opinions, nor their creed, nor dry doctrine, but Jesus Christ Himself, in all His convicting, converting and saving offices.

Doctrine divorced from Him, like a plucked rose, loses

much of its beauty and soon fades, but when radiating from Him as its center it is wonderful both in its beauty and its power. Even the doctrine of holiness thus divorced leaves its possessors Pharisaical, arbitrary, exacting and un-Christlike, but when received with Him as its source and center it unfolds a holy, symmetrical Christian life.

They press holiness. " Now when the apostles which were at Jerusalem heard that Samaria had received the word of God, they sent unto them Peter and John: who, when they were come down, prayed for them, that they might receive the Holy Ghost " (Acts viii. 14, 15).

They not only preached holiness, but, as in this instance, held special meetings for that purpose, wisely leading young converts to expect and receive the gift which fully sanctifies. Their example is a standing rebuke to ministers who condemn special meetings for this purpose on the plea that "all meetings should be holiness meetings," or for any other excuse. Pentecostal preachers realize that special definite prayer and instruction is needed at special epochs in the spiritual life, and that young converts who have received forgiveness should be led at once to possess their blood-bought inheritance among them that are sanctified. This is God's antidote to preserve them from backsliding. It is the kid wherewith they may make merry their friends. Possessing this, they will have no relish for the leeks and onions of worldly amusements.

Preachers who do not administer this divine antidote are accountable for the wreckage of young people on the rocks of worldly entertainments.

They are discreet. " But their plot became known to Saul. And they watched the gates also day and night that they might kill him; but his disciples took him by night, and let him down through the wall, lowering ᾱim in a basket '' (Acts ix. 24, 25). They realize that there are times when discretion is the better part of valor, and that flight instead of fight is the divine order. On this principle, the Master, on His advent to earth, was borne by Joseph from Herod's wrath to Egypt's welcoming asylum, and many times in His ministry withdrew Himself as the lightning of the wrath of His foes was about to leap upon Him. Dauntless Paul, brave before kings and princes, was humble enough to adopt this expedient when God so led. This discretion is the '' gift of wisdom'' which enables to do the wisest things in the wisest way. (See chapter on *Pentecostal Gifts.*)

Unsophisticated preachers mistake natural shrewdness and worldly shamming for their gift. They are no more related than the wiles of a fox to the movement of an angel. Some ministers profess to preach holiness in such a way as not to awaken opposition or persecution' and think this is an evidence of superior wisdom and discretion !

The preaching of holiness will awaken commendation instead of opposition if it is so presented that it does not unmask depravity and point to a perfect cure, nor press immediate decision, and urge its claims as a work of grace to be sought subsequent to conversion, through the blood of Jesus, and by the Holy Ghost.

Discreet brother, put this attachment on to your next holiness sermon and climax it with a joyous testimony of the possession of the present experience, and as earnest and as definite an altar call as you would make to sinners for pardon, and you will find in most places that your earth-born discretion will prove a poor arm to protect you from arrows that will certainly fly. Pentecostal discretion, while it fears no foes, is full of wisdom to defeat all foes and sometimes does it without a battle, and under cover of an apparent defeat. Calvary appeared to be Christianity killed, the sepulcher Christianity buried, and the ascension Christianity flying from the battle field, but each one of these were the triumphs of the highest wisdom in the victorious campaign of Christ against the devil. He who abandons himself to God has no need of worldly policy for the success of his plans, for God will guide him with counsels such as no man can gainsay.

Becoming "fools" in order to be "wise" is the act of the transfer of one's self from the counsels of men to the counsels of Omnipotence.

Pentecostal preachers have the "discretion" to do this, and thus become possessed of a wisdom as far above that which is born in human brains as the heavens are higher than the earth.

They are open-air preachers. The gospel wine burst the bottles of Jewish restriction and flowed over all the land. Salvation, like air and sunshine, can not be confined to frescoed walls. Many a chapel whose only organ is the wind whistling between the cracks is a temple of God, while many a costly cathedral is a rendezvous of unclean birds and a stench to God. Any place out doors or where God's true children meet to learn and do His will is holy ground, while churches whose steeples pierce the sky, as the sins of their false worshipers do the heart of God, where lust and pride, extortion, hypocrisy and selfishness, under the cloak of sanctity, meet and take the name of God in vain by empty, idle prayers and songs, are as repellant to Him as pagan shrines or the ridiculous antics of heathen fakirs and medicine men ; yea, even more, for the latter have no open Bibles, gospel light and faithful, warning ministers. Pentecostal preachers, like John by Jordan, Jesus on the mountain side, Paul at Mars' Hill, John Wesley on his father's grave, and the Salvation

Army in the crowded city streets, are perfectly at home when preaching in the open air. As they have no need of pulpit to preach, nor upon which to repose a dainty manuscript, they do not miss it ; as they have no false dignity to nurse, a box or barrel makes a fitting platform, and the sky canopied with the drapery of floating clouds or the dome of blue above, or perhaps gemmed with blazing worlds of light, each one the handiwork of Him whose gospel they proclaim, inspires them from above. Hence were every church on earth closed to them they would still have countless places of worship ever open and inviting them to come, and plenty of fresh air, with no expenses for sexton, gas, nor fuel, and no covetous officials worrying over soiled carpets and accumulating expenses.

There is no record of a gospel church building in all New Testament history. This shows, not that church buildings are needless, but that without churches, by utilizing places and opportunities which providentially open, the Pentecostal movement won its way and did more in half a century than a steepled, frescoed, wealthy unsanctified following has done in generations, and that God is independent of all such aids in planting His kingdom. Yet, if they did so much without a single church building, what victories might be won if the pulpits and pews of modern churches were filled with preachers and people with Pentecostal experiences. In the meantime, whether in the synagogues of the Jews, or their own pulpits, or that of their brethren, or in the open air, Pentecostal preachers can preach Jesus everywhere. Such adaptation, the gift and the gifts of the Spirit freely bestows upon them.

They are undignified preachers. For true Christly dignity, with the exception of their Master, the world has never seen their peers. But they are total strangers to the stiff, starchy, shroud-like, graveyard dignity which characterized the Pharisees of all centuries. They are so undignified as to weep, and shout, and laugh, and pray as occasion may demand. Their Master hung on a cross. Their first revival was called a drunken frolic, and they have been frequently mobbed because of their undignified irregularities. Pentecostal preachers can not be put into straight jackets nor bound with grave cloths. God has set them free, and none may bind them.

They are not reputation-nursing preachers. God will baptize no man with the Holy Ghost and fire until he has weened his reputation. That must be given absolutely to God. Pentecostal preachers all have done this. They are dead to all opinions contrary to God's will. Many hesitate at this point. Their reputation among ministers and members is an idol. To exchange it for the reputation which God will give if baptized with fire creates a struggle. They desire the baptism with the Holy Ghost, but not earnestly enough to make the exchange. They desire God, but must be a "good fellow, well met" with all of their associates. Blind to the fact that an all-loving, all-wise, all-powerful God can give a reputation among men and angels better than man can make, they stumble here, but ministers who have won their Pentecost had rather be of good reputation with the saints and angels of God, and with the Father, Son, and Holy Ghost, than with all earth and hell besides. They have seen a star which blinds them to all lesser lights, and, like their Saviour, they are glad to become of "no reputation," and "take upon themselves the form of servants," and become "obedient unto death," if thus they may please Him, and aid in bringing, not many unconverted members into the church, but "many sons to glory."

They are divinely-employed preachers. "Now when I

came to Troas for the gospel of Christ, and when a door
was opened unto me in the Lord, I had no relief for
my spirit, because I found not Titus my brother'' (II.
Cor. ii. 12).   We hear no complaint on their part, neither
of persecution, nor of poor appointments, nor of lack of
openings.   When rejected at city appointments they be-
take themselves unto country circuits with joy and
victory.   When stoned and left for dead at one appointment, they arise and open up another one.   Before this
class of men God always sets an open door which no man
can shut.

The gospel preacher who whines over what he con-
siders an oppressive appointment, advertises that he has
not the Pentecostal type.   Not that ecclesiastical oppression at this point may not be felt, but that victory will be
claimed over it, and other doors will be divinely opened.
When the Jews drove Paul from Palestine God gave him
a city appointment in the metropolis of the world, with
expenses all met, and an opportunity to sow the gospel
seed over a whole continent.   All Pentecostal preachers
whom men seek to thus circumscribe will find these
divinely opened doors.   When one door is shut and man
says, ''Step down,'' God opens another and says, ''Thou
art my beloved son, step up.''   ''Step up'' may to
blinded human eyes seem down, but to Pentecostal vision
all is plain and satisfying.

They believe in ''gifts of healing.''   They recognize
the gift of healing as a Pentecostal bestowment, and when
God bestows it, use it for the comfort of sufferers, and
advancement of the holiness movement.   Like the apostles, they do not give it undue prominence, neither do
they ignore or discourage its use.   (See chapter on *Pentecostal Healing.*)

They are pure preachers.   There is no record of any

of the apostles lapsing, or in any way forcing scandal upon the Church. The secret of their being so wondrously kept doubtless lay in the fact that they had received and kept the genuine baptism with the Holy Ghost and fire, which preserved them from evil. They could challenge those among whom they had labored how "justly and holily and unblameably" they had lived among them. Testimonies thus electrified by holy lives are among Christ's mightiest magnets to draw men to Himself. Cleansed from all filthiness of the flesh and spirit, they treated the "elder women as mothers and the younger as sisters, *with all purity.*"

Satan seeks to ditch God's ministers through improper intimacy of the sexes, and some have co-operated with him under this enchanted spell and thus courted disgrace and the wreckage of immortal interests.

Questionable mingling of the sexes under pretense of counsel, or other excuses, should be avoided. Contact at the altar should not be tolerated. Ministers holding and caressing the hands of women, while giving them altar or inquiring-room instructions, should be labored with for imprudent conduct.

This is a delicate subject, that needs mighty emphasis from pulpit and press, as no Samson is impervious to Satanic approach through this silken source.

Every Methodist minister publicly promises to "converse sparingly and conduct himself prudently with women." Much evil would be avoided if all would follow this rule.

Pentecostal preachers claim the victory over lust and every carnal appetite, else they were slaves instead of "free indeed."

They are fraternal preachers. "I had no relief for my spirit, because I found not Titus my brother" (II. Cor.

ii. 13). They loved each other. All selfish ambition for place and power was, with inbred sin, electrocuted at Pentecost. Hence they were free from wire-pulling and ecclesiastical politics, and we have no record of any effort on their part to influence votes for themselves to places of honor and profit. There was no backbiting among them. They loved and admonished one another as brethren, and delighted in these God-given companionships. They seldom labored alone, but each Paul had his Barnabas, and common sacrifices, and victories, and experiences knit them closely together, so that they were "willing to lay down their lives" for each other.

Their union was not cemented, nor conversation stimulated, by carnal jokes or Christless stories, nor by treating with beer nor tobacco, as with apostate preachers, but by mutual joys, sorrows, persecutions and triumphs. Nor did they extend their fraternal congratulations to the false prophets of their day, nor invite them to their pulpits as a minister in charge recently did the blasphemous champion of modern infidelity.

They are highly honored preachers. They covet no honorary degrees which many flaunt as Indians do the scalps they take, and which the Master has forbidden, but instead they each bear the dearer title of B. B.— Beloved Brother—which Christ Himself confers upon all who do His will, and doing it become members of the Royal House of God and co-heirs and rulers with His own Beloved Son, titles and degrees by the side of which those that church, or state, or fraternities can give are empty, bursting bubbles.

They are not man-pleasing preachers. "If I were still pleasing men, I should not be a servant of Christ" (Gal. i. 10). If Paul could not cater to worldly-minded men and retain his salvation, no one can. Serfdom to such influences is a certain mark that a preacher is not a servant of Christ.

They are divinely-certified preachers. "Ye are our epistle, written in our hearts, known and read of all men" (II. Cor. iii. 2). God sets His seal upon their ministry by souls saved and sanctified. Pentecostal preachers are used of God to accomplish these results, and though there may be places where they "can not do many mighty works because of unbelief," yet God will bless their efforts, so that their "leaf shall not wither," and whatsoever they may do "shall prosper."

A minister's success consists in his being completely loyal to God and to his gospel commission. If he is this, God is responsible for the fruitage, and whether the result be gladness, rejoicing, and three thousand converts, as when Peter preached at Pentecost, or madness, a shower of stones, and martyrdom, as under Stephen a little later, the one is equally as successful in God's sight as the other. But it must be remembered that Stephen saw "disciples multiply greatly" under his ministrations, before his transcendent promotion. A barren ministry is a Christless ministry. God does not send His ambassadors on empty errands, yet revivals in subtraction are as essential as in addition and multiplication. A Pentecostal pastor recently had one of two hundred subtractions. The tooth must be excavated before it is filled, or there will be trouble. One may excavate and another fill, and both rejoice together as co-workers in the victory. Pentecostal preachers are crowned with this kind of success. They do not need to be encouraged with the story of the man who preached twenty years with one conversion, and then said, "Here goes for another twenty years." They "sow in tears and reap in joy." "Being not weary in well-doing," in due season they "do reap" in souls saved, sanctified, edified, and God's will done. A converted cow-boy, who can neither read nor write, has been the means of the salvation and sanctification of several during a period of three months. Shall gospel ministers be less fruitful than he? Not if they are as reckless of their reputation, as humble and self-denying in their lives, as persistent in their efforts, and as full of faith and fire!

God will have His work done, and multitudes of laymen and women who are flexible in His hand are being advanced by him to positions which will astonish many of the "wise and prudent" when the general roll is called.

God may speak to them through visions. See Peter's experience in Acts x., and Paul's in Acts. xvi. 9. "And a vision appeared to Paul in the night; There was a man of Macedonia standing, beseeching him, and saying, Come over into Macedonia, and help us. And when he had seen the vision, straightway we sought to go forth into Macedonia, concluding that God had called us for to preach the gospel unto them."

If a minister should relate such an experience in most pulpits to-day Prejudice and Ignorance would arrest him at once and brand him a hair-brained enthusiast, yet he might be in the apostolic line. For God has declared that "visions" shall be given, and sainted men have had them and do still, and when ministers or others of Paul's piety and sense so declare it simply corroborates the fulfillment of prophecy. The liability of the abuse of visions by people who put a divine interpretation to the nightmare or to their own imaginations calls for caution at this point, but we must admit them as a promised part of the Pentecostal preacher's legacy or do violence to both prophecy and experience. The author has treated this subject more fully in his book on *Impressions*, which see.

They are joyous preachers. "About midnight Paul and Silas were praying and singing hymns unto God" (Acts xvi. 25). And this when sore with "many stripes," in a horrid "inner prison" with "feet fast in the stocks." Surely such men are in possession of celestial secrets. It would not be surprising if God himself should set them free if He must send a great earthquake to do it.

Every Pentecostal preacher reaches a place where many "stripes," social, ecclesiastical, or Satanic, may fall upon his back. When he is thrust into some "inner prison" of providential confinement, and his feet are made fast in the stocks of fettering circumstances over which he has no control, and it appears that all friends are lost and that God Himself has forgotten him, then look out for prevailing prayers! for glad hallelujahs! for songs of victory!

Weaklings weep and repine in such moments, and apostates are full of bitterness and retaliation; like wolves they shake off their sheep's skin then and growl and show their teeth! But these men move all worlds with their prayers and songs, and sometimes, like Paul and Silas, precipitate a great revival.

They are tempted preachers. Their Master, the Model Minister, Himself was sorely tempted. The first forty days of His public ministry was one prolonged conflict, in which He shows that Spirit-baptized humanity may be victorious at every point, and so resist the devil that he will fly and angels bright come down and comfort. Paul was in "heaviness through manifold temptations," but "more than conqueror." Carvosso, spiritual giant though he was, writes that he was "dogged by temptation."

Pure Phœbe Palmer wrote: "Temptations complicated and diverse abounded." Glowing Caughey, amid them, cried out: "If yonder heaven does not save me the sea will drown me!"

Sanctification does not exempt from temptation, but prepares for it. When the Holy Ghost fell upon Jesus, immediately the devil attacked Him. Pentecost was followed by bitter persecution. Satan hates fire-baptized preachers as no other persons. They are the officers of the army that is conquering him and wresting earth from his traitorous grasp. Hence every stratagem that fiends in earth and hell can devise for their perplexity, defeat and ruin is employed. He seeks to burn them at the stake of ridicule and censure, to torment them on the rack of false accusations, human and Satanic, to chloroform them with sensual gratification, to weaken them by magnifying his own powers and minifying their gifts and God's promises, and sometimes, as with Paul at Iconium, to smother them with an avalanche of popular applause. Every point in their armor will be tested by the devil, his imps and apostate preachers.

If for one moment they lay aside one piece of armor, that moment some poisoned arrow will pierce, and every gatling gun of hell will seem to be let loose upon them. But out of every temptation, whether from the "lying in wait of the Jews," or from "false brethren," or directly from the devil, God is able to deliver, and, to the chagrin of enemies and confusion of devils, to fully save from sin and crown with constant victory.

They are faithful preachers. "Wherefore I testify unto you this day, that I am pure from the blood of all men. For I shrank not from declaring unto you the whole counsel of God" (Acts xx. 26, 27). They are true to their commission and preach the whole gospel.

They are too true to neglect to probe a wound because of the pain thus caused when God commands, and the patient's life may depend upon their thoroughness. No preacher who eliminates hell, and holiness, and warnings of grievous wolves from the gospel, or preaches these truths so gingerly and indifferently as to stir no one, is a faithful minister. Pentecostal preachers "keep nothing back which is profitable" whether it pleases or not.

Women may be Pentecostal preachers. The prophetic psalm which declares "the Lord giveth the word; the women that publish the tidings are a great host" (Ps. lxviii. 11), was verified. Joel's prophecy also finds fruitful fulfillment that Spirit-anointed women should "prophesy." Philip the evangelist had four such daughters, and Paul not only recognizes woman's prophetic office as a preacher, but gives explicit instructions as to how she is to appear in her public ministrations. By her divine call to this sacred ministry, by her gifts and graces and fruitage, she has demonstrated the genuineness of her call, and is recognized among the most effective of Pentecostal preachers. (See Godbey's *Woman Preacher.*)

They are beloved preachers. "And they all wept sore, and fell on Paul's neck, and kissed him, sorrowing most of all for the word which he had spoken, that they should behold his face no more. And they brought him on his way unto the ship" (Acts xx. 37, 38). Multitudes whom they rescue from sin and Satan's power love them with God-given affection. Having "forsaken all," the Pentecostal preacher finds friends a hundred-fold, as the Master promised. These friendships are even sometimes dearer than nature's ties, which may have been alienated by devotion to Pentecostal truth, and become the "joy and the crown of rejoicing" of the Pentecostal preacher.

Self-called, formal, fruitless preachers are strangers to
such bonds, and have been known to vent their jealous
spite toward those whose ministry God has thus crowned,
in this way advertising their own spurious birth.

They are ready preachers. "Then Paul answered,
What do ye, weeping and breaking my heart, for I am
ready not to be bound only, but also to die at Jerusalem
for the name of the Lord Jesus" (Acts xxi. 13). Ready
always to preach, pray, live or die for God. A minister
who is not thus prepared, though schooled in all the lore
of earth, is not a Pentecostal preacher.

They are innocent preachers. "And when he was
come, the Jews which had come down from Jerusalem
stood round about him, bringing against him many and
grievous charges, which they could not prove" (Acts
xxv. 7). Though accused on every side, enemies could
not "prove" their complaints, and were compelled to
retreat.

Pentecostal preachers can say, "Receive us, we have
wronged no man, we have corrupted no man, we have de-
frauded no man." All who are not maintaining this
Pentecostal innocence dare God's lightnings and men's
censures, if they pose as Pentecostal preachers.

They are solicitous preachers. They have the salvation and sanctification of people on their hearts. The
prosperity of the Church is the passion of their souls.
How often this appears in Paul's Epistle to the Roman
believers—"I long to see you, that I may impart unto
you some spiritual gift, to the end ye may be established" (Rom. i. 11). "Be perfected; be comforted; be
of the same mind; live in peace; and the God of love
and peace shall be with you" (II. Cor. xiii. 11). "My
little children, of whom I am again in travail until Christ
be formed in you" (Gal. iv. 19). "Grieve not the

Holy Spirit of God" (Eph. iv. 30). "Always in every supplication of mine on behalf of you all, making my supplication with joy" (Phil. i. 4). "Epaphras, who is one of you, a servant of Christ Jesus, saluteth you, always striving for you in his prayers, that ye may stand perfect and fully assured in all the will of God" (Col. iv. 12). "And the God of peace himself sanctify you wholly; and may your spirit and soul and body be preserved entire, without blame at the coming of our Lord Jesus Christ" (I. Thess. v. 23).

Pentecostal preachers always feel this solicitude for the spiritual prosperity of the Church, and especially for the fruits of their own ministry, and this is one of the marks of the genuineness of their call. False prophets will have deep solicitude for the temporal prosperity of the Church, and often form strong social ties, and, like Simon Magus, may seek spiritual power as a means of advancement, but they are strangers to the tender solicitude which God's true preachers feel. They are like parents who labor for love; others are enemies, who work for selfish motives.

They are prayer-coveting preachers. "Finally, brethren, pray for us, that the word of the Lord may run and be glorified, even as also it is with you; and that we may be delivered from unreasonable and evil men: for all have not faith" (II. Thess. iii. 1, 2). I once heard a minister say as he began his sermon that it was customary for preachers to ask the people to pray while they preached, but he did not so desire. The sermon which followed was as dry as the winds from the desert.

Pentecostal ministers covet the prayers of the saints that the Word may do its work and that they may be delivered from "foolish controversy." They love to have special united prayer as often as possible for victory on the battle field.   Many of their greatest victories may be traced to the prevailing united prayer of devout saints. They know and magnify its power.

They are tested preachers.   '' And let these also first be proved; then let them serve as deacons, if they be blameless'' (I. Tim. iii. 10).   The Pentecostal rule was that all '' should be first proved '' before advanced, and then continued only on the condition that they be '' blameless.''   From this it is evident that the proving was not a test in solely intellectual but also in spiritual gymnastics. False apostles are only too glad to substitute the former for the latter.

They are well-balanced preachers.   They possess '' sound minds '' as well as sanctified hearts.   The worldly maxim, '' He is good for nothing else ; he will have to be a preacher,'' finds no sanction in the Word of God.

Under the Old Testament the best belonged to God, and any blemish disqualified for this sacred office.   Jesus chose none but sound men of sterling sense for his ambassadors.   There is not an instance after Pentecost of one of them being guilty of an unsound speech.   Full of sound common sense, they were saved from foolishness ; and full of Scripture and of the Holy Ghost, they were saved from all fanaticism, and their characters shine forth as the sun in the spiritual sky.

Pentecostal preachers belong to this class.   Under this name it may be that men have on one hand covered a shallow experience, and on the other hand some may have gone to fanatical extremes, but in either case there has been a diversion from the Pentecostal life, which has no duties nor delights which are not both reasonable and right.

They are studious preachers.   '' Neglect not the gift that is in thee, which was given thee by prophecy, with the laying on of hands of the presbytery. Be diligent in these things ; give thyself wholly to them ; that thy progress may be manifest unto all '' (I. Tim. iv. 14, 15). '' But shun profane babblings ; for they will proceed further in ungodliness, and their word will eat, as doth a gangrene '' (II. Tim. ii. 16, 17). Though possessed of both the gifts and the graces of the Holy Spirit, and also favored with the companionship of inspired men, yet they realized that, if they were to be preachers and teachers of the Word, they must have it in their hearts and heads. They were strangers to the fallacy that claims that those who have the Spirit need to search the Word no more, and to the folly that blindly believes that without such searching one can always ''open the mouth and God will fill it '' with the proper message, and to the laziness that depends upon chance texts, with no study nor preparation, where there are opportunities for it. The Pentecostal preacher realizes that he is a physician to souls, to diagnose their condition, and from the divine doctor-book to prescribe the gospel remedy.

The Bible alone, if prayerfully studied for a lifetime, would still have many infinite treasures in it undiscovered. He who neglects its study and the employment of the best available helps to the understanding of its truths, commits ministerial suicide. How can he bring forth '' things new and old '' unless he first enters the treasure-house and possesses them ? How can he wield the ''sword of the Spirit '' if he does not first have it '' well in hand ''? How can he prescribe for others if he has learned neither the symptoms nor the remedies? Hence the great Head of the Church commands every Timothy in every age to '' study to shew thyself approved unto God, a workman that needeth not to be ashamed handling aright the word of truth.'' No minister can

disregard this and be guiltless.   Because many are
carried away with the "culture craze" of substituting
a college course for the gift of the Holy Ghost is no excuse for others to neglect the study of the Word and all
that throws light upon it.

Shall I wear no armor at all because fools persist in
wearing one of straw? Shall I throw my weapons away
because some one substitutes a painted tin horn for a
sword? If I do, I will fall or fly from the field, while the
enemy laughs at my folly. John Wesley's advice to
ministers that they should cultivate the habit of study or
else "find some other employment" still holds good of
all who would be Pentecostal preachers.

A Word-neglecting ministry is a church-starving ministry, and God has no place for such in His employ.
It is as wicked to starve souls to spiritual death as to
send bullets through their bodies.

Pentecostal preachers revel in the study of the Word
and all that will make their ministrations thereof effective.

They are "loyal" preachers.   Not always to ecclesiastics nor to ecclesiasticism, when that comes between
them and God-given duty, but loyal to Christ in every
way and on every battle-field. Though the kingdom of
God, and the cause of Christ, His Son, are derided and
disclaimed by the throngs around them, yet they glory
in wearing the badge of the "reproach of Christ," and
lifting high his royal banner. Though bullets whiz and
demons hiss, and dead churchmen scorn, with faces firm
as flint, they press forward in the name and strength of
God, ready to do or die. We shall doubtless find that
such men, linked with Omnipotence, will do exploits, and
when the war is over be given bounties and positions in
keeping with the King they love and serve.

They are revival preachers.   They were the product

and promoters of the revival at Pentecost, and from thence they swept out cyclone-centers of revival power. All Pentecostal preachers love revivals. To promote them is their chief business, and by personal effort and by the employment of every lawful help they seek to propagate the experiences of salvation. They can no more rest in the mere routine of church-work than a fish could live without water.

A minister without Revivals is as sad a sight as a general who will fight no battles when the enemy is making advances on every hand. He should be retired either for cowardice or inability. Satan seeks no more pleasant sight than a minister firing the blank cartridges of polished sermons, and opposing genuine Holy Ghost revival of religion. (See chapter on *Pentecostal Revivals*.)

They are obedient preachers. When the apostles were candidates for this position they received an order not to "depart from Jerusalem," but to "wait for the promise of the Father." Though that appointment was a perilous one at that time, and many of them probably would, under the circumstances, have preferred some quiet college or a country church, yet they heeded the divine summons and tarried in the very center where the wolves were still red with the blood of their crucified Leader —tarried until the trolley of their faith touched the wire of fulfilled promise, and the electric current of the Holy Ghost filled and thrilled, and sent them out as samples of the kind of Pentecostal preachers God could make and will have to do His work. More trying appointments men never received. No official boards, no organized churches, no salary except stripes and stones guaranteed, no church buildings, yet each went to his appointed charge without a murmur and, in spite of an organized and murderous hunt on the part of pagans and of exasperated Jewish

wolves, they won converts by the thousand, and not one
whine is recorded in all their Pentecostal career.   Their
brethren in all ages of the Church have been marked by
the same spirit of obedience to the great Head of the
Church.

They are praying preachers.   "These all with one
accord continued stedfastly in prayer" (Acts i. 14).
In every difficulty they flew to God in prayer.   They
were graduates of kneeology.   They found what many
have not learned: that spiritual diamonds are found, not by
star-gazing nor sky-scraping, but on the knees.   The minister may polish his gun in the study or lecture-room, but
unless he loads it on his knees he will always miss the
mark.   Pentecostal preachers always are praying men.
One may give an entertaining lecture without prayer in
either preparation or delivery, but never an effective gospel sermon.

They are fire-baptized preachers.   "And there appeared
unto them tongues parting asunder, like as of fire; and
it sat upon each one of them" (Acts ii. 3).   The Bible
definition of a minister is not an icicle, to chill and kill,
nor a skyrocket, to surprise and amuse; but " a flame of
fire."   "And his ministers a flame of fire" (Heb. i. 7).
The minister " who lacks the fire," lacks the very thing
that constitutes a true preacher.   Spurious preachers are
fireless preachers, except when they glow with the foxfire of human enthusiasm or affected earnestness ; but
this enduement makes men feel like Whitefield, when he
said : " I would fain die blazing, not with human glory,
but with the love of Jesus."   They are the electric lights
of a lost world, salvation torches with which God spreads
the Pentecostal revival conflagration.   They love to be
like the wick of a lamp, hid and consumed by the flame
that feeds upon them.   The confessed and lamented cold-

ness in the churches is not a lack of methods or machinery, but of these "flames of fire." The devil tries to make the preachers think that true fire will burn them, or ostracize them, or make them unpleasantly conspicuous, or create unkind criticism, and so succeeds in making many remain little, sizzling, sputtering candles who should be flaming "like the sun when he goeth forth in his might." The Pentecostal chamber of earnest, obedient, determined, prayerful, believing faith for the falling of the promised fire is where these flames are kindled.

They are drawing preachers. Under their ministration the "multitude came together." A Pentecostal preacher, endued with Pentecostal gifts and graces, brings people together. He is a magnet that draws men. What the Church needs to gain an audience is, not higher steeples, nor softer pews, nor canaries in her choirs, nor cultured schoolmen, but Holy Ghost magnets in her pulpits. Some of the birds may fly out, it is true, when these men step in, and some of the goats may run to more congenial places, but people will be drawn, not only to the Church, but to Christ. It is being done to-day, but as too much paint destroys a magnet, so too much form, and ceremony, and starch is negativing the force of many pulpits that should be Pentecostal in their power to draw, and save, and sanctify.

They are mysterious preachers. Many were amazed, mystified, and maddened by their preaching (Acts ii.). So it ever is where Spirit-filled men proclaim Spirit-given messages. A ministry that lacks the mystery of the superhuman is not a Pentecostal ministry. One unaccustomed to such scenes can not sit under the ministry of such men, and feel the electrical currents come from heaven, and see the sobbing penitents, and hear the shouting of saints, and behold the opposition melt, without feeling, "What meaneth this?" Some, as of old, will be annoyed, and the evil disposed may as then declare that the whole company is "drunk on new wine," or "aflame with wild fire," but what is such a secret to the "wise and prudent" is revealed to all who have been initiated into the mysteries of the Pentecostal chamber.

In II. Cor. vi., Paul in a masterly manner throws upon the canvas a picture of a Pentecostal minister and writes out his credentials. In woeful contrast to most modern man-made pictures of preachers, there are no honorary degrees mentioned, no college curriculum alluded to, and no salary hinted at, showing that these things were not magnified then as now ; but the following facts shine out very clearly. Paul's picture not only includes himself, but embraces the whole Pentecostal class of which he was a member.

They are offenceless preachers. "Giving no occasion of stumbling in anything, that our ministration be not blamed" (II. Cor. vi. 3). They both condemn offences, and keep clear of them. Offensive to many, but offenceless toward all. This is clearly the Pentecostal standard, and if any one is below it the fault is not in the standard but in the man. An experience of holiness that breaks at this point needs remelting and recasting. Not that the Jews will not be offended and throw stones, but that they will have no rightful cause to do so, and if they accuse will have to "hire witnesses" to swear to "false charges." Better suffer a thousand losses than that blame should come to the ministry.

"*In much patience*" (II. Cor. vi. 4). An impatient preacher is condemned by his own conscience, by saints, sinners and God Himself. Impatience is the creaking of the hinges of the soul, which advertises that it needs salvation oil.   Pentecostal preachers see that the rust is off from their own hinges and that they are well lubricated with the anointing that abideth, before they attempt to administer this oil to others.   Patience is love tried and found true.   The true preacher finds plenty to try it, and needs and has "much patience."

"*In afflictions*."   God quenches the violence of the fire in every afflictive furnace, and they rejoice and are glad. They know that "afflictions" are the machines in which jewels of priceless worth are being "worked out and polished," and they patiently wait God's process until the "but for a moment" shall give place to a glorious eternity and "exceeding weight of glory."

"*In necessities*."   Feeling the gnawing of the rats of need is an apostolic mark that no preacher need despise. Yet he will do well to remember that for such rats God has a steel trap of promised supplies, which is sure to catch and kill them.   "My God shall fulfill every need of yours according to his riches in glory in Christ Jesus" (Phil. iv. 19).   Faith may be tested, but if true, the promise will be proved.   There is no record of a Pentecostal preacher having a house of his own, a bank account, or insurance policy.   They did not, as pastors and evangelists, stipulate for big pay, or any pay.   Such bartering has not the stamp of any Pentecost on it, ancient or modern.   Ministers who are moved to change their relation simply for more wool, will search in vain for a Pentecostal precedent.

"*In distresses*."   They suffer mental torture on account of the state of the Church, the obstinacy of sinners, the coldness of friends, the treachery of false brethren and the deprivations of home and friends, but they endure all with joyous patience for Jesus' sake.

"*In stripes*."   Lashes, blows, bullets and stones have

struck these brave heroes in all ages.   Thus God tries their faith, advertises to 'all worlds their heroism, and keeps cowards from their ranks.   Their stripes may come in the shape of censures or expulsions, and their blows and bullets from " lewd fellows of the baser sort," who are incited to such deeds by people who say they are Jews, but are not.   An ungodly official board beneath a minister and an unholy ecclesiasticism above are the two stones between which God allows some of His choicest ones who have grace to endure the process, to be polished into shafts which reflect with singular luster celestial light.   Many a Stephen, between these two mill-stones, has had his body crushed, while his soul exulted and was glad.

"*In imprisonments.*"   Philippian jails and Bedford prisons and cold Bastiles have no terror to these stalwarts. Many a prison house, in the past few years, has rung with the songs and shouts of victory from the lips of Salvation Army lads and lassies, who constitute so largely God's Pentecostal preachers of the present day.   These heroes of the cross will shine like the sun when theological scholastics, with their cherished titles, who have ridiculed them, shall have sunk into eternal obloquy. Preachers of this class, because of their testimony and preaching of holiness, have been banished to some mountain, or pine woods, or cheerless Patmos; but there they still prophesy and see still more glorious visions of Jesus and demonstrate the divinity of their course by the spirit with which they receive their sentence.   They are among the Pauline princes of Christ's Church in every age, and will sparkle and shine and shout and reign when their haughty, hard jailers have been forgotten.   Joyous patience in imprisonment and persecution is one mark of the Pentecostal credentials.

"*In tumults.*" The margin reads, in "tossings to and fro." Such men will be borne about by the waves of divinely-ordered and providential circumstances which may often to them seem inexplicable. They may be moved from their fields of labor when it seems to them without cause and before their work is there completed; but, like their Master, they triumphantly walk the rolling waves and do not sink, but sing—

> "My bark is wafted from the strand by breath Divine:
> Upon the helm there rests a hand other than mine.
> He holds me when the tempest smites; I shall not fall.
> If sharp, 'tis short; if long, 'tis light: He orders all."

If their providential appointment falls in a jail, the whole city is shaken and the jailer and his family saved. If on Patmos, burning messages, such as Revelation and "Pilgrim's Progress," like morning stars, burst from the place of exile. If in Babylonish captivity, conspirators are defeated and a king and kingdom converted. If in Egypt, a nation is saved from extinction and a dungeon becomes a stepping-place to a throne. They are P. P.'s (Patient Prisoners) of Jesus Christ, who, sharing now the reproach of the cross, will forever share with Him the imperishable honors of His coming kingdom.

"*In labors.*" They delight to spend and be spent in the service of their Redeemer. To them the minister is not a lord, to be paid, petted and worshiped, but a sower, to break soil, sow seed, and root up thorns and drive away fowls; a harvester, beneath scorching sun, to garner golden grain for God; and a householder, to prepare a feast and gather and entertain the hungry guests. Pentecostal preachers are not loiterers, but laborers, in God's vineyard.

"*In watchings*" against treachery on the part of open foes and false professors, and, also, against the

many grievous wolves that seek to destroy the sheep.
Such perils in all ages call forth the true minister's watchfulness. Without it, the pigeons of error will steal away
the grains of truth before they have had time to take
root.

"*In fastings.*"   Pentecostal preachers know the power
of observing religious fasts, and also have the grace to
practice them when the interests of the kingdom so demand.   Fasting, not feasting, was a mark of their genuineness.   One of the proofs of a spurious and defective
ministry to-day is the transposition of these acts.

"*In pureness*" of intentions, of heart and of life.
An impure preacher is not a Pentecostal preacher, for a
Pentecostal conversion and baptism sweeps away all im-
purities of heart and life. "God will not grime His
hands with unclean instruments."   Hence pureness is a
mark which all His true ministers bear.

"*In knowledge,*" not only of the history and doctrines
of Christianity, but the knowledge of Jesus as a personal
Saviour and Sanctifier.   Every Pentecostal preacher possesses this gold mine, and gathers priceless treasure
from its depths.

"*In longsuffering.*"   Pentecostal pastors "suffer long
and are kind."   Some of the kindest, sweetest men I
know have suffered long without a murmur.   Spurious
apostles can not do this, but will wince and wriggle and
retort unkindly.

"*In kindness.*"   They are kind men, even to their
foes.   No unkind act eclipses the glory of their Pentecostal sun.   They throw at their foes great lumps of
sugar in the form of a "God bless you!" where those
destitute of their experience would hurl the hard stones of
retaliatory retort.

"*In the Holy Ghost.*"   By His indwelling, His graces,

and His gifts, they give positive proof of the genuineness of their calling. A Pentecostal preacher without the Pentecostal baptism is like a furnace without fire. Paul well declares this enduement among the inseparable attendants of a Holy Ghost ministry.

"*In love unfeigned*," both towards God and man, friend and foe. All can not know as much or do as much as Paul, but all may *love* just as much, even with all the heart, fervently, constantly, and truly. Pentecostal preachers have this mark. Their love is "without dissimulation."

"*In the Word of Truth.*" Their lives are consistent with its privileges and requirements, and their preaching the echo of its truths. Pentecostal preachers proclaim, not their own conceits, but preach the Word, as God commands and a perishing world needs, not sections of it, such as will please, but the whole Word, in both its tenderness and its awfulness.

"*In the power of God*," which attended their ministrations in convicting, converting, sanctifying, judgment-dealing, wonder-working might. The ministry of Pentecostal preachers is attended by this divine energy, which makes enemies like Herod fall, wicked men cry, "What must we do to be saved?" and devils fear and fly. This is one of the marks which God stamps upon every Pentecostal certificate. It is the gift of "miracles," or as Dr. Godbey explains it in *Gifts and Graces* (which see), the gift of "manipulating dynamite." Whedon says it means "supernatural efficiency in word and deed."

"*By the armor of righteousness.*" Pentecostal preachers are righteous preachers. Right with God and man. Thus armed behind a coat of mail that men and devils can not pierce, they press to the forefront of the battle for God and truth. Without this armor they would quickly fall. It is not an imputed righteousness, but an imparted righteousness, and safely shields against every spiritual foe. The lack of this armor makes cowards where there should be conquering commanders. An experience that is destitute of right-being and right-living is a stupendous fraud. Only the upright in heart are divinely authorized to shout for joy. Is not one reason why there are not more shouting preachers because there are not more clad in this shouting armor? All had it on at Pentecost, and it is as needful now as then. But no man can wear it who is knowingly wrong in any particular.

"*By glory and dishonor.*" The glory which comes from loyalty to God, and the dishonor with which the world esteems people who are "crazy on the subject of religion."

"*Evil report and good report.*" Evil report among criticizing professors and devils, but good report among true believers here, saints and angels in heaven, and the Father, Son, and Holy Ghost, with whom the things "highly esteemed among men are an abomination."

"*As deceivers and yet true.*" Holiness-fighting ecclesiastics accused Jesus of being a deceiver, yet He was God incarnate. His ministers who follow Him fully may meet similar accusation from like sources, and yet be true heralds of the burning, shining truth of God.

"*As unknown, yet well known.*" Unknown in social circles, and ecclesiastical politics, and holiness-evading company, but well known among the saints of God on earth and all His family above. What Pentecostal preacher has not met acquaintances in places where they did not care to recognize him, lest they might be thought "partakers" with him? He was well known, yet appeared to be unknown. Yet the recognition which true preachers receive from the aristocracy of the skies is so marked that such treatment does not annoy them, but, on the other hand, they feel it an honor to be treated as their Master was.

"*As dying, and behold we live.*" This may include "dying" to sin and the world and "living" without them, but doubtless alludes primarily to Paul's being stoned to death in one place and arising and preaching with power in another. Thus Pentecostal preachers are sometimes stoned to death by criticism, calumny and persecution, until in certain circles they are considered "dead men," when, behold! they arise from their graves and "live" with greater might than ever. A successful pastor whom I know was thus killed and buried by being sent to an appointment two miles from any street-car line, but, behold, he lives! and is turning the world upside down.

"*As chastened and not killed.*" This class of preachers can receive chastisement from both God and man without being killed. They accept such discipline as sent or allowed by a loving Father to correct and to promote to deeper experiences and more abundant usefulness. Such men feel: " Let the righteous smite me, it shall be a kindness; let him reprove me, it shall be as oil upon the head." The gospel armor so completely encases that " no weapon formed against " such men " shall prosper."

"*As sorrowful, yet always rejoicing.*" Sorrowful over the ravages of the wolves, yet rejoicing over the sheep safely within the fold. Sorrowful over past defeats, yet rejoicing over present salvation and anticipated triumphs. Sorrowful over the acts of false professors, but rejoicing over the triumphs of true Christians. Sorrowful over the souls sinking in sin to hell, yet rejoicing over the wrecked ones that have been rescued.

"*Poor, yet making many rich.*" Poor in spirit, yet

possessors of exhaustless gold mines of spiritual wealth.
Poor in this world's goods, but making others infinitely
rich with spiritual possessions and titles and mansions and
crowns and kingdoms that will increase in glory forever !

"Having nothing."　No homes, no houses, no lands, no
worldly titles nor offices, and perhaps no guarantee of
support, yet as heirs of God and joint-heirs with Christ
Jesus, inheriting *" all things."*　For "all things are
yours ; and ye are Christ's ; and Christ is God's."
Their stock is not in the worthless dust of this earth,
which soon is to consume in final conflagration, but in
the eternal realities of a heavenly kingdom where, as
sons of God and joint-heirs with Jesus, they are to be
kings and priests forever.　As they have already secured
their positions and entered upon their royal duties, the
honors and offices of this world are to them as the flicker
of tallow candles to the possessor of electric lights and
stars and suns.　This is one of Paul's pictures of a Pentecostal preacher.　All who have the Pentecostal diploma
can meet these Pentecostal tests.

What is the privilege and duty of God's children towards these, His chosen and qualified representatives?

Satan hates them, the world may deride them, and
hypocrites will treat them as they did the Master when
he came.　God in his Word, as well as in the hearts of
His own true children, makes both duty and privilege
plain.

Do not reject them.　" He that heareth you heareth
me ; and he that rejecteth you rejecteth me : and he that
rejecteth me rejecteth him that sent me " (Luke x. 16).
They who scoff at God's true ministers scoff at Him, and
a doom as fearful as befell those who jeered at Elijah
will befall unless they repent.　Better tamper with
lightning rods in a thunder storm than to criticise God's

true preachers. Many churches have died because of rejecting and criticising some humble pastor whom God sent to them with messages from heaven.

The writer knows a church which was greatly blessed and built up under the ministry of young men, but some "despised their youth," and insisted upon having an "experienced" preacher. They got their wish, but he was as dry as a stick, and the church languished and longed for a minister with less experience on certain lines.

Joyfully welcome them. "Receive him therefore in the Lord with all joy; and hold such in honour" (Phil. ii. 29). What pastor has not fragrant memories of such welcomes? Such greetings multiply in proportion as the Pentecostal experience is received. The recollection of such faces which so greeted the writer in the pastorate often float through his mind like "spicy breezes," and this moment his eyes are moist at their memory. He would record some of their names, but for their number and modesty and his lack of space. God bless them.

He will never forget the melting emotions that filled his soul when returned to a pastoral charge as at his first public service he was greeted with the following lines, composed and read by a noble layman, long since promoted to Paradise, as expressing the feelings of the church. Such expressions are spontaneous from Pentecostal people toward Pentecostal pastors :

> " Welcome, thrice welcome, dear pastor, to-day,
> Gladly we greet thee ; for this did we pray,
> Again 'neath thy pastoral care to be fed,
> With ' meat in due season,' and life-giving bread.
> To listen as thou shalt the Scriptures unfold,
> And bring from God's treasury things new and old,
> Indeed is a favor ; a blessing from God ;
> A gift the Good Shepherd, himself, hath bestowed.

And while thou art tending the sheep of this fold,
Our prayers and our purses thy hands shall uphold."

Follow their godly example. "Brethren, be ye imitators together of me, and mark them which so walk even as ye have us for an ensample" (Phil. iii. 17). Ministers must walk so that it is safe for their members to follow them, or they are not true preachers. And members who neglect to follow such examples are under double condemnation. A member has no license to do what he would condemn in his minister. The professor who himself does the things which he condemns in his minister is a hypocrite.

Attend their ministrations. "Not forsaking the assembling of ourselves together, as the custom of some is, but exhorting one another; and so much the more, as ye see the day drawing nigh" (Heb. x. 25). Soldiers who would neglect to convene at the command of officers to hear their instructions, would be disciplined and punished. Ministers are the officers of Christ's army. Through them he has messages of great moment to every soldier. He who needlessly neglects these ministrations is guilty of wrong to himself, disrespectful to God's messengers, and offers an insult to the God who sends them, and commands attention to their words.

Sham believers have a whole hornet's nest full of excuses for neglecting this, to them, distasteful duty. To Pentecostal people it is most delightful. The real excuse is a heart that is wrong and the consciousness of sins that merit and may receive their just rebuke.

The duty of believers to hear every one who professes to be a gospel preacher or to recognize as such every compact of people that labels itself a "church," is another question which will be treated elsewhere. (See chapter on *Pentecostal Impostors and the Pentecostal Church.*)

Pray for them. "Now I beseech you, brethren, by our Lord Jesus Christ, and by the love of the Spirit, that ye strive together with me in your prayers to God for me; that I may be delivered from them that are disobedient in Judæa, and that my ministration . . . may be acceptable to the saints" (Rom. xv. 30, 31). God's people mightily aid their ministers by their prayers. Many ministers have been fully sanctified through the prayers of their people. For a people to withhold their earnest prayers from a minister is to rob him of one of the vital conditions of his successful ministry among them. The very fact that I have the assurance of a number of people daily praying for me makes me a stronger and better man. Pentecostal churches pray for their pastors.

Obey them. "Obey them that have the rule over you, and submit to them" (Heb. xiii. 17). Pentecostal preachers will exact no wrong or unreasonable thing from their people. They come with divine messages and divine authority, and to disregard it and them is an insult to the King and government in whose name they come. Converts who thus treat their ministers are simply sowing seeds of anarchy in their own hearts, which will bear a baleful harvest, not only in their own lives, but in those of their children.

Pray for the increase of their number. "Pray ye therefore the Lord of the harvest, that he send forth labourers into his harvest" (Matt. ix. 38). The need of the Church and of the world, above everything else, is ministers baptized with the Holy Ghost and fire. God sends them in answer to the prayers of His people.

Be charitable towards their infirmities. "That which was a temptation to you in my flesh ye despised not, nor rejected; but ye received me as an angel of God" (Gal.

iv. 14). Ministers are but men, and though they should
be saved from all sin, yet still they are full of human
infirmities, and weaknesses, and defects, which God's
people should deal kindly with. One of the most apostolic men in the Church was recently rejected by a proud
city appointment because of his mannerism, his unassum-
ing appearance, plain dress, and uncouth ways. So did
not the Galatians treat Paul, but received him, notwithstanding his infirmities, as an angel of God.

Love them. God's true people love Pentecostal
preachers. "For I bear you witness, that, if possible,
ye would have plucked out your eyes and given them to
me" (Gal. iv. 15). They greet with joy their coming,
weep over their departure, and are willing to pluck out
not only their dollars, but their very "eyes," if need be,
in their affection for them.

Support them. "Know ye not that they which minister about sacred things eat of the things of the temple,
and they which wait upon the altar have their portion
with the altar? Even so did the Lord ordain that they
which proclaim the gospel should live of the gospel"
(I. Cor. ix. 13, 14). God's plan calls them and sets them
apart solely to the work of the gospel ministry. It demands all their time and energies. They renounce all
secular pursuits by which they might earn a competency
for themselves and families, and covenant to God and the
Church to give themselves "wholly to the work of the
ministry." God commands that those who share the
spiritual blessings which they bring shall reciprocate by
supporting them, both while in active work and when
sickness or old age supersedes their activities. It never
has been a part of God's plan to require ministers to do
secular labor for a livelihood. He who gives all his time
to the Church should have all his real needs supplied by

her. The apparent exception of Paul supporting himself in no wise affects this rule. He did this voluntarily, glorying in so doing; but he repented when he realized its injurious educating influence upon the churches, and pleaded "forgive me this wrong." God sometimes allows men of their own free will to do this as a love offering to Him. He is thus crowning with victory the labors of hundreds of lay-workers on the Pauline self-supporting line who, with no salary, are everywhere kindling Pentecostal fires.

Such have bread to eat that others know not of, and "honey out of the rock" hid for them alone. God bless them. But it is wrong for God's people to allow these examples to divert them from their duty. This is plain. Unconverted church members neglect it, and often refuse to support a Pentecostal minister. They are like one man who refused one year to pay his "quarterage" because the pastor called upon them so seldom, and the next because he called so much that he could not afford to "board him" and to "pay quarterage," too.

"The laborer is worthy of his hire," and the church which shifts this duty is as guilty as a man who would refuse to pay his taxes. It was levied as a tax under the law, but is left to the free-will and choice of believers under the gospel. Shame on the man who is faithless because thus trusted. This support should always be paid as a debt due, not as a benevolence, any more than a school tax. There is no room in the gospel economy for the "donation" until all such dues are met in full. God's true people love to pay as able for this sacred purpose. All who neglect this and thus "sow sparingly," shall also "reap sparingly."

The contemptible compromise with the world in the shape of fairs, festivals and fandangoes to raise money for ministerial support is spurned by Pentecostal pastors and people. Instead of this they welcome the Scripture plan, and "on the first day of the week they lay by them in store as God has prospered them" for God's work. A collection or subscription does not spoil their piety, for they love to respond as able, and thus test the blessedness of the promise which declares: "God is able to make all grace abound towards you, that ye always, having all sufficiency in all things, may abound unto every good work."

Live churches, properly educated, respond to this call as naturally as a government feeds and uniforms and pays its officers. To neglect it is a sad type of disloyalty to Christ. "Thou shalt not muzzle the ox that treadeth out the corn." Woe unto him who by temporal neglect at this point would place the muzzle of temporal want upon God's oxen. Pentecostal preachers merit and should have such support.

All of the above, and other Scriptural rules pertaining to all of God's true ministers, the Spirit "writes on all truly converted hearts." To disregard them is to sow to the wind and to reap a whirlwind of dire consequences. To heed them is to sow seed that will ripen into a golden, glorious and eternal harvest.

They are well paid preachers. The Pentecostal preacher is divinely assured of certain and glorious rewards. Some are received now ; most are in the future. His name may not be lauded by the secular press, nor applauded by worldly papers. He may not receive the "cane" from questionable fraternities, nor a "gold watch," as some others do ; his salary may not be "paid in full," or at all ; but these things, to him, are chaff compared to his glorious rewards :

1. The approval of his own conscience and the

plaudits of the saints, angels, the Father, Son and Holy Ghost.

2. Exceeding great and precious promises, which will shine brighter when canes shall have been consumed by judgment-day fires, and watches have no time to measure.

3. Gold "tried in the fire," and priceless pearls and fruit of Canaan.

4. All daily "needs supplied," and the promise of white raiment that never will soil, a mansion that never will need repairs, and free access forever to the tree of life in glory.

5. The daily comforting companionship of Christ Himself sharing every joy and sorrow, and giving needed counsel, comfort, encouragement and strength.

6. "An hundredfold" in the present time, and glory measureless beyond.

7. The prayers and gratitude of "sons and daughters" in the gospel, and of others, to whom his ministry has been a blessing.

8. "A crown of glory that fadeth not away" "when the chief Shepherd shall appear."

9. The honor of having been in the front of the fight for Him, when all earth and hell were leagued in rebellion against their Lord.

10. Scars on the battle-field that will be badges of honor forever.

11. A part in the first resurrection, and the privilege of ministering with Christ in glorified body during His millennial reign on earth, and then forever. (See chapter on *Pentecostal Expectancy of Christ's Return.*)

12. Final and full vindication at the Judgment.

13. A prominent and eternal appointment in the New Jerusalem.

These and numberless other blessings from the rich treasure store of God's paying department are the privileges of every Pentecostal preacher, privileges more than a millionfold compensating for every sacrifice.

A picture of the joys and honors that certainly await them crowds itself upon the writer's mind. He seems to hear a fearful sound " like the voice of many waters," as to this wicked world the Son of God returns. In the twinkling of an eye His true ministers are clothed in immortality, and with all who love His appearing, arise with shouts of joy to meet Him "in the air." For each of them He bears a "crown of glory," which by angel hands is placed upon their radiant brows. "The marriage of the Lamb has come and His Bride hath made herself ready." Every minister, who, faithful to his Lord, endured unto the end, is there! What minglings! What greetings! What adorings!

Arrayed in white, their blood-bought bridal robes, and faces shining with the love they feel towards Him who has redeemed them, I seem to hear them sing: "Unto him who hath loved us and washed us from our sins in his own blood and hath made us kings and priests unto God and the Father, unto him be glory and dominion for ever and ever. Amen." But, see! Led by the royal Bridegroom, they all descend to earth, the birthplace of the Bride. To the land of the cross and sepulcher and Israel's awful apostasy, with the shining hosts who once proclaimed the Saviour's birth, triumphant now they come.

The feet of Him that once were pierced by cruel nails again as prophecy declared they should are resting upon Mount Olivet. The thorn-pierced brow is shining now with many star-gemmed crowns. No more the despised, rejected " Man of Sorrows," but the all-conquering "King of kings," who, with His Bride, has come to claim and hold His own. Earthly thrones crumble, and on their ruins His twelve apostles sit in seats divinely given, as was promised, "judging the twelve tribes of Israel," aided by every minister who "forsook all" for Jesus' sake ; with Him as kings and priests they jointly reign. "But they shall be priests of God and of Christ, and shall reign with him a thousand years" (Rev. xx. 6).

Satan, their foe and His, is bound and banished for a thousand years. Free from his damning influence, men yield to gospel claims. Great conventions and training-schools for Christian work conducted by Isaiah, Paul, Wesley, Finney and other mighty men of God abound. Under the leadership of Christ and the combined efforts of the preachers and evangelists of all centuries, unprec-edented revivals will break out. A nation will be born in a day. One shall chase a thousand, and two put ten thousand to flight, and the heavens and the earth shall be full of the knowledge of the Lord. Holiness will be popular. None but Pentecostal preachers will be in de-mand. Controversies over the status of evangelists in the Church and over woman's rights, which have so perplexed and befogged theologians here, will vex no more, but, as shining stars of light, they will dart on their world-wide missions with the glad consent and co-operation of all the officials and ecclesiastics of those days.

Pastors, if the interests of Christ's kingdom demand, can remain on their charges one thousand years. Satan and unholy governments and systems of religions will be cast out and banished. See Rev. xix. and xx. Think of it, a thousand years' pastorate of a Pentecostal preacher, with no devil to fight and every member of the official

board below and of the appointing power above saints
baptized with the Holy Ghost and fire !

Such an appointment would be a hell to a minister
that was not a possessor of holiness.   Yet such appointments await every Pentecostal preacher.   No wonder they
can shout and sing amid the poorest appointments of
earth, thus knowing that their time is coming and that
the grindstones of earth are simply sharpening them for
the harvests of millennial and eternal rewards.

Once worn, weary, misunderstood, reviled, persecuted
and oppressed, but now with bodies made like that of
their transfigured Lord, with lightning speed they fly
around the earth on new ministries of love and light and
joy.   Painless, deathless, hungerless, they will range the
old battle-field with prophets, apostles, and with the
King himself for one thousand years.   The popular
preachers of that time, not so far off methinks as some
suppose, will be the holiness preachers.   During all these
victorious years, there will be no one to caution them of
making holiness a "hobby," or to tell them that they
might have better appointments if they "would not
preach holiness so much and be so pronounced against
fairs and festivals."

Noble, loyal, royal, kingly men of God ! lift up your
heads with joy, for your kingdom and your crown is
near !

But, look ! the bright millennial years have passed
away.   Under their celestial sunshine, unblighted by the
frosts of sin, the solitary places were all made glad,
every desert blossoming like the rose, and earth, so long
the dark abode of devils and of demon men, is restored
to fairer than Paradisical beauty, the happy home of
God's true ministers and their joyous people.   Maddened by his long confinement under clanking chains

of darkness, Satan, full of fury, now returns, and with diabolical schemes, hatched in the high counsels of devils and apostate preachers in hell, makes another determined effort to wreck this ransomed world (Rev. xx. 7, 8). Followed by all the armies of hell, suddenly, as upon the fated, sinful cities of the plain, fire from heaven falls upon him and all his hosts, and, confounded, dismayed and imprisoned, under the charge of heaven's mighty police force, by a cyclone of righteous retribution, he is swept down into the outer darkness of fearful and eternal doom.

But look, what dazzling, glorious sight at the King's right hand! There, rank above rank, celestial spirits from every heavenly world circling out and up beyond the penetration of all mortal sight, I fancy that I see. While to the right of the King His ministers, true and tried in all the long war against sin and Satan, now are summoned to receive new installments of their great reward. Many of them have suffered on the cruel torture-rack, and others at the burning stake, while others still have been the victims of hate and ridicule, which made their lives on earth one lingering death. Some had been degraded in their ministry by leaders blind, because of loyalty to holiness and God. Prophets and apostles foremost, I seem to see among that throng. Polycarp and Knox and Latimer are there, and every minister who had the spirit of a martyr, which every Pentecostal preacher has. The hour of their final vindication now has come. They remember the bounding joy which filled their souls when first they felt the fullness of the Holy Ghost and the glad experiences bestowed when, in their early ministry, away back on the battle-field, when the sky was so black and men and demons raged around them. They remember the increasing raptures that rolled over their expanding spirits as kings and priests during the happy ministries of the glorious millennial reign, and doubtless marvel that any greater rewards can yet await.

Shining forth like the sun in the kingdom of the Father, they await His commands, henceforth to move in any orbit He may chose, His will, as in the past, to be their heaven.

He speaks, every word, I fancy, thrilling each as though addressed to him alone: "Come, ye blessed of my Father, inherit the kingdom prepared for you from the foundation of the world" (Matt. xxv. 35-46).

"Well done, good and faithful servant: thou hast been faithful over few things: I will make thee ruler over many things. Enter thou into the joy of thy Lord."

Open, swing the doors of the glorious eternity, and these veterans from earth's probationary pulpits and millennial ministries sweep up, attended by celestial escorts, to "inherit all things," and, thrilled by ecstasies inexpressible, to possess the ever-increasing joys, honors and glories of the new heaven and the new earth, where "there shall be no curse any more: and the throne of God and of the Lamb shall be therein: and his servants shall do him service; and they shall see his face; and his name shall be on their foreheads. And there shall be night no more; and they need no light of lamp, neither light of sun; for the Lord God shall give them light: and they shall reign for ever and ever" (Rev. xxii. 3-5).

Such is a part of the infinite reward of every true Pentecostal preacher.

Happy are all they whose names are thus enrolled.

PENTECOSTAL IMPOSTORS.

Up from the shades of night,
Transformed as angels bright,
In shining robes of light,
    They dare appear.

On in Satanic might,
Hating both God and right;
For sin they fiercely fight,
    Their master near.

When from his high estate,
Born of both pride and hate,
Down to his awful fate,
    Their leader fell.

Then earth he swore to take,
From Christ its Lord to break;
His own to ever make,
    And join to hell.

In their prophetic guise,
His agents, full of lies,
The souls of men surprise,
    And lead astray.

When Jesus shall appear,
Then, seized with awful fear,
They must their sentence hear,
    And flee away.

CHAPTER XIII.

PENTECOSTAL IMPOSTORS.

"For such men are false apostles, deceitful workers, fashioning themselves into apostles of Christ. And no marvel; for even Satan fashioneth himself into an angel of light. It is no great thing therefore if his ministers also fashion themselves as ministers of righteousness; whose end shall be according to their works" (II. Cor. xi. 13–15).

Satan brought about the fall by a fraud, and seeks to thwart redemption in a similar way. Hence his ministers are often found under the seeming garb of sanctity and of ecclesiastical office.

The above Scripture declares the existence of these impostors, that this is to be expected in the nature of the case, and that their final defeat is certain.

When earth, bright and beautiful, rolled from the great creational center with its joyous terrestrial passengers on its circle through the eternities, Satan saw it, coveted, and determined to wrest it from its Maker, subject it to his rule and annex it to his empire. Only one way seemed feasible whereby he could accomplish this, and that was to deceive its inhabitants, and thus inject sin. This he did through the agency of the serpent, who was the first false preacher, and the governmental ambassador from hell to earth. His plan was and is to supplant the kingdom of God with his own government. To do this the world over, he has tried to plant his systems of religion. Hence, his false ecclesiasticisms and false ministers fill the world, and wherever it serves best his hellish purposes, they throw out the stars and stripes of God's great celestial Union and profess to be its loyal officers. Thus they capture multitudes of people. This is Satan's most successful way of resisting Christianity, hence his plans must be unmasked, and the works whereby the agents of his counterfeit worship are known must be advertised.

How to detect and expose them is the subject of this chapter. The writer shrinks from the painting of the painful picture about to be portrayed, and is pained at the awful reality which makes such an exposure a necessity. Yet he rejoices that God unmasks these subtle foes, and, feeling divinely called, is glad to do his utmost to aid Him in the work.

Possibly by these lines some one of them may be undeceived and saved. This would be a great miracle of mercy, but the great good in view is to warn those who are imperiled by their wiles. The Scripture shows that their character is the same in every age, and that God has not left His little ones to their cruel mercies unwarned. He has declared in His Word certain marks which they bear, which all who are wise may read, and thus know and escape their snares.

The duty of exposing them, oft neglected for fear of being misunderstood and accused of wrong and bitter motives, rests upon every true minister. It was discharged by Jesus and by the apostles, and every true agent of God's kingdom must warn of these false prophets and their counterfeit gospel. Instead of this being censoriousness, as is falsely charged, it is a token of the deepest love.

If love compels to warn a man about to step upon a rotten bridge, or to go to sea in a sham ship, or to place his money in a bogus bank, much more does it when he is in danger of being swindled, by spiritual confidence men, out of his soul.

It is believed that there are as true men in the ministry of the evangelical churches to-day as were the apostles. Volumes of their virtues might be written, but the object of this chapter is not to eulogize them but to expose the frauds which are among the greatest hindrances to their work. Jesus was a Lamb to one class of people but a *Lion* to the religious hypocrites of His day, and His Gospel is the same as then.

It should be remembered that this chapter does not refer to honest ministers, though full of mistakes, if walking in all the light they have, but to the *false apostles*, who for the world's warning and the believer's safety God has branded with certain signs, one or more of which is upon each one of them. He who finds *any one* of these brands upon himself may well take warning. The dead and dying ecclesiasticisms of the day present a fruitful field for these deceptive foes of God and man, and no church is or ever has been exempt from their ravages. As a class their character is ever the same, so that their pictures as drawn by prophets, apostles and by Christ Himself, portrays those of to-day as accurately as those in olden times. Listen to what God Himself has said of them:

They are a source of intense grief to true preachers. "Concerning the prophets. Mine heart within me is broken, all my bones shake; I am like a drunken man, and like a man whom wine hath overcome; because of the Lord, and because of his holy words" (Jer. xxiii. 9). All true ministers thus deplore the harm to God and holiness which comes through the deceptive wiles of these impious impostors.

They are profane. One needs not to curse to be profane. All worship which does not come from the heart is profanity. He who takes upon himself uncalled the office of a minister of God is guilty of profaning the sacred office. Such were they and such are some to-day, for God says, "Yea, in my house have I found their wickedness" (Jer. xxiii. 11). Sermons against holiness, against the baptism with the Holy Ghost and other Bible doctrines, are the most obnoxious kind of profanity to God and to His true people.

"*They prophesied by Baal*" (Jer. xxiii. 13). Professing to be God's true ministers, yet they mingled in the rites of pagan worship. Their followers to-day dare to profess to be true ministers of Jesus Christ, and at the same time participate in disgusting rites of worldly orders which ignore regeneration, break the Sabbath, murder men who break their rules, and parade in all the pomp of pagan pageantry. Ministers are known to neglect their flocks for such company, and by gay regalia, carnal companionships and addresses seek to please the worldly minded, and thus, as then, to "prophesy by Baal."

"*They commit adultery*" (Jer. xxiii. 14). By lustful thoughts and lustful looks, and doubtless by many abominable private vices they were guilty of this gross sin. Also by compromise with the enemies of God, of the still "more horrible" sin of spiritual adultery. If public exposures are any index to covert sin there has been yet no reformation in their ranks as to this vice.

They are deceitful. "And walk in lies" (Jer. xxiii. 14). Their very position was a lie, and in order to hold it they were compelled to form the habit of lying. The same is true now. Men declare under the most solemn circumstances that they "expect to be made perfect in love in this life," and then preach that it is an impossibility. They vow to preach and defend all the truths of

the Bible and to drive away all erroneous and false doctrines, and then not only neglect to do so but sow the same.

They are self-sent preachers. "I sent not these prophets,
yet they ran" (Jer. xxiii. 21). God sends none but honest,
regenerate men to preach His Word. He who has not a
divine call to preach, dares God's lightnings if he pre-
sumes to do so. Like a self-sent Senator to Congress,
he can have no recognition or support from the government which he thus insults.

They substitute their own words for God's message. "I
spake not unto them, yet they prophesied" (Jer. xxiii. 21).
True ministers, like Jeremiah, get their messages from
God. Others, like Baalam, select the subjects which
they think will best please the people. They are like a
telegraph messenger, who would forge a telegram, and
collect and appropriate the dues on it. Woe to preacher
and people when this is the case!

They are arbitrary preachers. They forbade Peter
and John preaching in their church, and their children
treat modern Peters in a similar way. "I explained in
the evening, at Fonmon, though in weakness and pain,
how Jesus saveth us from our sins. The next morning
at eight, I preached at Bolston, a little town four miles
from Fonmon. Thence I rode to Lantrisant, and sent to
the minister to desire the use of his church. His answer
was, he should have been very willing but the bishop
had forbidden him. By what law? I am not legally
convicted, either of heresy or of any other crime. By
what authority, then, am I suspended from preaching?
By bare-faced arbitrary power" (Wesley's Journal,
Vol. I., page 245). In every age they manifest a
like spirit towards Pentecostal preachers.

They steal their sermons. "I am against the prophets,
saith the Lord, that steal my words every one from his

neighbour'' (Jer. xxiii. 30). Stolen sermons and stolen editorials are robbing, as really as breaking into banks or pilfering pockets, and a God-given mark of an apostate priesthood. God's ministers can get their messages from Him, without thus robbing each other.

They do not heed or declare the warnings of the Word. God commands, '' Hearken to the sound of the trumpet,'' but they said, '' We will not hearken '' (Jer. vi. 17). Refusing to warn of the consequence of sin, the peril of neglecting salvation, and the awfulness of rushing up to the Judgment and down to hell unprepared, is an unmistakable mark of a spurious ministry, that must meet the multitudes it has ruined, at the Judgment, and with them depart into the everlasting darkness prepared for the devil and his ministers.

They are '' time-servers.'' Such preachers pander to the palates of the people, instead of presenting the Gospel food commanded by God. One of their excuses, especially in city churches, for not preaching a Pentecostal Gospel, is that ''times have changed, and something else is better''; but failure is indelibly written upon every substitute for the glorious old Gospel of the Son of God.

They are covetous, and give false comfort. Covetous in desiring the reverence and reward of true ministers when playing the part of false. Dealing falsely in encouraging people to believe they are saved when not even regenerated, and to think they are prepared for soul-saving when unsanctified, and by crying, '' Peace, peace,'' to seekers who have not met the conditions of salvation, and to whom God does not speak peace. A young man under deep conviction, recently arose in meeting, and all broken down, confessed his sins and desire to lead a different life. The pastor told him he '' need not feel so bad,'' that he was '' not so bad '' as he thought, etc.

False comfort! "Peace, peace; when there is no peace" (Jer. viii. 11).

Their presence is a test to God's true people, who should refuse to listen to them. "Thou shalt not hearken unto the words of that prophet, or unto that dreamer of dreams: for the Lord your God proveth you, to know whether ye love the Lord your God with all your heart and with all your soul" (Deut. xiii. 3). Preachers who have any of the marks mentioned in this chapter, forfeit both the support and the respect of men and the smile of God, who has revealed no method of reclaiming such offenders.

They are stubborn. God commanded, "Ask for the old paths," but they refused saying, "We will not walk therein" (Jer. vi. 16). The Bible way of holiness they would not go. Like their brethren to-day, they discarded the religion of their fathers, and substituted their own notions for the Word divine.

They are blind, ignorant, dumb, and even dissipated (Isa. lvi. 10–12). "Blind," falling into the ditch of sin and leading others there, "without knowledge" of the first principles of experimental salvation. "Dumb" as to the great dangers of sin and privileges of redemption. "Dreaming, lying down, loving to slumber," instead of making pastoral calls and seeking the lost sheep, and those who need a pastor's care. And yet professing to be representatives of Him who "laid down His life for the sheep!"

They are insatiable. "Yea, the dogs are greedy; they can never have enough" (Isa. lvi. 11). No salary so large but they desire its increase, no position so high but that they build ladders for a higher one, and summon all under their influence to help build them. Enough time and money and brains are expended on such ladders to save the world, if it could be saved by that sort of effort.

They are popular with godless people. "A wonderful and horrible thing is come to pass in the land; the prophets prophesy falsely, and the priests bear rule by their means; and my people love to have it so: and what will ye do in the end thereof?" (Jer. v. 30, 31). A minister's popularity may be the measure of his faithlessness to God. "'His people are all unanimous in requesting his return another year," may simply be a notice of a worldly church and compromising preacher. Thus it was in Jeremiah's day, and thus it is in places that you can doubtless name. It is impossible to be popular with Heaven's King and government, and also with worldlings at the same time.

A woman may be a false prophetess (Neh. vi. 14). Few women are recorded as filling this high office in the devil's kingdom. Though first to fall, she has not been first to thus perpetuate pandemonium. The baleful influence of this class of Satan's ambassadors is forceful and fearful, wherever it is felt.

They fill the land with spurious professors who live in sin. "And they strengthen the hands of evildoers, that none doth return from his wickedness" (Jer. xxiii. 14). Opposition to God, righteousness and holiness intrenches itself behind this diabolical fortification.

They cause others to err. "For they that lead this people cause them to err; and they that are led of them are destroyed" (Isa. ix. 16). False teachers unsettle the weak, and by their example lead them from purity to unrighteousness; thus "causing them to err." Godlessness in dead churches is largely attributable to this source.

Their formal ministrations are unacceptable to God. "To what purpose cometh there to me frankincense from Sheba, and the sweet cane from a far country? Your burnt offerings are not acceptable, nor your sacrifices pleasing unto me " (Jer. vi. 20).   No amount of oratory, culture, worldly wisdom, ecclesiastical prestige, experience in filling worldly churches with worldly members, drawing crowds, pipe organs, costly choirs, tall steeples, frescoed walls, nor cushioned pews can be palmed off on God in place of loyalty to Him.

They destroy the Church.   " Many shepherds have destroyed my vineyard, they have trodden my portion under foot, they have made my pleasant portion a desolate wilderness " (Jer. xii. 10).   Spurious pastors will turn the Church of the living God into a clique of colliding factions, or a crowd of feasting, fashionable formalists, or a cold and clammy corpse, thus transforming what should be " the pleasant portion " into " a desolate wilderness."

They are boldfaced.   " Were they ashamed when they had committed abomination?   Nay, they were not at all ashamed, neither could they blush " (Jer. vi. 15).   The unblushing audacity with which some modern ministers preach and at the same time drink beer, or are slaves to tobacco, or tell smutty stories, or jolly jokes, or break their word, or oppose holiness, proves that this generation is not extinct.

They were subject to a death penalty.   "And that prophet, or that dreamer of dreams, *shall be put to death*; because he hath spoken rebellion against the Lord your God, which brought you out of the land of Egypt, and redeemed thee out of the house of bondage, to draw thee aside out of the way which the Lord thy God commanded thee to walk in.   So shalt thou put away the evil from the midst of thee " (Deut. xiii. 5).   Their crime was and is so great against both God and man that He has attached to it the severest possible penalties.

Their prosperity is short. " Wherefore their way shall be unto them as slippery places in the darkness: they shall be driven on and fall therein: for I will bring evil upon them, even the year of their visitation, saith the Lord" (Jer. xxiii. 12). Thus in prosperity, destruction visits them.

They must eat "wormwood and gall" instead of the honey and wine of Canaan. "Therefore, thus saith the Lord of hosts concerning the prophets: Behold, I will feed them with wormwood, and make them drink the water of gall: for from the prophets of Jerusalem is profaneness gone forth into all the land" (Jer. xxiii. 15). Rejecting a Canaan experience, they are compelled to live on Babylonian diet.

They may do wonderful works. Those of Egypt did to defeat Moses and confirm a false and Satanic religion, and in the final arrest and arraignment of these impostors before the Judgment they are represented as even there flaunting the claim of devil-dislodging, wonder-working power in the face of the Supreme Judge. Mormonism, Spiritualism, Christian Science, Catholicism and Paganism are replete with instances of the sick healed and other "wonderful works" done by the "false prophets" of these corrupt systems. Hence the New Testament test of the genuineness of its ministers is not miracle-working power, but the possession of the Spirit of Christ.

Though promoted, they finally fall. "Therefore they shall fall among them that fall: at the time that I visit them they shall be cast down, saith the Lord" (Jer. vi. 15). In the midst of their delusive prosperity God visits, and by affliction, by exposure, or death, tears off their mask, and exposes their hypocrisy.

They are accountable for the wreckage caused by their

ministry. "I sent not these prophets, yet they ran: I spake not unto them, yet they prophesied. But if they had stood in my council, then had they caused my people to hear my words, and had turned them from their evil way, and from the evil of their doings" (Jer. xxiii. 21, 22). This class of preachers doubtless includes ministers who may have been truly called in the beginning, but have compromised, lost their salvation, but still cling to their offices. Every untrue minister must remember that God holds him accountable for all the results of his unfaithfulness. The present awful spiritual condition of many in the churches is due largely to an unfaithful ministry. Let the preachers of the evangelical churches alone receive the Holy Ghost and press a Holy Ghost gospel of full salvation for one year only, and what a mighty transformation would follow. Yet the number that do this is so few, that when one does, he is in many places accounted singular, cranky and extreme, while such preaching should be the rule instead of the exception. The flimsy excuse given for not preaching entire sanctification because so many hate it, or misrepresent it, or have a fanatical stamp of it, will never shield the ministry at the Judgment. If such errors exist it is the result largely of the failure of the pulpit to do its duty, and it is both cowardly and useless to make that result an excuse for continuance in such a treasonable course. It is an apron of fig leaves that fails to cover the wickedness of the culprit behind it. I would rather be the most savage heathen in the heart of Central Africa, than the divine who professes to be a minister of God, and yet neglects to preach the Gospel as God has given it and commands it to be preached.

They are guilty of soul-murder. "When I say unto the wicked, O wicked man, thou shalt surely die, and thou dost not speak to warn the wicked from his way; that wicked man shall die in his iniquity, but his blood will I require at thine hand'' (Ezek. xxxiii. 8). All who are guilty of this crime are murderers of the deepest dye. Before this awful charge shams must shake, and quake, and sink.

Their victims perish with them. ''And they shall bear their iniquity: the iniquity of the prophet shall be even as the iniquity of him that seeketh unto him'' (Ezek. xiv. 10). Thus deceiver and deceived will sink together into the pit, there to taunt each other forever for their mutual misery. No congregation then will be too small to satisfy, for the larger the congregation, the deeper will the preacher be buried beneath its reproaches. This will be one of the sparks of the eternal fire of the impostor's punishment.

Such is the Old Testament picture of clerical impostors. Frightful as it is, we may find that the New Testament photograph is even more severe. He who paints the lily and the rainbow, and also the storm-cloud's solemn blackness, has stopped to paint and leave in the Gospel gallery a perfect picture of these deceptive officers of him whose works He came to destroy. Knowing that they would seek to devour His sheep, He warns them in no uncertain tones. His first message to these men was a burning rebuke and startling exposure of their true character. He fearlessly emphasized the following facts in regard to them:

They are blind preachers. '' Ye blind: for whether is greater, the gift, or the altar that sanctifieth the gift?'' (Matt. xxiii. 19). They were fond of splitting hairs, and substituting tradition for Scripture; and so blind they could see nothing but a '' devil '' in John the Baptist, and a '' wine-bibber '' in the true Messiah. Their chil-

dren treat the possessors of Bible regeneration and sanctification to-day as their fathers did our Saviour. They
see no good in Holy Ghost revivals or revivalists.

They are jealous preachers.   John and Jesus drew the
multitudes, leaving them with empty pews to listen to
their empty words.   Hence their rage and denunciation.
Great salvation revivals provoke the same class in the
same way to-day, and by public and private opposition
they advertise that they belong to the seed of the serpent
which hisses such work, instead of the seed of the woman
which rejoices over it.

They rejected Jesus.   Although He walked, talked,
preached, prophesied, died, and rose again before their
eyes.   Their children to-day are repeating their history.
They quibble over or oppose sanctification, instead of getting and preaching it, and are so blind that they see
nothing but "devils," "wild-fire," "fanaticism" and
"extravagance" in a genuine Pentecostal revival.

They are salary-seekers.   More concerned about what
they shall receive than what they may impart (Luke
xvi. 14).

They itch for office.   Unless constantly ascending the
ecclesiastical ladder they are glum.   They bring all the
prestige of the position which they have, to secure
further ecclesiastical promotion (Matt. xxiii. 6).

They are lovers of titles and honorary degrees, often
agonizing to get them, and feeling aggrieved if not
addressed by their titles.   They prefer these to the degree of "Brother," which the government of God confers upon all who "do the will of God."   Not meeting
the condition of the latter, they hold the former with the
tenacity of a hungry dog a marrowless bone (Matt.
xxiii. 7–10).

They are festival-going preachers, "loving the uppermost rooms at feasts,'' and place-seeking preachers, '' loving the chief seats in the synagogues.''

They are title-seeking preachers. '' To be called of men, Rabbi, Rabbi.'' Dandyish attire, and love of feasting and festivals, scrambling for place, and working for honorary degrees instead of saving souls, are divinely-revealed tokens of a spurious ministry (Matt. xxiii. 7–12). The preacher who magnifies the titles of the schools above those of the kingdom, and culture above entire sanctification, has alarming symptoms of a fatal disease.

They are salvation-hindering preachers. '' Ye shut the kingdom of heaven against men: for ye enter not in yourselves, neither suffer ye them that are entering in to enter '' (Matt. xxiii. 13). They are the '' dog-in-the-manger '' class, who will not themselves eat, but snap at those who would. Such a ministry is one of Satan's most effectual barriers to the door of salvation. Such preachers do not have genuine revivals themselves, but find fault and throw stones at those who are having them, thus declaring their own apostasy.

They persecute the Holiness Movement. (See Acts iv. 1, 2.) If pastors, they frown upon profession of holiness; if on the Appointment Committee, they threaten preachers who are true to it with removal. They call those who possess and confess Pentecostal piety ''cranks,'' '' fanatics,'' '' extremists,'' etc., stoning them with such terms or something harder (Acts. vii. 57, 58).

They are ostentatious preachers. They ''sounded a trumpet '' before them that they might '' have glory of men '' (Matt. vi. 2). The trumpet family of preachers in all ages has thus advertised its lineage; but blow and bluster for self-glory can not be accepted for tears and toil for Christ and humanity. It makes infinite difference whether one blows the Gospel trumpet for the glory of God, or a brazen trumpet for the glory of self.

They are rewarded preachers. "Verily I say unto you, They have received their reward" (Matt. vi. 2). They seek the glory of a large following, and of the earthly honors and rewards of their offices, and receive them.

They are hireling preathers. "He fleeth because he is a hireling, and careth not for the sheep" (John x. 13). Working for an earthly reward, when the hope of that vanishes, they have no incentive to labor. It matters not whether the reward be a living or a salary or a promotion, the hireling cares more for that than for the sheep, and when " he seeth the wolf " of any one or thing that jeopardizes personal interests, he leaves the flock and looks out for himself.

They are unexemplary preachers. "For they say, and do not" (Matt. xxiii. 3). Destitute of salvation from sin, they are the servants of sin, and fail to practice even the low standard which they feel compelled to preach. Hence, to follow their example is to share their doom.

They are dressy preachers. "For they make broad their phylacteries, and enlarge the borders of their garments" (Matt. xxiii. 5). The high silk hats of many modern clergymen are highly suggestive of this text.

They are offended by the truth. The truth burns them. Hence they resist it, and seek for a pretext under which to oppose it. (Matt. xv. 12.)

They are exposed by Christ. Jesus possessed none of the sentimental gush which would allow sin, under any circumstances, to continue its damning work unrebuked. Hence, He unmasked them, that all might see their true nature. This is a part of the work of the Holiness Revival Movement, and accounts for the bitter persecutions and opposition which Pentecostal ministers meet from certain quarters. Sin does not propose to be exposed without a fight, whether intrenched behind a saloon or a sham profession.

They are hypocritical preachers. "For a pretence make long prayers" (Mark xii. 40). Thus this class of men vainly and blasphemously use the most sacred act as a mantle to hide their true characters.

They are proselyting preachers. "Ye compass sea and land to make one proselyte" (Matt. xxiii. 15). Greed for numbers and zeal for denomination lead these impostors to great activity in gaining church members, sometimes conducting so-called revivals which would deceive the very elect. They insist upon "baptism," or "church-joining," instead of regeneration and entire sanctification. They burn incense to statistics and glory in numbers, caring more for a crowd than for souls saved, sanctified and edified. (See chapters on Pentecostal Conversions and Pentecostal Revivals.)

They may be "cultured" preachers. These whom Christ rebuked were graduates from the best theological schools of their day, and well versed in Scripture lore. Men of their class to-day are possessed of similar advantages, and, like them, emphasize the college curriculum above the Pentecostal diploma and the results which follow its possession.

They are proud preachers. Proud of their ancestry, their church property and prestige, their education and position in the nation, they were so full of human conceit and strut that they had no place for Jesus, nor disposition to hail the message of an humble carpenter, and accept of a religion, the foundation principles of which embrace repentance and self-surrender. Hence, to save a conceit they lost a kingdom, a crown, and the Christ of creation. Their seed is advertising its lineage and falling into the same ditch to-day.

They are Scripture-rejecting preachers. "Ye seek to kill me, because my word hath not free course in you" (John viii. 37). Hatred to God and holiness and Holy Ghost testimony and witnesses is born and fostered by rejecting the Word of truth. False apostles do this, and hence Hate, Envy, Malice and Persecution find friendly shelter within their hearts. A Spirit-filled evangelist recently preached a series of truthful, soulful, loving Holy Ghost sermons in a certain church. His messages, by many, were rejected, and he was cursed instead of blessed. Howbeit, some believed and were baptized with the Holy Ghost.

They are time-serving preachers. They claim that because times have changed preaching also should, thus by their own confession admitting that they seek to please the age in which they live, instead of God. Apostolic preaching has been the only kind that has defeated the devil in all ages of the world. True preachers understand that the times must conform to God instead of He to them. This class of ecclesiastics are the weather-vanes of popular opinion, the sham physicians who prefer to see their people perish rather than prescribe the true remedy for them.

They are neglectful preachers. "Woe unto you, scribes and Pharisees, hypocrites! for ye tithe mint and anise and cummin, and have left undone the weightier matters of the law, judgement, and mercy, and faith: but these ye ought to have done, and not to have left the other undone" (Matt. xxiii. 23). They excelled most of their grandchildren in that they were fastidious about paying their tithes, which these usually withhold from God. These, however, are of the same mind in neglecting the weightier matters of the law, "judgement, mercy and faith." Now, as then, they refuse to preach God's judgments, or declare them in such a way as to take the edge off, and do not insist on the conditions of mercy being met, and omit justification and sanctification by "faith." These "weightier matters" often are utterly ignored, and even derided! How unlike the true Gospel minister! "By their fruits ye shall know them."

They are impure preachers. "Woe unto you, scribes and Pharisees, hypocrites! for ye cleanse the outside of the cup and of the platter, but within they are full from extortion and excess. Thou blind Pharisee, cleanse first the inside of the cup and of the platter, that the outside thereof may become clean also" (Matt. xxiii. 25, 26). It is to be kept in mind that the Pharisees were largely the preachers of Christ's time. They were like their representatives now — very tenacious about fine architecture, temple adornments, faultless apparel, cleanliness and other outside observances, but defenders of a sinning religion. They did not believe in any theory of religion which makes men perfectly clean and pure. Their religion is a whitewash instead of a washwhite religion. Without, the whitewash of an empty profession; within, "extortion and excess," and all the fruits of a carnal heart. Christ commanded them to "cleanse first the inside of the cup," which they refused to do, but full of "extortion and excess," they ridiculed His doctrine and resisted Him, as do their children now. Though "beautiful" without, "beautiful" sermonettes, "beautiful" church buildings and adornments, "beautiful" social qualities, "beautiful" select audiences, yet within full of putrefaction and wickedness. Their congregations, like themselves, become dead spiritual skeletons, and full of all the uncleanness of worldliness, hypocrisy and sin. A fearful picture, but true to life.

They are saint-worshiping preachers, worshiping dead saints, and persecuting and murdering living ones. "Woe unto you, scribes and Pharisees, hypocrites! for ye build the sepulchres of the prophets, and garnish the tombs of the righteous, and say, If we had been in the days of our fathers, we should not have been partakers with them in the blood of the prophets. Wherefore ye witness to yourselves, that ye are sons of them that slew the prophets" (Matt. xxiii. 29, 30). They will erect monuments to Fox and Wesley, and kindred saints, and laud them to the skies, but at the same time murder their theology and persecute their true followers. All who have open eyes know that this class of false prophets still live, and that the "deeds of their fathers" still they do. That Christ was describing this class of preachers in all ages, as well as those in His presence, is seen from the fact that He charges them with the murder of all saints in all time. They are now and ever have been the leaders and instigators in the criticism, ostracism and death of men and women who are cleansed, filled, used and kept by the Holy Ghost.

They are testimony-suppressing preachers (John xii. 42, 43). They are opposed to Holy Ghost testimonies, and when in their power have been known to put such witnesses "out of the synagogue"! (John ix.). They always make them feel unwelcome. People are being constantly excluded or ostracized to-day by such preachers for this reason. Names could be given if needful. If such testimonies were more frequent, such exclusions would doubtless be more numerous.

They are flaw-hunting preachers (Mark xiv. 55, 56). They even secured false witnesses to swear to what they had sought, but failed to find, in our Saviour, and they adopt the same course with His followers. They are the buzzards of all ages, flying over beautiful, faultless flowers, trees and forests to seek carrion, and finding none are furious, and too often manufacture it. They never oppose true ministers under the charge of being too holy, but always, as with Jesus, seek for some defect or technicality, or false accusation, to accomplish their diabolical deeds. Such action in a certain quarter now is a forceful reminder that this breed of buzzards is still about their unholy business.

They are exposed preachers. "Therefore by their fruits ye shall know them" (Matt. vii. 20). It is all in vain for such men to try and deceive God's true saints. They know thorns from peaches, and brambles from grapes. A fruitless or a brambly ministry is its own advertisement of its true nature.

They are Christ-crucifying preachers. "Now when morning was come, all the chief priests and the elders of the people took counsel against Jesus to put him to death: and they bound him, and led him away, and delivered him up to Pilate the governor" (Matt. xxvii. 1, 2). They rejected Jesus and put him to death, and with brazen faces professed to do it in the interest of truth and religion, thus capping the climax of their infamy, hypocrisy, and sin. Because He did not come and live and reign in the regal splendor they demanded of the Christ, they rejected Him. Their followers now treat the Holy Ghost, and those in whom Christ is incarnated, in the same spirit. They let the Barabbases of worldliness and worldly members in their churches go without a censure and persecute people who are filled with the Holy Ghost, thus joining with their fathers in bringing upon themselves "all the righteous blood shed upon the earth," and like their fathers, they do this in the interest of religion! And like them, they are rushing down to an eternal hell, from whose fires the phylacteries and honors of offices will prove no protection.

Our Saviour was sentenced by the ecclesiastical officials of the Church. They doubtless were full of self-justification of the act, and of congratulation that the "wildfire" which had so frequently burned their fingers was at last quenched.

They are cowardly preachers. "They feared the multitudes" (Matt. xxi. 46). Knowledge of the rottenness of their cause made cowards of them, so that they lacked the courage which the preaching of the Gospel required. Too cowardly to warn their people of the sins that are damning them, and to declare to them the fullness of redemption that would save them, together they sink down to their eternal doom.

They are testimony-trimming preachers. "They said therefore unto him, What did he to thee? how opened he thine eyes?" (John ix. 26). They were faced with the fact of a mighty work of God, and could not disprove the man's testimony, therefore they did their best to get him to trim it down so that Christ would get no glory from it. A vivid picture of the way the same class of preachers tamper with the testimonies to an uttermost salvation and insist upon unscriptural terms that will keep the knowledge of the divine work from man, and the glory from God.

They are devil-born preachers. "Ye are of your father the devil, and the lusts of your father it is your will to do. He was a murderer from the beginning, and stood not in the truth, because there is no truth in him. When he speaketh a lie, he speaketh of his own: for he is a liar, and the father thereof" (John viii. 44). They

are the devil's most successful officers in his campaign to
capture and hold this world as an annex to hell, and
Christ Himself declares that they are devil-born. By
their loyalty to their father, by their substitution of a
sinning religion in the place of a Gospel that saves from
sin, and by the multitudes of damned souls with which
they have peopled hell, they have proved their right to this
God-given title. Christ utters the most startling warnings against them. He denounces them as " wolves " in
sheep's clothing, " serpents," " vipers," " blind guides,"
" whited sepulchres," " children of the devil," " hypocrites," " children of hell," and " murderers. " He publicly declares that their end shall be awful beyond description, that they shall receive " greater damnation," and
that they can not " escape the damnation of hell." Should
there ever be a contest for the highest seats of honor in
pandemonium because of service rendered on earth, this
class of men will doubtless be able to present the greatest
number of victims, and ascend to the highest seats at the
right hand of Satan.

They are threatening preachers. "And they, when they
had further threatened them, let them go, finding nothing how they might punish them " (Acts iv. 21). It
takes no brains nor religion to threaten, and this race of
shams, when defeated in argument, confounded by facts,
and answered by fire, have a way of "threatening"
which might intimidate men like themselves, but which
has no terrors to God's fire-baptized children.

They are character-arresting preachers. "And they
stirred up the people, and the elders, and the scribes, and
came upon him, and seized him, and brought him into
the council " (Acts vi. 12). They dread men who, like
Stephen, are full of the Holy Ghost. They are opposed
to such evangelists conducting revival meetings, for

they know that such men will tear off their masks, and that the gift of the Holy Ghost received by the Church will defeat hell. Hence, the knowledge of it must be suppressed. So Stephen, like Jesus, is arrested, false charges prepared, and he is summoned before an ecclesiastical court for condemnation, not for trial. These vipers never give a man a trial unless it is a mock one, a farce in which they carry out their cooked purposes. Their murder of Stephen and stoning of many since, prove the continuance of their right to the title of betrayers and murderers, which they so long have held—betraying the cause of Christ, and stoning, mocking, and murdering many of His true followers.

They are jealous preachers. " But when the Jews saw the multitudes, they were filled with jealousy, and contradicted the things which were spoken by Paul, and blasphemed" (Acts xiii. 45). Holy Ghost preachers often draw great multitudes of people to their ministration. This was and is the secret of much of the " contradicting and blaspheming" which their ministrations provoke. It is but the howling of wolves in sheeps' clothing over the loss of sheep which they had hoped to destroy.

They are crafty preachers. " But the Jews urged on the devout women of honourable estate, and the chief men of the city, and stirred up a persecution against Paul and Barnabas, and cast them out of their borders" (Acts xiii. 50). Such preachers, when possible, try to effect their purposes by using for a cat's-paw " devout and honourable" persons who are under their seductive influence. This gives their action an appearance of sanctity, and shields them from opprobrium which otherwise might fall upon them.

They are rabble-exciting preachers. " But the Jews, being moved with jealousy, took unto them certain vile fellows of the rabble, and gathering a crowd, set the city on an uproar; and assaulting the house of Jason, they sought to bring them forth to the people '' (Acts xvii. 5). When it serves their purpose they unite with '' vile fellows of the rabble '' sort to stop a Holy Ghost work. There is a hellish affinity between these two classes. Both serve the same master, and, though they hate each other, they unite when it serves their own selfish purposes to stop a genuine work of grace. Rotten eggs from the mob are born of rotten hearts among the Jews. It was the Jewish hierarchy, not the soldiery, that drove the nails and thrust the spear when Jesus was crucified.

They are "quick-tempered" preachers. Again and again they flew in a rage, and unless providentially hindered, would have killed God's ministers as they did Jesus and Stephen. This is one of the marks of Pentecostal impostors. They are easily provoked. They get mad at a word, miffed at a slight, and retaliate as soon and as much as they dare. True preachers not yet fully sanctified may feel this temper, but they control it; or if it masters them for a moment, they quickly repent, confess, weep and apologize; but these do not control their temper only from a sense of fear and pride. It rules them and continually goads to hot, hasty words, acts, and sometimes blows. If they do not throw stones as at Stephen, they often do words that are harder than stones. Sometimes they even do this publicly, and then fear lest it get into the newspapers as coming from Christian ministers.

They are accursed preachers. ''Though we, or an angel from heaven, should preach unto you any gospel other than that which we preached unto you, let him be anathema '' (Gal. i. 8). Thus God's lightning leaps upon all compromise preachers who eliminate entire sanc-

tification, judgment, hell and other vital Gospel truths
from their sermons.   If the nurse who knowingly withholds unpalatable, though essential remedies, to please a
patient is guilty, much more are Gospel nurses who thus
jeopardize immortal souls.   Men may praise, but God says
"accursed."   In II. Timothy, third chapter, Paul declares
that their existence in profusion shall be a special sign of
these very days, and emphasizes many marks by which
they may be recognized.

Selfish.   "Lovers of self."   Selfish in their homes with
their families, and in their dealings with their fellow-man.

"*Lovers of money.*"   Eagerly, selfishly desiring that
which belongs to others; big appointments, big pay and
big patronage; measuring opportunities by the money in
them, instead of by their spiritual worth.

"*Boastful*" of their own gifts, possessions, churches
and achievements, and even of their success in hindering
holiness.

"*Haughty.*"   Proud of lineage, place, reputation.
Too proud to go to an altar for salvation, and to confess
their need of heart-cleansing.

"*Disobedient to parents.*"   Lacking parental reverence
and obedience, with all other Christian graces.

"*Unthankful*" for mercies offered, redemption extended, and the baptism of fire promised.

"*Unholy,*" and teaching that holiness is impossible
in this life, but that one while in the body must sin "in
thought, word, and deed."

"*Without natural affection*" toward the members of
their own family, thus transforming homes that should
be Edens into icehouses of bickering and strife.

"*Slanderers,*" accusing God of the spurious gospel which they preach, and his saints of "fanaticism"
and "wildfire" and "disloyalty."

' *Without self-control*,'' their passions and tempers running away with them like wild and unmanageable horses, often resulting in humiliating scandals.

'' *Fierce* '' in their opposition to a movement like primitive Pentecost and to those who propagate its experiences. They manifested their ''ferociousness'' towards Paul, and their children do towards all who are Pauline in their experiences, preaching, profession and aggressiveness. Peter rebuked them by saying, '' Behold, ye despisers, and wonder and perish.'' It is impossible for one to be so good as to appease this class of persons. The brighter goodness shines the more bitter their feelings towards it. If Jesus and Stephen could not escape their scorn and arrows, it is useless for others to seek to do so. A test of genuineness of real goodness is that this class despise it. Like swine, they prefer mire to diamonds.

'' *Traitors*,'' Judas-like, betraying Jesus and holiness often for less than thirty pieces of silver.

''*Headstrong*.'' Full of human arguments and sophistry, philosophizing about the Gospel, instead of preaching it. Their messages cobwebs from their own minds, instead of fire from God; ''brainy '' preachers instead of '' heart '' preachers.

'' *Puffed up*,'' instead of humble-minded. Flying the kite of their own intellectual conceits, instead of delving into the rich mines of Gospel truth. Preaching great SELF, instead of a great GOSPEL. Pleasing the cultured few of high social and financial standing, and condescending not to '' men of low estate.''

'' *Lovers of pleasure*, more than lovers of God.'' For their own pleasure, yielding to '' fleshly lusts, which war against the soul,'' seeking worldly society, desecrating the Sabbath day, causing needless pain and labor to others in many ways, taking ease instead of being in "labours abundant," feasting instead of fasting, indulging instead of self-denying, and in kindred ways walking contrary to God and to the good of others, for the gratification of self.

"*Holding a form of godliness*, but having denied the power thereof." This sentence proves that churchlings, and not non-professing worldlings, are being here pictured. They are formalists, who deny the power of God to save from sin and impart vital godliness. The power of godliness is the power of the Holy Ghost in the soul, eliminating everything contrary to it, and imparting the mind that was in Christ, so that its possessor can "walk as Christ walked." Every professor that denies this, is related to this class.

Truth resisters. "And like as Jannes and Jambres withstood Moses, so do these also withstand the truth." This comparison with false preachers shows that this description, while it may apply to the pew, yet has especial reference to false ministers. By resisting the truth, they throw away the key which unlocks the treasures of salvation, and thus rob themselves of all the riches which Christ has purchased for them, for "only those who willeth to do His will," shall know of the doctrine.

Corrupted in mind. The source of their false lives and bogus ministry lies in a corrupt, unregenerate heart. This is the source of all designed opposition to Bible holiness. A corrupt heart, as in the beginning, is always making an apron of fig leaves to keep out the light of God's Word, and cover its own nakedness. When a minister fights Pentecostal holiness, you may know that either he does not understand what it is, or else he is a hypocrite, hiding some sin.

They are in demand. "For the time will come when

they will not endure the sound doctrine; but, having itching ears, will heap to themselves teachers after their own lusts '' (II. Tim. iv. 3). These words show that these Pentecostal impostors would flourish, even as they do, and that people of kindred carnality would desire them in their pulpits and take measures to get them there. Bishop Walden, at a preachers' meeting recently, in an earnest plea for vital piety in the churches, said that the most persistent advisers of bishops in regard to appointments are not the '' spiritual members of the churches, but the trustees; the men who want a drawing card to fill the pews.'' Thus they seek to '' heap to themselves teachers '' who will pander to their worldly plans.

They are exposed preachers. '' But they shall proceed no further: for their folly shall be evident unto all men, as theirs also came to be'' (II. Tim. iii. 9). No screen can hide them and no cloak can permanently cover their hypocrisy, foolishness and sin. By some sudden outburst of passion, or surprise of opportunity, or test in trial, the veneering will crack off and expose the true character. Peter, divinely inspired, also painted and hung in the Bible gallery a picture of these clerical traitors. II. Peter ii. so strikingly pictures them that it might fittingly be called the Impostor Gallery. Mark the close resemblance between this photograph and those drawn by Old Testament writers, by Jesus and by Paul.

They are false prophets. They bring in '' destructive heresies.'' Every heresy that has cursed the Church has been fostered by some of their number.

They are popular. '' Many shall follow their lascivious doings,'' even whole churches of unregenerated members, and by reason of them '' the way of the truth shall be evil spoken of.'' Holiness is derided through their influence.

They are carnal preachers. They walk after the flesh, yielding to carnal appetites. Lust, Ease, and Feasting are their cherished companions.

They are defiant preachers. They " despise dominion." They do not labor with or discipline their unruly members, and themselves defy apprehension. " Self-willed," they persist in their sinful ways, and are not afraid to rail at " dignities," of God's way of salvation, and of the Holy Ghost Himself. A minister in this city, referring to the Holy Ghost, said that he wanted no " Ghost" in his church.

They are lustful preachers. " Having eyes full of adultery." Lustful in their private lives, and worldly in all their ways.

They are established preachers. They " can not cease from sin"; they preach and practice a sinning religion, which is always the religion of the devil. They entice " unstedfast souls," who, mistaking them for true ministers, and their utterances for divine messages, are ensnared and bewildered. " Having a heart exercised in covetousness," shows that their evil has crystallized into character.

They are further characterized as,—

Dissemblers. " Spots and blemishes, revelling in their love feasts while they feast with you." " Children of cursing; forsaking the right way, they went astray."

Disappointing. " Springs without water."

Agitated. " Clouds that are carried with a tempest" (A. V.).

Slaves. " Bondservants of corruption."

Their doom is here declared to be,—

Impending. " Whose sentence now from of old lingereth not, and their destruction slumbereth not."

Certain. " Reserved against the day of judgement and destruction of ungodly men."

Deserved. "Creatures without reason, born mere animals to be taken and destroyed."

Eternal. They are "mists driven by a storm; for whom the blackness of darkness hath been reserved."

Jude, too, was not faithless in warning the Pentecostal Church of the strategems of these generals of Satan, and adds his picture to the striking ones already seen in the gallery of the Word. He declares that they are,—

Foretold. "But ye, beloved, remember ye the words which have been spoken before by the apostles of our Lord Jesus Christ; how that they said to you, In the last time there shall be mockers, walking after their own ungodly lusts."

Crafty. "Crept in privily." Cunning and deceptive; under a profession of loyalty, they steal into position. "Turning the grace of our God into lasciviousness," they use position, gifts and influence to secure selfish ends.

Audacious. "Denying our only Master and Lord, Jesus Christ," both the privileges and benefits of redemption, and the right of God's people to possess and proclaim them.

Sacrilegious. "Defile the flesh"—God's temple—by pandering to its appetites.

Seditious. They set at naught both God's dominion over them and His power to fully sanctify the Church.

Disrespectful. They respect neither God nor His rightful rulers.

Unreasonable. They "rail at whatsoever things they know not,"—the conscious experiences of salvation.

Carnal. "Walking after their lusts," yielding to lustful appetites and impulses, and living sinning lives.

Blatant. "Their mouth speaketh great swelling words" against God's holy people and the truth.

Partial. " Showing respect of persons for the sake of advantage," pandering to the rich for their influence and money.

Mockers. Accusing God's people of being "drunk on new wine," or of similar inconsistencies.

Separatists. " Make separations" from those who are baptized with the Holy Ghost and ·fire, holding conferences and conventions on everything but the great Pentecostal issue. It is a significant fact that many ministers can not be induced to go to holiness meetings or conventions, much less to hold them.

Complainers. " These are murmurers, complainers," constantly complaining about their surroundings and treatment, and the holiness people, their meetings, professions, expressions and actions.

Sensual. " Having not the Spirit." Destitute of the Spirit themselves, and opposing its manifestations in others. Jude further declares that they are,—

Hopelessly doomed. " Set forth unto this condemnation."

Dangerous. " Hidden rocks in your love-feasts."

Disappointing. " Clouds without water."

Presumptuous and greedy. "Shepherds that without fear feed themselves."

Murderers. " Woe unto them! for they went in the way of Cain."

Hirelings. "And ran riotously in the error of Balaam for hire."

Blasted. " Autumn trees."

Doubly dead. " Without fruit, twice dead, plucked up by the roots."

Barren. Their ministrations attended by no conversions or sanctifications.

Restless.   "Wild waves of the sea, foaming out their own shame."

Out of their orbits.   "Wandering stars, for whom the blackness of darkness hath been reserved forever."

Sentenced.   That upon them God will "execute judgement," when He comes "with ten thousands of his holy ones."

Punished.   That their punishment shall be like that of Sodom and Gomorrah and of the angels which kept not their first estate, but who are "kept in everlasting bonds under darkness unto the judgement of the great day."

Great prudence and care is needed at this point not to err either on the side of severity or compromise. Satan would have us believe that they do not exist to-day, so that we will be unprepared to resist them. Beware of this fallacy. They still live and are carrying on their wicked work. They are the devil's spies in the uniform of loyal officers, the Benedict Arnolds who seek to betray the Church into the hands of her enemies.

The treatment they should receive from true believers is made very plain by Scripture precept and example. Its voice must be heard and heeded.

Test them.   "Beloved, believe not every spirit, but prove the spirits, whether they are of God: because many false prophets are gone out into the world" (I. John iv. 1). If there are doubts as to their genuineness, apply the tests which God has given. The Word of God is the standard by which the impostor is to be tested. If his life and teachings do not stand its tests he is a fraud.

Be watchful.   "Take heed lest there shall be any one that maketh spoil of you through his philosophy and vain deceit, after the tradition of men, after the rudiments of the world, and not after Christ" (Col. ii. 8;

see also Eph. v. 6, and Matt. xxiv. 4). This is evidently a warning to believers against the corrupting influence of worldly philosophizing ministers, who substitute their "philosophy" and "vain deceits" for a "Thus saith the Lord."

Avoid them. "Now I beseech you, brethren, mark them which are causing the divisions and occasions of stumbling, contrary to the doctrine which ye learned: and turn away from them" (Rom. xvi. 17). True preachers cause division of believers from worldlings and hypocrites, but these cause divisions "contrary to the doctrine" of the Bible, and believers are imperatively commanded to "avoid them." No amount of eloquence or geniality on their part can be an excuse for not heeding this warning.

Forsake them. "Cease, my son, to hear the instruction that causeth to err from the words of knowledge" (Prov. xix. 27, A. V.). A positive commandment not to attend their ministrations.

Refuse to support them. "If any one cometh unto you, and bringeth not this teaching, receive him not into your house, and give him no greeting: for he that giveth him greeting partaketh in his evil works" (II. John 10, 11). All preachers who are destitute of the experience and "teaching of Christ," are thus stigmatized by God Himself, and their reception and support is positively prohibited. He who in any way aids them, thereby becomes a co-partner with them in their wickedness. If the mines of wealth which are thus squandered on false ministers could be turned into their rightful channels, the financial question of the conquest of this earth for God would be settled in a day.

Do not apologize when they are offended at the truth. "Then came the disciples, and said unto him, Knowest thou that the Pharisees were offended, when they heard this saying? But he answered and said, Every plant which my heavenly Father planted not, shall be rooted up. Let them alone: they are blind guides. And if the blind guide the blind, both shall fall into a pit" (Matt. xv. 12–14). "Let them alone" is our Saviour's advice under all circumstances. Keep living, and testifying, and spreading a Holy Ghost experience, and God will root them up, and they, with all their blind followers, "shall fall into a pit" which they have digged for others. Howbeit this does not forbid merited warnings and rebukes given them, as Christ and Paul gave, when God so leads. The wolf must be thwarted in his efforts to steal the sheep, though not appeased when he howls over the erection of the fold to protect them. A proof of the defectiveness of much that is labeled Christianity to-day, is seen in that it is too charitable to expose and denounce the wolf, and even apologizes to him when he is displeased. A genuine Pentecostal minister will expose him and make him as uncomfortable now, as when his hideous howls rent the atmosphere in Pentecostal days.

Turn away from them. In Paul's exposure of them to Timothy (II. Tim. iii. 5), he says, "From these also turn away." God's purpose with such men is not for His people to win them by increasing their revenues and number of hearers, of which they are so greedy, but to warn them of the peril of their course by the withdrawal of the co-operation of His people. God's people are divinely commanded to allow Pentecostal impostors to prophesy to their spurious followers, or to empty seats. David evidently had this thought in mind when he said, "I have not sat with vain persons, neither will I go in with dissemblers. I hate the congregation of evil-doers, and I will not sit with the wicked." A loyal man can not feel comfortable in a camp of traitors, unless he is there to expose them. It is worse to support a spiritual traitor than a political enemy. Treason against God, in a minister, is a crime as black as hell. The thunderbolts of God Almighty fall on all who are thus guilty, and all who knowingly support them.

Keep the alarm-fires burning. Wolves are afraid of fire. It defeats and maddens them. One is safe from them when under its protection. The baptism with the Holy Ghost and fire is God's safeguard against spiritual wolves. They are afraid of it. They will call it wild-fire, fanaticism, and all sorts of names in their desperation, but it exposes their nature, defeats their plans, and saves the Church from their ravages. Keep the holy fire burning.

The claim that these impostors were confined to Scripture times is a ruse of the devil. "Things which are equal to the same thing are equal to each other." Those then and now both equal the description God gives of that class of impostors, and hence equal each other.

Prophecy declared that they shall exist in great profusion, and this prediction is fulfilled.

Ministers who fail to warn their people of them are guilty of an awful crime.

God's people must be true to the foregoing teachings of Scripture or come under condemnation.

The wolf family and their defenders try to screen themselves behind the following specious sophistries:

1. "The Bible says 'Judge not,' and this course makes every man a judge." Scripture never contradicts itself. "Judge not" prohibits attributing false motives when the facts are not known, or condemning when the fruits are not discerned. But the Saviour expressly declares this class of people are "known by their fruits,"

and commands His sheep to "beware" of them. He does the judging and commands us to do the "bewaring" and "avoiding."

2. "Such action is uncharitable." Then Jesus was guilty of this offense, and all who expose criminals should be censured. True charity shoots the tiger and protects the threatened victim.

3. They also seek to make a breastwork of Matt. xxiii. 2, 3, which says: "The scribes and the Pharisees sit on Moses' seat: all things therefore whatsoever they bid you, these do and observe: but do not ye after their works; for they say, and do not." They forget that a literal obedience to this commandment would have led to the rejection of Jesus and many other wicked acts. The early Church, in direct violation of their counsels, preached and taught Pentecostal truth, hurling into their faces the bold declaration: "Whether it be right in the sight of God to hearken unto you rather than unto God, judge ye: for we can not but speak the things which we saw and heard" (Acts iv. 19, 20).

4. "This will cause divisions." God who commands it will care for the consequences. It doubtless will lead to accessions to churches which are on a New Testament basis of Scriptural piety and practice, or the establishment of such churches where they do not now exist. If Christian people heed the advice of Scripture in this matter, Pentecostal impostors will have smaller congregations, and Pentecostal preachers larger ones. Why not? Formal and worldly professors withdraw their support and attendance from the latter. A part of God's compensation doubtless is that His people so do with the former.

To recognize their authority in the sense demanded by those who apologize for them would coffin Christianity, turn Pentecosts into spiritual graveyards, crucify the example of Jesus and the apostles, and violate repeated commandments to the contrary.

Satan has many similar sophistries by which he seeks to place and keep these agents of his own in Christian pulpits. The only true course believers can take is to follow Scripture and be loyal to God. Many, compromising at this point, have lost their experience and become partakers of the evil deeds of their destroyers.

May God keep us all full of faith and holy fire, saved, sanctified, preserved, and guided by His perfect will. Then we will be able to detect every device of the devil to divert from the path of duty, and become "more than conquerors through Him that loved us."

As I contemplate the character, deeds and doom of these soul-murdering minions of the pit, the following picture of their fearful fate appears before me, in which the experience of one of their number vividly portrays that which is about to fall upon them all.

I seem to see him on his dying bed. The past, with all of its golden, but neglected opportunities, haunts him like a horrid night-mare. The future, still more appalling, chills his very soul with horror. Tormenting memories of duties neglected, souls deceived, and God betrayed, goad him almost to madness.

"A dreadful sound is in his ears," for "in his prosperity the destroyer has come upon him,"—"trouble and anguish make him afraid." The brittle thread of his earthly life suddenly breaks, and with a frenzied shriek of hopeless despair and dread, his soul passes from his body down to its dreadful doom. As his tortured spirit drops into the fearful abyss of lost souls, which is to be his home until the final sentence shall be passed at the day of judgment, all hell is moved to meet him at his coming. Satan, seated upon his throne, exclaims, "Be-

"THREE DEMON SPIRITS HOVER."

hold, one of my most successful generals from the black battlefields of earth." Then I seem to hear a mighty chorus shouting, "Alcohol slew its thousands, Lust its tens of thousands, but this Preacher and his confederates have slain their millions."

I leave his spirit for a little time to the demoniacal reception of those dire realms and return to the place that was his home, the locality where he so long had preached. Among the many who congregate there out of respect to his memory and to sympathize with his friends, I see a number holding high political positions both in church and State. Within the spacious room where his body is awaiting the last attentions which man can give, three demon spirits hover. The name of one is the World, the second the Flesh, and the third, with his black wings shading the coffin, is the Devil.

The World sobs, " He was my truest friend; how hard it is for us to part." The Flesh whispers, "How can I spare him; he always yielded to my wishes." Satan sighs at losing such a general, yet exultant over the victories he had won, is heard to say, " He served me well." He looked at me suspiciously and said, "You can be of no service here." Out of curiosity I lingered near until the hour for final obsequies at last arrives. I seemed to see a vast concourse of people following the costly casket. It was borne by Dr. Formality, Dr. Worldliness, Dr. Flattery, Dr. Self-Righteousness, Dr. Egotism and Dr. Deception, all boon companions of the deceased. Then followed his widow, leaning upon the arm of Dr. Hypocrisy, a twin brother of the departed. Dr. and Mrs. Pride, Dr. and Mrs. Loose Morals, Dr. and Mrs. Vanity, Dr. and Mrs. Love the World, all near relatives, and many more whose names I have not time to record were among the mourners. Then came the various

fraternities of which he had been a member, and one of
which had charge of the funeral.

He had requested that his funeral sermon be preached
by his uncle, Dr. Elymus Compromise, the most popular
preacher in the land.   The hymn sung would have been
appropriate over the body of a Paul-or a Wesley. The text
was from II. Tim. iv. 7: "I have fought the good fight,"
etc.   When the text was announced and the hymn,
"Servant of God, well done," was being sung, Satan's
face wore a fiendish, gleeful expression, as if he were enjoying a farce after his own heart. I fancied that he
said: "I can well afford to lose my best worker for such
a closing scene as this."

After the departed had been extolled as the embodi-
ment of all virtue, his soul was "consigned to the grand
lodge above and his body to its last resting place."

As I turned to take a last look at the newly-made
grave, upon its headstone fancy painted these startling
words:

HE AWAITS THE RESURRECTION OF DAMNATION.

Suddenly I seem to see the heavens open and Jesus
Christ, the Saviour of this world, with all His glorious
white-robed host, appear to take vengeance, in flaming fire,
upon those who know not God, and to reign in joy forever.

Pentecostal Impostors, beneath the burning reproach of
the multitudes whom they have betrayed, and the brightness of the glory of Him whose gospel they have belied,
appalled with awful fear, seek to fly from His presence.
The day has come, long foretold by Jeremiah when he
said, "Howl, ye shepherds, and cry; and wallow yourselves in ashes, ye principal of the flock: for the days of
your slaughter are fully come, and I will break you in
pieces, and ye shall fall like a pleasant vessel.   And the

shepherds, shall have no way to flee, nor the principal of the flock to escape. A voice of the cry of the shepherds, and the howling of the principal of the flock! for the Lord layeth waste their pasture.'' Their fearful, final, agonizing, despairing doom is at hand. ''And the beast was taken, and with him the false prophet that wrought the signs in his sight, wherewith he deceived them that had received the mark of the beast, and them that worshipped his image: they twain were cast alive into the lake of fire that burneth with brimstone '' (Rev. xix. 20).

They are ridiculed by Satan, who has deceived them, and whose willing dupes they were, and cursed by the multitudes of souls who have lost heaven, with its eternal enjoyments, and are doomed to hell, with its unspeakable anguish, through their perfidy.

The centuries of Satan's incarceration (Rev. xx.) quickly pass on earth, but seem like endless cycles to those imprisoned spirits in the caverns of the lost.

The final judgment nears. Scenes exceedingly grand and awful suddenly startle and appall all who are not prepared. I seem to hear the clash of colliding universes, the shout of the angels, the trumpet of doom, and the despairing shrieks of the lost as the voice of the Judge, in final judgment, is now heard from the throne. Graves fly open and multitudes are suddenly summoned, their resistance all in vain, to appear and hear their final sentence.

At the right and back of the Judge, as far as eye can reach, I seem to see celestial spirits which have come from every world to view this awful scene. Nearest the throne, the flower of all the heavenly hosts, are God's true ministers and the blood-washed throngs whom they have won for Him upon earth's battlefields. The Saviour

King, for whom they suffered while below, with words as sweet and tender as those He spoke to Mary weeping over her brother dead, with a welcome more to them than all the universes that fill His infinite domain, says: "Come, ye blessed of my Father, inherit the kingdom prepared for you from the foundation of the world." With angelic escorts and songs of everlasting joy upon their heads, I seem to see them fly to their celestial rewards and appointments, to unfold in all that brings richest enjoyment, glory, honor, and usefulness forever. But oh, the inexpressible sight at the left of the judgment throne! All the catastrophies of floods, and earthquakes, and famines, and fires, and tortures of earth combined would be no parallel to the unutterably agonizing spectacle of the deceived and deceivers who now must drink the bitter cup which they themselves have filled. They plead for rocks and mountains to fall upon them and hide them from Him whose law they have broken, whose gospel they have perverted, whose saints they have persecuted and sought to deceive, and whose promises and threatenings they have spurned. Of all the lost spirits who writhe there amid the tortures of that hour there are none whose guilt is greater or punishment more severe than that of Pentecostal Impostors.

In the same spirit of deception with which they have deluded the myriads of earth, and with audacity bold and defiant, they even here attempt to deceive their Maker. Just as the final sentence is about to be pronounced upon them that will banish them to their long-merited exile, they rise and say: "Lord, Lord, did we not prophesy by thy name, and by thy name cast out devils, and by thy name do many mighty works?" Thus by this last recorded speech of their existence they multiply their infamy and set the seal upon the justice which would outrage heaven and right if it revoked their doom.

Then follows their long dreaded sentence from the Judge, "Depart from me, ye cursed, into the eternal fire which is prepared for the devil and his angels," and quickly, by heaven's executives they are marshalled to the gates of eternal doom, behind which the livid flames of eternal fire leap to welcome and torment them. These gates open upon their massive hinges and then close forever, as down, down, down they sink in frenzied rage, cursing themselves, cursing each other, cursing their Maker and the devil whose willing tools they were, and whose victims they are to be forever "where their worm dieth not, and the fire is not quenched.'

It is a great comfort to the writer that, while preparing this book for the press, the "God that answereth by fire" has spoken not only to his own heart, but that a Revival through the aid of "Pentecostal Preachers" has been in progress in connection with our work. There have been two services per day for four months, in which many have been swept into the experiences of salvation herein magnified. Our "Colportage" Holiness Library has also been launched, through which many have been blessed.

This, with correspondence and other duties, has precipitated an unusual pressure of labor; but through it all Jesus has wonderfully helped, led, and illuminated.

"Now the God of peace, who brought again from the dead the great shepherd of the sheep with the blood of the eternal covenant even our Lord Jesus make you perfect in every good thing to do his will, working in us that which is well-pleasing in his sight, through Jesus Christ; TO WHOM BE THE GLORY FOR EVER AND EVER.

"AMEN."

www.ingramcontent.com/pod-product-compliance
Lightning Source LLC
Chambersburg PA
CBHW051748040426
42446CB00007B/271